Women Writers of Children's Literature

Women Writers of Children's Literature

Edited and with an Introduction by

Harold Bloom

CHELSEA HOUSE PUBLISHERS

Philadelphia

Pied Piper of Hamelin, 1957.14. The Pierpont Morgan Library, New York. Gift of Mrs. George Nichols.

CHELSEA HOUSE PUBLISHERS

EDITOR-IN-CHIEF   Stephen Reginald
MANAGING EDITOR   James D. Gallagher
PRODUCTION MANAGER   Pamela Loos
PICTURE EDITOR   Judy Hasday
ART DIRECTOR   Sara Davis
SENIOR PRODUCTION EDITOR   Lisa Chippendale

WOMEN WRITERS OF ENGLISH AND THEIR WORKS:
  Women Writers of Children's Literature

SERIES EDITOR   Jane Shumate
CONTRIBUTING EDITOR   Marya Bradley
SENIOR EDITOR   Therese De Angelis
COVER DESIGNER   Sara Davis
EDITORIAL ASSISTANT   Anne Hill
INTERIOR DESIGNER   Alison Burnside

First Printing
1 3 5 7 9 8 6 4 2

Library of Congress Cataloging-in-Publication Data

Women writers of children's literature / edited and with an
  introduction by Harold Bloom.
        p.   cm. — (Women writers of English and their works)
  Includes bibliographical references.
  ISBN 0-7910-4486-6 (HC). — ISBN 0-7910-4502-1 (PB)
  1. Children's literature, American—Women authors—History and criticism. 2. Children's literature, English—Women authors—History and criticism. 3. Children's literature, American—Women authors—Bibliography. 4. Children's literature, English—Women authors—Bibliography. I. Bloom, Harold. II. Series.
PS490.W66   1997   97-28610
810.9'9282'082—dc21   CIP

Contents

The Analysis of Women Writers

Harold Bloom

I APPROACH THIS SERIES with a certain wariness, since so much of classical feminist literary criticism has founded itself upon arguments with that phase of my own work that began with *The Anxiety of Influence* (first published in January 1973). Someone who has been raised to that bad eminence—*The Patriarchal Critic*—is well advised that he trespasses upon sacred ground when he ventures to inquire whether indeed there are indisputable differences, imaginative and cognitive, between the literary works of women and those of men. If these differences are so substantial as pragmatically to make an authentic difference, does that in turn make necessary different aesthetic standards for judging the achievements of men and of women writers? Is Emily Dickinson to be read as though she has more in common with Elizabeth Barrett Browning than with Ralph Waldo Emerson?

Is Elizabeth Bishop a great poet because she triumphantly meets the same aesthetic criteria satisfied by Wallace Stevens, or should we evaluate her by criteria she shares with Marianne Moore, but not with Stevens? Are there crucial gender-based differences in the representations of Esther Summerson by Charles Dickens in *Bleak House,* and of Dorothea Brooke by George Eliot in *Middlemarch*? Does Samuel Richardson's Clarissa Harlowe convince us that her author was a male when we contrast her with Jane Austen's Elizabeth Bennet? Do women poets have a less agonistic relationship to female precursors than male poets have to their forerunners? Two eminent pioneers of feminist criticism, Sandra Gilbert and Susan Gubar, have suggested that women writers suffer more from an anxiety of authorship than they do from influence anxieties, while another important feminist critic, Elaine Showalter, has suggested that women writers, early and late, work together in a kind of quiltmaking, each doing her share while avoiding any contamination of creative envy in regard to other writers, provided that they be women. Can it be true that, in the aesthetic sphere, women do not beware women and do not suffer from the competitiveness and jealousy that alas do exist in the professional and sexual domains? Is there something in the area of literature, when practiced by women, that changes and purifies mere human nature?

I cannot answer any of these questions, yet I do think it is vital and clarifying to raise them. There is a current fashion, in many of our institutions of higher education, to insist that English Romantic poetry cannot be studied in the old way, with an exclusive emphasis upon the works of William Blake, William Wordsworth, Samuel Taylor Coleridge, Lord Byron, Percy Bysshe

Shelley, John Keats, and John Clare. Instead, the Romantic poets are taken to include Felicia Hemans, Laetitia Landon, Charlotte Smith, and Mary Tighe, among others. It would be heartening if we could believe that these are unjustly neglected poets, but their current revival will be brief. Similarly, anthologies of 17th-century English literature now tend to include the Duchess of Newcastle as well as Aphra Behn, Lady Mary Chudleigh, Anne Killigrew, Anne Finch, Countess of Winchilsea, and others. Some of these—Anne Finch in particular—wrote well, but a situation in which they are more read and studied than John Milton is not one that is likely to endure forever. The consequences of making gender a criterion for aesthetic choice must finally destroy all serious study of imaginative literature as such.

In their *Norton Anthology of Literature by Women*, Sandra Gilbert and Susan Gubar conclude their introduction to Elizabeth Barrett Browning by saying that "she constantly tested herself against the highest standards of male-defined poetic genres," a true if ambiguous observation. They then print her famous "The Cry of the Children," an admirably passionate ode that protests the cruel employment of little children in British Victorian mines and factories. Unfortunately, this well-meant prophetic affirmation ends with this, doubtless its finest stanza:

XIII
They look up with their pale and sunken faces,
     And their look is dread to see,
For they mind you of their angels in high places,
     With eyes turned on Deity.
"How long," they say, "how long, O cruel nation,
     Will you stand, to move the world, on a child's heart,—
Stifle down with a mailèd heel its palpitation,
     And tread onward to your throne amid the mart?
Our blood splashes upward, O goldheaper,
     And your purple shows your path!
But the child's sob in the silence curses deeper
     Than the strong man in his wrath."

If you read this aloud, then you may find yourself uncomfortable, on a strictly aesthetic basis, which would not vary if you were told that this had been composed by a male Victorian poet. In their selections from Elizabeth Bishop, Gilbert and Gubar courageously reprint Bishop's superb statement explaining her refusal to permit her poems to be included in anthologies of women's writing:

> Undoubtedly gender does play an important part in the making of any art, but art is art and to separate writings, paintings, musical compositions, etc., into sexes is to emphasize values in them that are *not* art.

That credo of Elizabeth Bishop's is to me the Alpha and Omega of critical wisdom in regard to all feminist literary criticism. Gender studies are precisely that: they study gender, and not aesthetic value. If your priorities are historical, social, political, and ideological, then gender studies clearly are more than justified. Perhaps they are a way to justice, or at least to more justice than women have received throughout thousands of years of male domination and aggression. Yet that is a very different matter from the now vexed issue of aesthetic value. Biographical criticism, like the different modes of historicist and psychological criticism, always has relied upon a kind of implicit gender studies and doubtless will benefit, as other modes will, by a making explicit of such considerations, particularly in regard to women writers.

Each volume in this series contains copious refutations of, and replies to, the traditionally aesthetic stance that I have advocated here. These introductory remarks aspire only to a questioning, and not a challenging, of feminist literary criticism. There are no longer any Patriarchal Critics; they are all dinosaurs, fabulous beasts fit for revival only in horror films. Sometimes I sadly think of myself as Bloom Brontosaurus, amiably left behind by the fire and the flood. But more often I go on reading the great women writers, searching for the aesthetic difference that yet may prove to be there, but which has not yet been found.

Introduction

SO VARIED ARE THE DOZEN women writers discussed in this volume that neither their genre nor their gender can be said to hold them together. Louisa May Alcott, the only one among them who died in the 19th century, wrote what is still the most popular work of its kind, *Little Women*. G. K. Chesterton, observing that women were more realistic than men, praised Alcott for anticipating literary realism. Whether or not one agrees with Chesterton that women "pit their realism against the extravagant, excessive, and occasionally drunken idealism of men," it does indeed seem to me that women writers of children's literature are frequently more realistic than their male rivals.

Something of this tendency can be seen by contrasting Ursula K. Le Guin's visionary fictions for children to those of J. R. R. Tolkien and C. S. Lewis. Le Guin's *A Wizard of Earthsea* and its three sequels fuse realism and fantasy as intricately as does her masterpiece for adults, *The Left Hand of Darkness*. Unlike Tolkien and Lewis, who always wrote as Christian moralists, Le Guin shrewdly blends naturalism and pre-Christian magic into a cosmos that seems very much our own. Critics continually note Le Guin's ecological concerns, and it may be her largest achievement that ecology and fantasy are allied, rather than antithetical to one another, in her fiction.

It is odd to compare Le Guin to the author of *The Tale of Peter Rabbit* and *The Tale of Squirrel Nutkin*, yet Beatrix Potter has something of the same relation to Lewis Carroll that Le Guin has to Lewis and Tolkien. Like Carroll, Potter sees her visionary spaces and characters from a child's perspective, and though she cannot rival Carroll in an absolutely original vision, she has a private realism almost as menacing as his uncanny happenings and personages. An unnerving traditionalist, Potter seems to me very close in spirit to the Yahwist or J writer, the earliest author of the Hebrew Bible. The J portions of Genesis in particular gave Potter her salient stances and situations. I am largely alone in believing that the J writer was a woman, but there is a direct sense, as Potter shows, in which the J narrative is the fundamental text of what we now term children's literature.

P. L. Travers is the principal heir of Beatrix Potter, and the Mary Poppins books provide their own fusion of realism and the magical. Grotesques and daemonic figures abound in the world of Mary Poppins, who herself is a benign spirit of the wind, as well as a governess, and so an emblem of moral control. Like Potter, Travers returns us to the imagination of the J writer, where the mundane and the divine scarcely can be distinguished. The oddity of the Mary Poppins books is that they are stronger as what might be termed realistic mysticism than they are as literary narratives. Travers takes her stories and characters wherever she can find them, from the Bible to J. M. Barrie, but she infuses them with a weird addiction to what children ultimately want: a safe haven after imaginary voyagings. I call this addiction or obsession "weird" because Travers herself is profoundly ambivalent about these moral home-comings. Chesterton may have been right that women writers are more real-istic than male fantasists, yet Travers allows just enough of the extravagance of idealism to invade her work so that we learn to overlook her literary weak-nesses. Perhaps a new wave of women writers of children's literature will arrive with the millennium, and we will see other masters of realistic fantasy as accomplished as Le Guin.

Louisa May Alcott
1832 – 1888

LOUISA MAY ALCOTT was born on November 29, 1832, the second daughter of Abigail May and Amos Bronson Alcott, with whom she shared a birthday. The Alcotts were living in Germantown, Pennsylvania, where Bronson was trying to realize his Transcendentalist vision and educational methods in a small school. This project failed after a year and proved to be one of many of his unsuccessful attempts to translate his philosophical views into even slightly profitable practices, failed attempts that would take the family from Pennsylvania to various parts of Massachusetts and would exact an enormous toll upon the family's—and especially Abigail May's—well-being. Abigail was frequently required to support the family by sewing, a task that would be shared by Louisa and her older sister, Anna; Louisa vowed in her journal to help keep the family afloat.

All the Alcott daughters (two more girls were born after Louisa) were encouraged to keep journals from the time they could write. Their journals, however, were not private, but open to the scrutiny and morally improving commentary of their parents. The discipline of writing for Louisa was thus a conflicting exercise—at once a stage for expression and yet also a confessional in which to exorcise desire and achieve moral self-restraint. Although Louisa's upbringing was starkly spartan, one bright element was the frequent presence of authors Emerson and Thoreau in the Alcott home. Emerson not only encouraged Louisa's writing but helped her set up a little school in which she taught, among others, his children. It was for his daughter Ellen that Louisa wrote what were to be her first published tales: *Flower Fables*.

In 1848 Alcott started to make money by publishing stories and poems in newspapers and journals. She published her first poem in *Peterson's* magazine under a pseudonym; her *Flower Fables* came out in 1855. From this time on, Alcott wrote to support her family; her most lucrative projects in this period were what she called her "blood and thunder" romances and thrillers, published under the pseudonym A. M. Barnard. The pressure to produce was intensified by the staggering debts the Alcotts incurred in medical bills for their younger daughter, Beth, who died after much suffering in 1858.

During the Civil War, Alcott volunteered at the Union Hotel Hospital in Washington as a nurse. Although she later published *Hospital Sketches* about her experiences, her work there was brief, for she contracted scarlet fever and had to return to her family. The medicine with which she was treated caused her to suffer vertigo, headaches, joint aches, dyspepsia, and insomnia for the rest of her life. With the end of the war, however, Alcott celebrated the publication of her novel *Moods* (1865). Critics, including the young Henry James, praised the novel—though James faulted its conventionality and artifice. Nevertheless, Alcott's success was such that she could travel to Europe.

In 1867 one of Alcott's publishers at Roberts Brothers asked her to write a story for girls, and out of this effort came the works that would make Alcott famous and financially independent for the rest of her life. *Little Women*, based upon the story of Louisa's own family, came out a year later and was immediately popular. Within a year, she published a sequel to satisfy the overwhelming desire of her readers to learn the fates of the "little women" as they matured. In the years that followed, Alcott came to be known as "The Children's Friend," for she published volumes of stories for young girls and boys and continued to write sequels to her March family story.

Although she had won fame and financial security, Alcott never seems to have had a lover. She took over her mother's role of supporting the family, and when her mother died in 1877, Louisa herself was so ill from caring for her that her older sister, Anna, had to nurse her (and her father) back from grief. Two years later, Louisa's younger sister, May, died after childbirth, leaving her daughter in Louisa's care.

With her niece as an audience, Alcott continued to write stories for magazines, though she suffered from increasing attacks of vertigo and insomnia. She published the last of the March family stories, *Jo's Boys*, in 1886. Two years later, while tending her dying father, Louisa suddenly became ill. She died March 6, 1888, two days after the death of her father.

Critical Extracts

HENRY JAMES

It is sometimes affirmed by the observant foreigner, on visiting these shores, and indeed by the venturesome native, when experience has given him the power of invidious comparison, that American children are without a certain charm usually possessed by the youngsters of the Old World. The little girls are apt to be pert and shrill, the little boys to be aggressive and knowing; both the girls and boys are accused of lacking, or of having lost, the sweet, shy bloom of ideal infancy. If this is so, the philosophic mind desires to know the reason of it, and when in the course of its enquiry the philosophic mind encounters the tales of Miss Alcott, we think it will feel a momentary impulse to cry Eureka! Miss Alcott is the novelist of children—the Thackeray, the Trollope, of the nursery and the school-room. She deals with the social questions of the child-world, and, like Thackeray and Trollope, she is a satirist. She is extremely clever, and, we believe, vastly popular with infant readers. In ⟨*Eight Cousins; or The Aunt-Hill*⟩ her latest volume, she gives us an account of a little girl named Rose, who has seven boisterous boy-cousins, several grotesque aunts, and a big burly uncle, an honest seaman, addicted to riding a tilt at the shams of life. He finds his little niece encompassed with a great many of these, and Miss Alcott's tale is chiefly devoted to relating how he plucked them successively away. We find it hard to describe our impression of it without appearing to do injustice to the author's motives. It is evidently written in very good faith, but it strikes us as a very ill-chosen sort of entertainment to set before children. It is unfortunate not only in its details, but in its general tone, in the constant ring of the style. The smart satirical tone is the last one in the world to be used in describing to children their elders and betters and the social mysteries that surround them. Miss Alcott seems to have a private understanding with the youngsters she depicts, at the expense of their pastors and masters; and her idea of friendliness to the infant generation seems to be, at the same time, to initiate them into the humorous view of them taken by their elders when the children are out of the room. In this last point Miss Alcott does not perhaps go so far as some of her fellow-chroniclers of the nursery (in whom the tendency may be called nothing less than depraved), but she goes too far, in our opinion, for childish simplicity or parental equanimity. All this is both poor entertainment and poor instruction. What children want is the objective, as the philosophers say; it is good for them to feel that the people and things around them that appeal to their respect are beautiful and powerful specimens of that they seem to be. Miss Alcott's heroine is evidently a very subjective little girl; and certainly her history will deepen the subjective tendency in the little girls who read it. She "observes in a pensive tone" that her health is considered bad. She charms her uncle by telling him, when he intimates that she may be vain, that "she don't think she is repulsive." She is sure, when she has left the room, that people are talking about her; when her birthday arrives she "feels delicate about mentioning it." Her conversation is salted with the feminine humor of the period. When she falls from her horse, she announces that "her feelings are hurt, but her bones are all safe." She certainly reads the magazines, and perhaps even writes for them. Her uncle Alec, with his crusade against the conventionalities, is like a young lady's hero of the "Rochester" school astray in the nursery. When he comes to see his niece he descends from her room by the water-spout; why not by a rope-ladder at once? When her aunts give her medicine, he surreptitiously replaces the pills with pellets of brown-bread, and Miss Alcott winks at the juvenile reader at the thought of how the aunts are being humbugged. Very likely many children are overdosed; but this is a poor matter to tell children stories about. When the little girl makes a long, pert, snubbing speech to one of her aunts, who has been enquiring into her studies, and this poor lady has been driven from the room, he is so tickled by what would be vulgarly called her "cheek" that he dances a polka with her in jubilation. This episode has quite spoiled, for our fancy, both the uncle and the niece. What have become of the "Rollo" books of our infancy and the delightful "Franconia" tales? If they are out of print, we strongly urge that they be republished, as an antidote to this unhappy amalgam of the novel and the story-book. These charming tales had, relatively speaking, an almost Homeric simplicity and "objectivity." The aunts in "Rollo" were all wise and comfortable, and the nephews and nieces were never put under the necessity of teaching them their place. The child-world was not a world of questions, but of things, and though the things were common and accessible to all children, they seemed to have the glow of fairy-land upon them. But in 'Eight Cousins' there is no glow and no fairies; it is all prose, and to our sense rather vulgar prose.

    —Henry James, [Review of *Eight Cousins; or The Aunt-Hill*], *Nation* 21 (14 October 1875): 250–51

G. K. CHESTERTON

Little Women was written by a woman for women—for little women. Consequently it anticipated realism by twenty or thirty years; just as Jane Austen anticipated it by at least a hundred years. For women are the only realists; their whole object in life is to pit their realism against the extravagant, excessive, and occasionally drunken idealism of men. I do not hesitate. I am not ashamed to name Miss Alcott and Miss Austen. There is, indeed, a vast division in the matter of literature (an unimportant matter), but there is the same silent and unexplained assumption of the feminine point of view. There is no pretence, as most unfortunately occurred in the case of another woman of genius, George Eliot, that the writer is anything else but a woman, writing to amuse other women, with her awful womanly irony. Jane Austen did not call herself George Austen; nor Louisa Alcott call herself George Alcott. These women refrained from that abject submission to the male sex which we have since been distressed to see; the weak demand for masculine names and for a part in merely masculine frivolities; parliaments, for instance. These were strong women; they classed parliament with the public-house. But for another and better reason, I do not hesitate to name Miss Alcott by the side of Jane Austen; because her talent, though doubtless inferior, was of exactly the same kind. There is an unmistakable material truth about the thing; if that material truth were not the chief female characteristic, we should most of us find our houses burnt down when we went back to them. To take but one instance out of many, and an instance that a man can understand, because a man was involved, the account of the quite sudden and quite blundering proposal, acceptance, and engagement between Jo and the German professor under the umbrella, with parcels falling off them, so to speak, every minute, is one of the really human things in human literature; when you read it you feel sure that human beings have experienced it often; you almost feel that you have experienced it yourself. There is something true to all our own private diaries in the fact that our happiest moments have happened in the rain, or under some absurd impediment of absurd luggage. The same is true of a hundred other elements in the story. The whole affair of the children acting the different parts in *Pickwick*, forming a childish club under strict restrictions, in order to do so; all that is really life, even where it is not literature. And as a final touch of human truth, nothing could be better than the way in which Miss Alcott suggests the borders and the sensitive privacy of such an experiment. All the little girls have become interested, as they would in real life, in the lonely little boy next door; but when one of them introduces him into their private club in imitation of *Pickwick*, there is a general stir of resistance; these family fictions do not endure being considered from the outside.

All that is profoundly true; and something more than that is profoundly true. For just as the boy was an intruder in that club of girls, so any masculine reader is really an intruder among this pile of books. There runs through the whole series a certain moral philosophy, which a man can never really get the hang of. For instance, the girls are always doing something, pleasant or unpleasant. In fact, when they have not to do something unpleasant, they deliberately do something else. A great part, perhaps the more godlike part, of a boy's life, is passed in doing nothing at all. Real selfishness, which is the simplest thing in the world to a boy or man, is practically left out of the calculation. The girls may conceivably oppress and torture each other; but they will not indulge or even enjoy themselves—not, at least, as men understand indulgence or enjoyment. The strangest things are taken for granted; as that it is wrong in itself to drink champagne. But two things are quite certain; first, that even from a masculine standpoint, the books are very good; and second, that from a feminine standpoint they are so good that their admirers have really lost sight even of their goodness. I have never known, or hardly ever known, a really admirable woman who did not confess to having read these books. Haughty ladies confessed (under torture) that they liked them still. Stately Suffragettes rose rustling from the sofa and dropped *Little Women* on the floor, covering them with public shame. At learned ladies' colleges, it is, I firmly believe, handed about secretly, like a dangerous drug. I cannot understand this strange and simple world, in which unselfishness is natural, in which spite is easier than self-indulgence. I am the male intruder, like poor Mr. Laurence and I withdraw. I back out hastily, bowing. But I am sure that I leave a very interesting world behind me.

—G. K. Chesterton, "Louisa Alcott" (*Nation* 1907), reprinted in *Critical Essays on Louisa May Alcott*, ed. Madeleine B. Stern (Boston: G. K. Hall and Company, 1984), 213–14

PATRICIA MEYER SPACKS

The difference between boy and girl is strongly marked in *Little Women*. It is spelled out in an account of Meg's twins, a boy and a girl, who from infancy define themselves according to sex:

> At three, Daisy demanded a "needler," and actually made a bag with four stitches in it; she likewise set up housekeeping in the sideboard, and managed a microscopic cooking stove with a skill that brought tears of pride to Hannah's eyes, while Demi learned his letters with his grandfather. . . . The boy early developed a mechanical genius which delighted his father and distracted his mother, for he tried to imitate every machine he saw, and kept the nursery in a chaotic condition, with his "sewin-sheen" . . . ; also a basket hung over the back of a big chair, in which he vainly tried to hoist his too confiding sister, who, with feminine devotion, allowed her little head to be bumped till rescued. . . . Of course, Demi tyrannized over Daisy, and gallantly defended her from every other aggressor; while Daisy made a galley slave of herself. . . . A rosy, chubby, sunshiny little soul was Daisy, who found her way to everybody's heart, and nestled there.

This distribution of virtues seems invented for the purpose of being attacked by feminists: a textbook example of damaging assumptions about the nature of the female, and of the way a girl learns to be charming because she's not allowed to be intelligent or inventive. The patterns of life for bigger girls and boys in the book are what one might predict from this version of babyhood.

Little Women is usually remembered, sometimes even referred to in print, as a study of four girls with an absent father. In fact, the father is on hand for half the narrative. He provides spiritual advice to his daughters (his tone and language eerily identical with his wife's), confiscates the wine at Meg's wedding, teaches his grandson the alphabet: guide, rebuker, pedagogue—man. Yet he seems invisible: in a deep sense this is a women's world. On the other hand, there is no doubt about which sex really *does things*. The novel—one hesitates to call it that, since the narrative complexity is on the level of a child's story:

all, of course, it purports to be—exhaustively examines the feminine role of "taking care," yet makes clear from the outset that the masculine kind of taking care—providing financial and serious moral support—is the kind that counts. The girls dispute about who is to have the privilege of buying their mother some new slippers. Jo wins, saying, "I'm the man of the family now papa is away, and *I* shall provide the slippers, for he told me to take special care of mother while he was gone." Unfortunately for her psychic well-being, she can only temporarily occupy the comforting role of "man of the family"; her father returns to supplant her.

The book is not one an adult is likely to reread with pleasure, yet children—even college students—still respond strongly to Jo as a fictional character. And the pure didacticism that governs the narrative gives it special clarity as a revelation of nineteenth-century feminine assumptions about feminine nature and possibility. Louisa May Alcott's ideas about what women should and can be, and what men naturally are, shape the simple narrative structure, which moves from one "lesson" to another. These pieces of didacticism reveal how completely women can incorporate unflattering assumptions about their own nature, using such assumptions as moral goads.

—Patricia Meyer Spacks, *The Female Imagination* (New York: Avon Books, 1972), 120–22

JANE VAN BUREN

⟨Alcott⟩ said of herself:

> I think my natural ambition is for the lurid style. I indulge in gorgeous fancies and wish that I dared inscribe them upon my pages and set them before the public. . . . How should I dare to interfere with the proper grayness of old Concord?—And my favorite characters! Suppose they went to cavorting at their own sweet will, to the infinite horror of dear Mr. Emerson. To have had Mr. Emerson for an intellectual God all one's life is to be invested with a chain armor of propriety. . . . And what would my own good father think of me . . . if I set folks to doing the things that I have a longing to see my people do? No, my dear, I shall always be a wretched victim to the respectable traditions of Concord. ⟨*Behind a Mask*, 1975, xxvi⟩

The constant inner warfare within Louisa's mind became the material for her fiction. Thus, writing became an exquisite means to project out the inner dramas which partly inhibited her potency and will. This process was highly complex and exacted a high price for Louisa's generative self.

I would like to suggest that literary work is an imaginative rendering in which one aspect of the self communicates with another. Fictional characters are thus often the manifest and transformed version of the content of unconscious structures. The characters of the moral mother and the femme fatale can be seen to carry the inherent meaning of the mother from both mythic and cultural perspectives. In their representation of the polar opposition of good and evil, they also display the mind's attraction towards splitting complex data into opposites.

These selves and their relationships can be seen in Alcott's two main types of works: (1) the sentimental domestic novel, written in sympathy with her good moral-mother self and directed at children, and (2) the pseudo-Gothic tale, created out of her destructive aspects, as well as out of the rebellion against and collaboration with her inner tyrants. She is best known for her domestic stories, and only recently, through Madeline Stern's splendid scholarship, have we become acquainted with the Gothic tales. In the 1860's Louisa wrote in both genres, although the Gothic style thriller predominated during this period. In the 70's, there followed a period in which the Gothic tales were seldom written. When she allowed herself to write in this exciting style, and almost always when the main character was a rebellious femme fatale, Louisa frequently wrote anonymously. She dubbed her thrillers "necessity stories," as both she and her fictional alter ego, Jo, wrote them to bolster the family budget. However, as the use of the pseudonym implies, the writing of "lurid tales" brought forbidden and tainted satisfaction.

—Jane Van Buren, "Louisa May Alcott: A Study in Persona and Idealization," *The Psychohistory Review* 9, no. 4 (Summer 1981): 288–89

ALFRED HABEGGER

Half a century ago Pierre la Rose and Katharine Anthony drew attention to the paradox that young Henry James's review of Louisa May Alcott's first and only serious adult novel, *Moods*, scoffed at her use of the same heroine he himself would build so many novels around: "We are utterly weary of stories about precocious little girls. In the first place, they are in themselves disagreeable and unprofitable objects of study; and in the second, they are always the precursors of a not less and unprofitable middle-aged lover" ⟨*The North American Review*, July 1865, 276⟩. It seemed odd to la Rose and Anthony that the man who wrote this surly dismissal would in time create a number of precocious girls of his own—Isabel Archer, Verena Tarrant, the governess at Bly, Maisie Farange, Nanda Brookenham. James's first novel would in fact introduce its heroine by twice calling her *precocious* (*Watch and Ward* 238, 241). Even stranger, as Anthony noticed, every one of these girls would fall in love with the older man James claimed to be so weary of. "The mutual influence" of James and Louisa May Alcott "was perhaps stronger than anyone realizes" ⟨*Louisa May Alcott*, 1938, 180⟩, Anthony guessed, correctly, even though influence in the old sense doesn't capture the rich network of connections between the two writers. The fuller truth 〈. . .〉 is that *Moods* assisted young James in defining his response to a large group of novels by women, and thus made it possible for him to absorb their stories and character-types in his own narratives. Another way of saying this is that through Alcott's fiction James had full access to the secret fantasy-life that helped generate it, and that his own fiction records the contours of his distaste for what he found there.

    —Alfred Habegger, "Precocious Incest: First Novels by Louisa May Alcott and Henry James," *The Massachusetts Review* (Summer/Autumn 1985): 233–34

ANGELA M. ESTES AND KATHLEEN MARGARET LANT

Louisa Alcott found herself 〈. . .〉 confronted with conflicting impulses: on the one hand, Alcott—educated under tutelage of Emerson and Bronson Alcott—craves freedom and the power of self-assertion for both herself and her characters; on the other hand, she feels strongly the pressure to meet the needs of her young readers and the demands of her publishers. In Alcott's most famous novel for children, therefore, woman's development toward membership in the acceptable female sphere is rendered in a surface narrative; to reveal the complex, dangerous truths of female experience, the self-assertive drives toward womanly independence, Alcott (resorting to one of the ploys she uses frequently in the thrillers—disguise) must incorporate a subtext. Thus, in *Little Women*, Alcott, employing both a surface narrative and a subtext to disclose an extended vision of feminine conflict, presents a vision of female experience at once innocuous and deadly. What appears at first to be a conventional and somewhat sentimental tale of the innocent trials of girlhood—what we have mistaken for a "feminine" novel of domestic education—is, on closer examination, another of Alcott's lurid, violent sensation stories. For in presenting the conflict between appropriate womanly behavior and the human desire for assertiveness and fulfillment, Alcott finds herself forced to wage war upon her protagonist, Jo. Young Jo—fiery, angry, assertive—represents all that adult Jo can never be, and for this reason young Jo must be destroyed. Thus, while the surface narrative achieves some closure, while it implies a moderately "normal," well-integrated future for Jo, the horrifying subtext of *Little Women* reveals that for an independent, self-determined Jo, no future is possible. 〈. . .〉

    Ironically, Jo's last self-assertive act is the burning of her writings, the destroying of her own self—her self-reliant, self-expressive, and self-authenticating being. This ultimate act of self-annihilation comes as no surprise, however, to the reader who has been alert to the subtext of the novel. For this alternate text has foreshadowed the enforced self-mutilation that is Jo's fate. One of Jo's first acts of self-effacement in order to become a proper "little woman" occurs early in the novel when Jo cuts off her cherished long hair, selling it to obtain money for her mother to visit her sick father in the army. Jo's comments about her sacrifice reveal that it is much more than a noble act of charity. For the shearing of her hair is Jo's attempt to atone for her selfish acts—"I felt wicked" (147)—and to curb her self-assertive behavior: "It will be good for my vanity" (146). The subtext reveals, however, the destructive consequences of the attempt to suppress a woman's self-reliant impulses, as Jo relates her feelings after cutting off her hair: "It almost seemed as if I'd an arm or leg off" (148).

Jo is repeatedly associated in the novel, in fact, with self-mutilation. Throughout the novel, Beth cares for Jo's cast-off "invalid" doll—appropriately named "Joanna" (56)—a lobotomized amputee symbolic of the fate of the "tempestuous" Jo herself: "One forlorn fragment of *dollanity* had belonged to Jo, and having led a tempestuous life, was left a wreck in the ragbag, from which dreary poorhouse it was rescued by Beth and taken to her refuge. Having no top to its head, she tied on a neat little cap, and as both arms and legs were gone, she hid these deficiencies by folding it in a blanket and devoting her best bed to this chronic invalid" (36). Here Beth hides the "deficiencies" of "Joanna" even as Alcott later uses the persona of Beth to "hide" the "deficiencies" of the incorrigible Jo. And twice in the novel Jo must mutilate her writing—the sole means she has to express her true self—in order to conform to the demands of others. First she mutilates her works, her "children," to please her editors, "feeling as a tender parent might on being asked to cut off her baby's legs in order that it might fit into a new cradle" (314). Then she completely destroys her works for Professor Bhaer. ⟨. . .⟩

By the end of the novel Jo has no rebellion, no self, left. Jo's mind, earlier filled with divided but vital and authentic impulses, is now—like the doll Joanna's head—vacuumed out and replaced with Beth's one-dimensional, selfless personality. Alcott can finally resolve the problems and conflicts engendered by the clash of Jo's independent personality with her required role in woman's sphere only by excising and replacing Jo's character.

Careful to leave no trace of blood in this children's novel, Alcott quietly substitutes for Jo an impersonation of the perfect "little woman," the dead and selfless Beth. And when Jo agrees to marry Professor Bhaer, her words affirm the success of Alcott's endeavor: "I may be strong-minded, but no one can say I'm out of my sphere now" (433–34). Jo has indeed been forced into her proper "sphere," but to do so, Alcott has had to perform a lobotomy on her. While in the surface narrative Jo seems to learn the lessons of little womanhood, the subtext of the novel reveals Alcott's Procrustean intent: Jo may begin life as a young "madwoman in the attic," but Alcott kills off this madwoman, leaving only the "angel in the house" (217).

—Angela M. Estes and Kathleen Margaret Lant, "Dismembering the Text: The Horror of Louisa May Alcott's *Little Women*," *Children's Literature* 17 (1989): 101, 118–20

ANN B. MURPHY

Biographies exploring the darker side of Alcott and reinterpreting her complicated family, as well as ongoing feminist work retrieving, recuperating, and reenvisioning American literature and cultural history, have all contributed to the scholarship on Alcott during the past two decades. Yet the text of *Little Women* remains something of a tarbaby, a sticky, sentimental, entrapping experience or place rather than a knowable object—and thus a fitting emblem of its own subversive content, which resists women's objectification and seeks a new vision of women's subjectivity and space. Some critics begin by directly recognizing the extraordinary power this work had for them and others in childhood. Others approach the novel with more apparent detachment, focusing on its repressive domesticity. For most of us, however, *Little Women* is a troubling text, a childhood icon that still resonates with images of positive female community, ideal and loving motherhood, and girlhood dreams of artistic achievement. Our reactions to the incarceration of Meg in claustrophobic domesticity, the mysterious, sacrificial death of good little Beth, the trivialization of Amy in objectifying narcissism, and the foreclosure of Jo's erotic and literary expression, are inextricably connected to our memories of our own struggles against these fates.

Not surprisingly, then, there is remarkable disunity in the contemporary reappraisals of the meaning and significance of Alcott's novel. Indeed, the disagreement is so pervasive and individual opinions so frequently contradictory, within and between essays, as to suggest both the abiding and seductive power of this text for many female readers, and the rich plenitude of its still unexplored critical possibilities. ⟨. . .⟩

The power of *Little Women* derives in large measure from the contradictions and tensions it exposes and from the pattern it establishes of subversive, feminist exploration colliding repeatedly against patriarchal repression. Like the log cabin quilt pattern Elaine Showalter uses to explore the underlying structure of *Uncle Tom's Cabin*, *Little Women*, too, is constructed on a "compositional principle . . . [of] contrast between light and dark," between exploration and entrapment, desire and denial, expression and repression. What Showalter terms the "symbolic relationship to boundaries" ⟨"Piecing and Writing," 1986, 235⟩ in the quilting pattern perfectly expresses the narrative pattern in *Little Women*, which consistently moves us to the outer boundaries of representational fiction in its effort to depict a resolution beyond the either/or constraints of the author's culture.

The text is constructed of contrasting pieces that depict both the female narrative of ethical development and its dark, insidious alternative of static female saintliness; both the passionate quest for a reconciliation of desire with separation and its darker suggestions about maternal eroticism, coercion, and socialization, both the artist's search for authentic female voice and its painful shadowing image of the failure of existing forms to express that voice. In each voyage or pilgrimage—each pattern of female quest—Alcott moves the narrative simultaneously to the borders of possibility in patriarchal culture and to the deep core of yearning for maternal oneness. This book is passionately memorable for young girls because it warns of the dangers that lie ahead— domestic incarceration, narcissistic objectification, sacrificial goodness, and the enforced silencing of voice, eroticism, and anger—and partly because it offers an alternative vision of adulthood-in-community, of female subjectivity, and above all of female oedipal narrative, restoring the lost, maternal presence in our lives.

The sites where Alcott's narrative flounders, where the shape of her textual pattern crashes against the absolute nature of her culture's borders, are the sites we are still exploring today. If her novel fails fully to sustain an image of resolution that transcends either/or choices, her failure suggests much that remains real and enduring in our own experience.

—Ann B. Murphy, "The Borders of Ethical, Erotic, and Artistic Possibilities in *Little Women*," *Signs: Journal of Women in Culture and Society* 15, no. 3 (Spring 1990): 563–64, 584–85

ANGELA M. ESTES AND KATHLEEN MARGARET LANT

Our attention and our sympathy are focused in "Fancy's Friend" on young Fancy, who is vacationing at the seashore with her Aunt Fiction and Uncle Fact. Fancy is not a particularly gregarious youngster, and she finds that her best friend during the summer is a mermaid—the creation of her own imagination—who becomes visible to the entire community. Aunt Fiction, an imaginative and accepting woman, deems the young mermaid, Lorelei, charming, but Uncle Fact—a logical, rigorous, "grim, grave, decided man" (218)—finds her a threat to all he stands for and believes in. The conflict in the story involves Uncle Fact's insistence that Fancy relinquish her cherished friend— since, in his view, she represents only a childish escape into the world of fantasy—and take her place in the world of reality and fact. Fancy ultimately defers to Uncle Fact's demands and loses her Lorelei—her friend—forever. ⟨. . .⟩

Uncle Fact is merciless in his attack. He convinces Fancy that Lorelei was never a mermaid, but was instead "a real child" and that Fancy only "fancied" (229) her coming to life from the shells that Fancy had arranged. A few moments later, Fancy herself admits, "I suppose I *must* give up my Fancy" (230). ⟨. . .⟩ Alcott's language is revealing: Uncle Fact is not simply talking Fancy out of her imagined relationship with an illusory being; he is—in making Fancy reject this relationship—causing Fancy to give up some part of herself. She "fancied" (229) Lorelei into being by projecting herself and her desires upon the world. The use of a verb that is a form of her very name implies that her activity in creating Lorelei is an intense expression of her identity—is, in fact, equivalent to her identity. In creating Lorelei, in telling the story of their relationship, then, Fancy lives most authentically for and through herself. In giving Lorelei up, she is giving up her essential self. ⟨. . .⟩

⟨. . .⟩ With Lorelei, Fancy possessed both self and relationship; in giving Lorelei up, Fancy abnegates self for the sake of connection with Uncle Fact:

> While her uncle said these things, all the beauty seemed to fall away
> from her friend, all the sweetness from their love, and all her faith in
> the little dream which had made her life so happy. Mermaids became
> treacherous, unlovely, unreal creatures; and Lorelei seemed like a
> naughty, selfish child, who deceived her, and made her do wrong
> things. (232)

Deploring her connection with what she now perceives as an "unlovely, unreal creature," Fancy agrees to renounce Lorelei. "I'll give her up," she cries, and Lorelei's destruction is brought about by the very language Fancy uses: "As the last word left Fancy's lips, a long, sad cry sounded through the room; Lorelei sprung in, gave her one kiss, and was seen to run swiftly toward the beach" (233). In structuring Fancy's betrayal and renunciation of Lorelei in this way— that is, by emphasizing the effects of the words Fancy uses—Alcott is foregrounding the performative powers of language, the ability of language to alter and shape reality.

With "the wreck of her friend" (233), the relationship and the story are ended. As Fancy accedes to Uncle Fact's view of the world, she silences herself ("Fancy never spoke of it" [233]) and loses her most intimate connection ("her dearest playmate" [234]). ⟨. . .⟩ By these means, the lovely view of the world and the opportunities for self-expression that Fancy's creation of Lorelei has made possible are lost forever. ⟨. . .⟩ The short story suggests that the only way Fancy could have successfully preserved her relationship with Lorelei would have been to maintain her belief and her faith in her own story, in her own version of events; without the help of Aunt Fiction, she could not do that. She needed someone to accept, to believe in, and to tell her story.

This is perhaps why Alcott placed "Fancy's Friend" at the end of her *Aunt Jo's Scrap-Bag* series. Alcott seems, in this work, to emphasize the vitality, the importance of stories for young girls, for it is their stories that create and validate a world that entitles them to both self and intimacy. If we search for Fancy's "friend" in the story, we must say, of course, that it is Lorelei, the being

who could enable Fancy to preserve self and imagination. But, even more con-
vincingly, it is Alcott herself, "the children's friend" as she was known for much
of her life, who is Fancy's true friend. Alcott—as author of stories for girls—
offers a guide to young girls on how to enter adulthood successfully, with their
imaginations and selves intact.

> —Angela M. Estes and Kathleen Margaret Lant, "'Unlovely, Unreal Creatures': Resistance
> and Relationship in Louisa May Alcott's 'Fancy's Friend,'" *The Lion and the Unicorn* 18, no. 2
> (December 1994): 155, 168–69

Elizabeth Young

In the fiction of Louisa May Alcott, ⟨. . .⟩ the Civil War functions as both historical ground and literary figure. On the one hand, the multiple fevers of war
provide an overarching metaphor for the topsy-turvyness Alcott experiences
as woman and as writer. On the other hand, the civil wars Alcott sketches
within her fictional plots symbolically reconstruct the nation itself, intervening in the process by which public understanding of the war had been shaped
by corporeal and domestic metaphors from the start. In the work of Alcott,
nation and individual are linked by a reversible double metaphor, wherein the
warring body politic symbolically fashions the female psyche, and the female
psyche allegorically reconstructs the fractured nation. This double metaphor
suggests both the centrality of the Civil War to nineteenth-century American
women writers such as Alcott and the importance of these writers to contemporary constructions of the war and its aftermath.

These two narratives are themselves related. Alcott's representations of
women in nineteenth-century American culture show how the female psyche
is excessively disciplined and how that psyche finds a measure of resistance in
the carnivalesque disruptions of Civil War. Her representation of the male-led
nation, by contrast, suggests that the Civil War body politic is too topsy-
turvy, and that it requires for its rehabilitation a full dose of discipline. In this
movement between discipline and carnival, gender is the key explanatory
term, at once cause and effect. For what animates *Hospital Sketches*, and indeed
all of Alcott's writings, is the project of finding female authority in a nation
whose public realms of power—political, military, medical—are definitionally
male. Her fictional solution to this problem is to recombine masculine and
feminine qualities in both male and female bodies, thereby reconfiguring relations of power between the sexes. In *Little Women* and its sequels, Alcott ener-
gizes female discipline with male freedom and tempers male agency with
female restraint. The result is a utopian world, Plumfield, which reinvents the
masculine nation by modeling it upon the disciplined female self.

These fictional strategies have a complex yield, both within Alcott's texts
and in the larger cultural landscape they help to illuminate. In highlighting the

role of female self-discipline, Alcott's work not only expands the political dimensions of women's fiction, but also helps to alter a critical map of nineteenth-century American culture in which masculinity has long held sway. As her private writings show, nineteenth-century disciplinary intimacy was an emphatically gendered mode, and self-denial emerged in particularly concentrated form as a feature of female development. Alcott's writings suggest that if we foreground self-control over self-reliance as the governing trope of nineteenth-century subjectivity, then women turn out to be as central to the former as they are excluded from the latter. When Emersonian self-reliance characterizes the era, women are excluded from its cultural center; but when self-control dominates a nineteenth-century model of the self, women set the terms of selfhood. Alcott's women—from Tribulation Periwinkle and Jo March to the topsy-turvy Louisa of her own letters and journals—are not only quintessentially self-regulating women, but paradigmatic Victorian subjects.

—Elizabeth Young, "A Wound of One's Own: Louisa May Alcott's Civil War Fiction," *American Quarterly* 48, no. 3 (September 1996): 467–69

Bibliography

Flower Fables. 1855.

Hospital Sketches. 1863.

The Rose Family. A Fairy Tale. 1864.

On Picket Duty and Other Tales. 1864.

Moods. 1865.

The Mysterious Key, and What It Opened. 1867.

Morning Glories, and Other Stories. 1868.

Kitty's Class Day. 1868.

Aunt Kipp. 1868.

Psyche's Art. 1868.

Louisa M. Alcott's Proverb Stories. 1868.

Little Women or, Meg, Jo, Beth and Amy. 1868.

Little Women or Meg, Jo, Beth, and Amy. Part Second. 1869.

Hospital Sketches and Camp and Fireside Stories. 1869.

Little Women or, Meg, Jo, Beth, and Amy. Parts I and II. 1869/70.

An Old-Fashioned Girl. 1870.

Little Men: Life at Plumfield with Jo's Boys. 1871.

Aunt Jo's Scrap-Bag. My Boys. 1871.

Aunt Jo's Scrap-Bag. Shawl-Strips. 1872.

Work: A Story of Experience. 1873.

Aunt Jo's Scrap-Bag. Cupid and Chow-Chow. 1874.

Eight Cousins; or The Aunt-Hill. 1875.

Silver Pitchers: and Independence, A Centennial Love Story. 1876.

Rose in Bloom. A Sequel to Eight Cousins. 1876.

A Modern Mephistopheles. 1877.

Aunt Jo's Scrap-Bag. My Girls. 1878.

Under the Lilacs. 1878.

Aunt Jo's Scrap-Bag. Jimmy's Cruise in the Pinafore. 1879.

Jack and Jill. A Village Story. 1880.

Becky's Christmas Dream. 1880.

Our Little Newsboy. 1880.

Moods. A Novel. 1882.

Proverb Stories. 1882. Later retitled *Kitty's Class Day.*

Aunt Jo's Scrap-Bag. An Old-Fashioned Thanksgiving. 1882.

Spinning-Wheel Stories. 1884.

Lulu's Library. Vol. I. A Christmas Dream. 1886.

Jo's Boys and How They Turned Out. A Sequel to Little Men. 1886.

Lulu's Library. Vol. II. The Frost King. 1887.

A Garland for Girls. 1888.

Lulu's Library. Vol. III. Recollections. 1889.

Louisa May Alcott: Her Life, Letters, and Journals. 1889.

Behind a Mask: The Unknown Thrillers of Louisa May Alcott. 1975.

A Modern Mephistopheles and A Whisper in the Dark; Plots and Counterplots: More Unknown Thrillers of Louisa May Alcott. 1976.

A Double Life: Newly Discovered Thrillers of Louisa May Alcott. 1988.

Frances Hodgson Burnett
1849 – 1924

FRANCES HODGSON BURNETT was born November 24, 1849, the third child of Eliza Boond and Edwin Hodgson, a prosperous silversmith and ironmonger in Manchester, Great Britain. Before Frances was four, Edwin died, so Eliza Hodgson moved with her five children to a less expensive neighborhood where she could rely on family help. The arrest of all shipment of cotton from the United States during the Civil War soon precipitated a depression in the Manchester economy. The Hodgsons suffered the effects of this shift, so in 1865 Eliza Hodgson accepted her brother's invitation to join him in Tennessee, where prospects seemed better.

The relief the Hodgson family sought, however, was slow in coming. The family settled in a village outside Knoxville, and, while Frances's older brothers went to work for a jeweler in the city, Frances earned a little money by teaching. The neighbors nearest to the Hodgsons were the Burnett family, whose youngest son, Swan, would later marry Frances. In the meantime, Frances started trying to publish some of the stories she had made up to entertain the younger children and herself. In 1868 she sent off two manuscripts; *Godey's Lady's Book* was accepted, and this was the beginning of Frances's change in fortune. Indeed, the archetypal story of a shift in a good person's fortune, revealing his or her innate nobility, appealed deeply to Frances; she would recast this tale in each of her greatest novels for children. By 1870, when her mother had died and her brothers had proved unable to support the family, Frances took on the task.

Frances's success as a published writer was such that by 1872 she could make a trip to England—a practice she would continue throughout her life. Upon returning, she married Swan Burnett, who was studying to become a doctor. She gave birth to their first son, Lionel, in 1874, and to their second, Vivian, several years later. She continued to be productive, publishing many stories in periodicals, but Swan was not yet successful, and the family suffered financial worries, settling not in Europe, as Frances might have preferred, but in Washington, D.C. Although *That Lass o' Lowries* was published and reviewed favorably in 1877, Frances suffered from depression. She became absorbed in theosophy, spiritualism, and Christian Science and published a number of popular adult novels, which gave her some financial, though not literary, success and allowed her to make frequent trips away from her family and Washington's extremes of climate.

The end of Frances's financial troubles came in 1886, when *Little Lord Fauntleroy*, based partly on her son Vivian, was published and became a best-seller in England and the United States. The additional sales of Fauntleroy paraphernalia and the many adaptations of the book combined to create a sizeable fortune. This wealth freed Frances to make trips to Europe more frequently, not only in the interest of her health, but also in the need to separate herself from her husband. While in England in 1887, she met a number of London's literati and actors, among whom was the young physician and aspiring actor Stephen Townesend, whom Frances later would marry. Her contact with this new set inspired her to take up playwriting; and, though she continued to make yearly trips between the United States, Italy, and England, she was gradually making England her home. Burnett's second immensely successful children's novel, *Sara Crewe* (later revised and retitled as *A Little Princess*), was published in 1888.

In 1890, Lionel was diagnosed with consumption. Terrified that her sensitive son could not bear the knowledge of his impending death, Frances spent the remaining months of his life trying to shield him, touring with him from one spa to another all over Europe, accompanied by Stephen Townesend. Her grief and guilt over Lionel's death in December of 1890 colored all that she wrote thereafter—most notably, *The Secret Garden* (1911). The novel was also inspired by the country house Frances rented in Kent after her divorce from Swan in 1898. Although she married Townesend, the marriage was brief: in 1907 she moved permanently to Long Island.

There Burnett continued to write stories, some of which she contributed to *The Children's Magazine*, for which Vivian was an editor. She published her last well-known children's novel, *The Lost Prince*, in 1915. The final years of her life she spent in her garden, only occasionally writing. She died on October 29, 1924.

Critical Extracts

FRED INGLIS

The Secret Garden ⟨. . .⟩ catches and intensifies in its central image all the energy which the Victorians directed at the home. The garden cherishes those strong, glad, positive qualities which were driven from the man's business world and left to the tender but passive care of the mother. But Frances Hodgson Burnett has a greater ambition for her book. She seeks not only to cherish the values of the garden, but to imagine them restored to the new public life of an ideal social order. 'An ideal social order' is just a slogan, of course, and yet ⟨. . .⟩ implicit in every good story we tell to our children (setting aside the story-tellers who are rancid with cynicism) is the moral: 'Look, this is how the world ought to be. Try to make it like that when you're grown up. We haven't managed it, we older ones; perhaps you will.' Whatever has happened to the idea of beauty and happiness in adult art, our children must keep faith with their radical innocence. That is our own, and the novelist's, act of faith for the future. It expresses our faith that our children will *have* a future.

But *The Secret Garden* ⟨. . .⟩ seeks to imagine the finest life possible and to use it to criticize and improve the life being lived around it at the time. Frances Hodgson Burnett wrote straight from the well-springs of Romanticism; the influence of the Brontës is felt on every page of the novel. She takes the great convictions of the Romantics that the 'nature', not, so to speak, of Edmund but of Edgar and Cordelia, needs only to be given a breathing-space to express itself in pure and excellent lives. But she turns certain expectations back to front in order to celebrate this commonplace. First, sensing (in 1911) the oppression and etiolation of family life, she removes her hero and heroine from their parents' care by making one an orphan, and the other, Colin, abandoned by his widower father in despair. She gives the children an ideal mother in Mrs Sowerby, instinctively sagacious, upright, compassionate; and in a brilliant insight makes Colin into a hypochondriac hysteric, thus providing a real consequence and a metaphor for the distortions wrought by Victorian family life. Frances Hodgson Burnett reinvents a pagan Garden of Eden for the children where culture is detached from labour and returned to creativeness, and which Dickon, the Pan-boy, tends and understands in the name of the mystery which Romanticism sought to keep intact from science. In this Eden, nature dissolves class—gardener and Pan-boy share the broadly human vocation of nursing the invalid boy to straight health, and helping the queer, difficult, yellow-faced little girl back into her natural fresh-cheeked shape.

I have spoken as though the book were a dull diagram from an old myth-kitty. In fact, it is alive and quick, full of warm, sympathetic strength of feeling. The Sowerby family are at times too close to picture-postcard peasants for comfort, but the great joy which anybody must feel as spring swings round again is marvellously recreated for the little girl who has never seen it and has known only the arid limitlessness of the Indian plains:

> Mary was at his bedside again.
> 'Things are crowding up out of the earth,' she ran on in a hurry.
> 'And there are flowers uncurling and buds on everything and the
> green veil has covered nearly all the grey and the birds are in such a

> hurry about their nests for fear they may be too late, that some of
> them are even fighting for places in the secret garden. And the rose-
> bushes look as wick as wick can be, and there are primroses in the
> lanes and woods, and the seeds we planted are up, and Dickon has
> brought the fox and the crow and the squirrels and a new-born lamb.'
> ⟨. . .⟩

The great strength of this book is the life it gives to these moving common-
places. Mrs Burnett starts from the positives of Romanticism and goes on to
turn these positives into solid details—the garden itself combines the ideal
remembered holiday in a golden age, potent to children and adults alike, with
a classless, reasonable, and joyous Utopia of the future.

   —Fred Inglis, *The Promise of Happiness: Value and Meaning in Children's Fiction* (Cambridge:
   Cambridge University Press, 1981), 111–13

PHYLLIS BIXLER KOPPES

The secret garden is the central georgic trope, the unifying symbol of rebirth
in Burnett's novel. A closer examination of her use of the garden demonstrates
how well she was able to meld themes and motifs from fairy tale, exemplum,
and pastoral tradition into a coherent mythic statement. First, the garden is the
place where the children work and observe the magic of change and new life
which the seasons bring in nature and in themselves. But the garden's symbolic
meaning is intensified in a number of other ways. For example, the garden represents that which is dead or apparently dead in the past. The sickness of the
garden clearly suggests the illness and ill-temper which the children put
behind them. The garden is also associated with Colin's dead mother: it was
her favorite place and the occasion of her death; Colin's father, Archibald
Craven, had the garden locked up because it reminds him of the past. But the
garden also represents the redemptive magic which can infuse the present and
future. According to Mother Sowerby, Colin's mother is still watching over
him, especially in the garden. It was Colin's mother who magically initiated
the plan to bring him to the garden by sending the robin to show Mary the
hidden key and door ⟨1911, 273–74⟩. ⟨. . .⟩

   Burnett's garden becomes representative of redemptive forces in the present and future also because she identifies it with the children as well as with
Colin's mother. Like Mary, the garden has suffered neglect because nobody
wanted it—it too is an "orphan." Also, both children are ten years old, and the
garden has been locked ten years, since Colin's mother died shortly after he
was born. The children, like the garden, are gifts which the dead mother has
given to the present and future. Archibald Craven must accept all of these gifts
if he is to live joyfully in the present and future.

Finally, Burnett connects the garden with human rebirth by making it a georgic "landscape of the mind." One character says that being inside the garden is like being in a dream (p. 127). A recurring metaphor for what happens to the garden as well as to the characters is "waking up" or "awakening." Details such as the garden's secrecy and its "wild" rather than "tidy" appearance (p. 134) further suggest the unconscious mind. Unfortunately, Burnett sometimes allows this part of her symbolism to become too conscious, especially in a chapter in which she describes the power of the mind, the dangers of locking it up, and the necessity of replacing the weeds of bad thoughts with the plants of beautiful thoughts (pp. 353–355). More often, however, Burnett allows her fictional garden to speak for itself so that in its apparent artlessness it seems less a "gardener's garden" than "a wilderness of growing things" (p. 208).

Because Burnett has invested the secret garden with so much symbolic meaning, she can use it to make the family reunion at the end of her exemplum about power something more than just a sentimental cliché. The garden gives her not only a setting for this scene but also a vivid image of what her story suggests about rebirth. As Archibald Craven gets near the walled garden in search of his son, he hears "the laughter of young things, the uncontrollable laughter of children who were trying not to be heard but who in a moment or so—as their excitement mounted—would burst forth." And the garden's secret does "burst forth" in the person of a healthy Colin followed by his playmates; through the door now "flung wide open," Colin makes an "unseeing dash" "full speed" toward his father (pp. 369–370). Throughout the novel, Burnett has stressed that the garden can come back to life not because of its secrecy, but because of that which can somehow find a way inside its locked walls: the powers of nature and the helpful work of human beings. Now Burnett uses the walled garden to show that the marvelous change of rebirth is a secret that cannot be kept, that a community of the reborn has the ability—indeed, the inner necessity—to expand and include the world outside.

—Phyllis Bixler Koppes, "Tradition and the Individual Talent of Frances Hodgson Burnett: A Generic Analysis of Little Lord Fauntleroy, A Little Princess, and The Secret Garden," Children's Literature 9 (1981): 203–4

ELIZABETH LENNOX KEYSER

During Colin's lectures ⟨in The Secret Garden⟩, "Mistress Mary" is described as feeling "solemnly enraptured" and listening "entranced" (pp. 241–42). Although we are doubtless meant to be as charmed by Colin as the other characters are and to see in his domination of the little group the promise of his future manhood, we are in fact disenchanted to find Mary little more than a worshipful Huck to the antics of Colin's Tom Sawyer. Yet Mary and Huck are the truly imaginative and convincing children who do not, like Colin and Tom, need the stimulus of books in order to have real adventures and solve real problems. Huck's escape from Pap and his flight down the river with Jim, Mary's discoveries of Colin and the garden, and, above all, her self-discoveries, make Tom's "evasion" and Colin's "magic" anticlimactic. And just as Jim loses stature because of the indignities inflicted on him by Tom, so the roles of Martha and Ben Weatherstaff, so important to Mary's development, diminish. Martha, as remarkable in her way as Dickon and their mother, simply disappears from the final chapters; but since she is the first person for whom Mary feels anything like trust and affection, it is hard to believe that Mary would forget her. Ben, like Mrs. Sowerby a party to the secret in the garden, is treated condescendingly by Colin—and by the author. When Ben makes a joke at the expense of Colin's "scientific discoveries," Colin snubs him, a snub which Ben—acting out of character—takes humbly (p. 245). But at least at the end of Twain's book we are left with its true hero. In *The Secret Garden* Burnett shifts from Mary's to Colin's point of view shortly after the scene in which Mary confronts him with his cowardice and hypochondria. From there on Mary slips into the background until she disappears entirely from the final chapter. The novel ends with the master of Misselthwaite and his son, Master Colin, crossing the lawn before their servants' admiring eyes.

Perhaps the analogy between Mary and Huck can do more than suggest why the final third of *The Secret Garden* is so unsatisfying. Huck is a memorable, even magical, creation not only because he is a very convincing boy (so is Tom, for that matter), but because he is, at the same time, unconventional. He resists being civilized in a way that Tom, for all his infatuation with outlaws, does not. Mary, too, is a more memorable creation than Colin because she is both recognizably human and refreshingly different. ⟨I believe this difference lies⟩ in her freedom from sex-role stereotypes. (This, of course, is why girls have always found Jo March so appealing, especially in Part 1 of *Little Women*.)

From the first Mary is an independent, self-contained, yet self-assertive child. Unlike Colin, she discovers and enters the secret garden all by herself, and she defies adult authority in order to find, befriend, and liberate Colin. Unlike her mother, she is never vain of her appearance; she is proud when she finds herself getting plump, rosy, and glossy-haired, but only because these are signs of her growing strength. When she receives a present from Mr. Craven, she is delighted to find books rather than dolls, and she works and exercises in the garden along with Colin and Dickon. She does not wish to have a nurse or governess but seems to thrive on an active life out-of-doors. Early in the relationship with Colin she is the leader, and even when he is able to run about, it is she who, on a rainy day, suggests that they explore his house. Colin, when we first meet him, is a hysterical invalid, and his father, as the name "Craven" signifies, is a weak and cowardly man, still mourning after ten years his dead wife and, in doing so, neglecting their living son. It is as though Burnett so generously endowed Mary at the expense of Colin and his father that she had to compensate for it by stressing Mary's disagreeable traits and exaggerating Colin's charm. And in the final chapter Colin's ascendancy suggests that if he becomes a "mon," as Ben predicts, then Mary will have to become a woman—quiet, passive, subordinate, and self-effacing. Huck at the end of *Huckleberry Finn* cannot escape civilization; Mary cannot escape the role that civilization has assigned her.

—Elizabeth Lennox Keyser, "'Quite Contrary': Frances Hodgson Burnett's *The Secret Garden*," *Children's Literature* 11 (1983): 8–10

U. C. KNOEPFLMACHER

The expression of anger by female writers has become of increasing interest to literary critics. We are now far more aware of the rich implications—cultural, biographical, artistic—that this subject entails, especially for our understanding of nineteenth-century women writers who faced simultaneously new freedoms and new restraints on their creativity. Still, when, in *The Madwoman in the Attic*, Gilbert and Gubar insist on separating the "decorous and ladylike facade" of Jane Austen or Maria Edgeworth from the more overt (and hence somehow more valued) depiction of aggressive impulses by those who "'fell' into the gothic/Satanic mode" ⟨1979, 101⟩ even the most comprehensive discussion of the subject remains slightly distorted.

The decorous and lady-like women who dominated the field of Victorian children's literature ⟨. . .⟩ were hardly gothic Satanists. As gentlewomen writing for middle-class juveniles, they, even more than an Austen or an Edgeworth, needed to maintain restraint and decorum. Paradoxically, the mode of fantasy also freed the same aggressive impulses that their fictions ostensibly tried to domesticate. Especially after 1865, with the playful anarchy of Lewis Carroll's *Alice's Adventures in Wonderland* before them as a foil as well as a model, women writers began to portray little girls who were allowed to express hostility without the curbs on female rebelliousness that had been placed earlier, in children's literature as well as in adult fiction. The fairy-tale realms depicted in ⟨. . .⟩ Burnett's *The Secret Garden* (1911), and in Burnett's earlier, less well-known, but delightful fantasy, "Behind the White Brick" (1874), thus serve a double purpose. The surreal setting is enlisted, on the one hand, to mute the hostile behavior of girls on the road to socialization and maturity; on the other hand, however, it permits their creators to turn their own satiric

energies against the deficiencies or complacencies of a society that frowned
on expressions of female anger.

    —U. C. Knoepflmacher, "Little Girls without Their Curls: Female Aggression in Victorian
    Children's Literature," *Children's Literature* 11 (1983): 14–15

PHYLLIS BIXLER

According to ⟨Elizabeth Lennox⟩ Keyser, *The Secret Garden* reflects Burnett's
own "ambivalence about sex roles" ⟨"'Quite Contrary,'" 1983, 12⟩; like women
writers such as the Brontës, George Eliot, Louisa May Alcott, and Mrs.
Humphry Ward, Burnett was uncomfortable with the self-assertion of her
writing career and chastened herself by chastening "her self-assertive female
characters" (10). Even more, by ending her book with a description of "the
master of Misselthwaite with his son, Master Colin," Burnett "seems to be
affirming male supremacy" and suggesting "a defense of patriarchal authority".

    Keyser has described a response to characterization in *The Secret Garden*
which, I have discovered, other readers share; and the gender-role conflicts
Keyser identifies as the source of Burnett's portrayal of Mary and Colin are
easily documented by looking at Burnett's other fiction as well as her life
⟨. . . .⟩ However, if one is to explain why *The Secret Garden* continues to fascinate readers and elicit critical explication, if one is to describe the deeply
female voice many readers hear in the text, one must move beyond "Images of
Women" criticism, as Toril Moi has observed. One must look not only at the
book's portrayal of individual characters but also at its configurations of characters and webs of symbolic imagery. ⟨. . .⟩

    ⟨In chapter 25,⟩ Mary makes a discovery that begins to reveal one of the
most important secrets in Burnett's masterpiece, a secret fully revealed in the
next two, concluding chapters: The "Magic" power at work in both house and
garden is Colin's dead mother. Mary notices in Colin's room that the curtain
over the portrait of his mother is now open; this curtain provides yet another
link to the garden, since it has been earlier described as "rose-colored" (132;
ch. 13), while the ivy covering the garden door has, in turn, frequently been
called a "curtain." Colin has shown Mary the portrait the night Mary found
him; he had told Mary that he kept the curtain closed because he hated his
mother for dying, because she smiled too much when he was miserable, and
because "she is mine and I don't want everyone to see her" (133; ch. 13). Now
that Colin is healthy and happy, however, it does not make him "angry any
more to see her laughing" (267; ch. 25). Apparently, his garden experience of
a power larger than his own has made him more willing to share. Finally, perhaps Colin is no longer driven by anger at her death because he senses that
she is still somehow alive in his room. He tells Mary how, two nights ago, the

moonlight had come in the window and made him pull the curtain's cord; it "felt as if the Magic was filling the room," he says, and he associates this Magic with his mother by adding that she "must have been a sort of Magic person." Mary's reply suggests that Colin's mother is alive in his room also in that her own soul at last shines through his face. Viewing the mother's laughing portrait, Mary tells Colin, "You are so like her now . . . that sometimes I think perhaps you are her ghost made into a boy." "If I were her ghost—my father would be fond of me," Colin observes (267; ch. 25).

Colin's observation points toward the final reunion of son and father in the garden, where his mother's Magic, now acknowledged in the manor, had first begun its work. The garden and garden community members have for some time been her living hands. It was because her orders to tend the garden preceded Archibald Craven's orders to have it locked that Ben Weatherstaff continued to prune the garden after she died (229; ch. 22). Similarly, it was Colin's mother who told Mary and Dickon to bring Colin to the garden, according to Mother Sowerby (217; ch. 21). Now, in a chapter titled "It's Mother," Colin's mother is given not only hands but voice by Mother Sowerby, who finally visits the children in the garden. ⟨. . .⟩

The final chapter, "In the Garden," describes Archibald Craven's return as a reprise of the earlier, more fully dramatized experiences of Colin and Mary. Without his knowing it, the garden had been at work within the father while it had worked within the son; he began to feel its "awakening" power while gazing at a forget-me-not on the same day Colin first entered the garden and declared, "I am going to live forever" (285–86; ch. 27). ⟨. . .⟩

Some of the deepest satisfactions Burnett's masterpiece affords can be explained if one perceives that the reunion that occurs when Craven reaches the garden is not just paternal but maternal. The book's configuration of characters and webs of imagery ⟨suggest⟩ that it is the soul of Colin's mother that has been transforming the garden and the house with nurturant power; now, ⟨in the final chapter,⟩ language of birth suggests that garden, and perhaps also house, are her maternal body. As the "rose-colored" curtain has recently been opened to reveal her portrait in the house, the door to the garden is now "flung wide open, the sheet of ivy swinging back"; "the uncontrollable moment" has arrived; with "quick strong young breathing," "a boy burst[s] through it at full speed and, without seeing," dashes "almost into his [father's] arms" (294; ch. 27).

By perceiving house and garden as images of not only the transforming power of nature and a mothering community but also of a mother's nurturant body, one uncovers a secret plot within *The Secret Garden* that breaks through its patriarchal sociology. Keyser points to this plot when she includes the following in her description of what she remembered of the book before rereading it to write her article: "I remembered Mary exploring the winding paths and gardens within gardens, and indoors the winding corridors with their many locked rooms" (2). At some level, the reader, along with Mary, Colin, and finally even Archibald Craven, reenacts the usually repressed desire to explore the secret mysteries of the mother's body as well as her soul. It may be this plot which above all identifies *The Secret Garden* as what the French feminists call *écriture féminine*.

> —Phyllis Bixler, "Gardens, Houses, and Nurturant Power in *The Secret Garden*," in *Romanticism and Children's Literature in Nineteenth-Century England*, ed. James Holt McGavran, Jr. (Athens: The University of Georgia Press, 1991), 208–9, 220–23

JERRY PHILLIPS

In the bestowal of an orphan's fate to Mary Lennox, *The Secret Garden* pays homage to the fundamental concern of much nineteenth-century fiction: the displaced person within. Yet, in another way, the text asks many difficult questions about a figure who might well be the index of our troubled modernity: the migrant, the refugee, the exile—the displaced person without. In this century of great travels, the fortune of nations—the rise and fall of hegemonic economic powers—has led to an unprecedented cultural mix of ethnicities and races and cultures and religions throughout every continent of the globe. Thus, the displaced person without, the stranger in search of a home, is an awesome reflection on problems of social identity in the contemporary world. A few of these problems can be reached through the principle of the allegorical inference in *The Secret Garden*.

Mary Lennox is an English child born, and raised to nine years old, far from England's shores. Her predicament is testing, beguiling; she is a foreigner who leaves home, which is not home, and returns, in a manner of speaking, to a native land she has never actually known. Little wonder, then, that the confusion of cultural values, which is the ideology of British colonialism, radically disorients Mary's sense of place in the world. The children of the English clergyman taunt Mary because she has to ask, "where is home?" They know that "home" is "England, of course" (8–9). Mary's failure to recognize her true point of origin eloquently conveys the double bind she is caught in: England is the home of meaning in her world, and yet the notion of "home" seems meaningless. ⟨. . .⟩ For the great ideological issue inherent in the literary discourse of the child orphan is, of course, the crucial and exorbitant question of assimilation—how is it to be done and is it desirable? *The Secret Garden* is a relentlessly complex meditation on just this issue.

At the center of *The Secret Garden* is an anatomy of social hierarchy, a laboratory of class relations: the great country house. The trope of the great house is a mainstay of Victorian fiction, particularly the gothic romance with its heightened interest in declining aristocracy. The gothic romance enabled prose fiction to delve into sexual, religious, psychological, and political controversies—"deep" troublesome areas that social realism, for one reason or another, would often balk at or avoid. In the initial characterization of Misselthwaite Manor, the great house in which Mary is to reside, the action of the text is placed on the edges of a gothic stage. En route to England, Mary learns that her uncle, Mr. Archibald Craven, "lives in a great, big, desolate old house in the country and no one goes near him. . . . He's a hunchback and he's horrid" (9). On Mary's arrival in the mother country, Mrs. Medlock, the housekeeper, gives her a description of the house itself: "a grand big old place in a gloomy sort of way. . . . The house is six hundred years old, and it's on the edge of the moor, and there's near to a hundred rooms in it, though most of them's shut up and locked. And there's pictures and fine old furniture and things that's been there for ages" (13). Although Mr. Craven is a victim of rumor and the target of much exaggeration, the basic tenet of the gossip is valid: the master of Misselthwaite Manor has ceased intercourse with the world. Since the accidental death of his young, attractive wife, Archibald Craven has renounced all but the most basic of familial and social duties; he lives only for the past. He is a man of lost ambitions who is locked inside his own secret world of grief. Mr. Craven may not be a "hunchback"; but, in Burnett's eyes, he is just as surely incapacitated by his refusal to let the past die. Burnett implies that a "gloomy" old house, strongly suggestive of the dead weight of history, is the natural objective correlative for Mr. Craven's damaged psyche. For, no less than a lonely heart, the manor is packed with forgotten treasures that are largely inaccessible. Thus, I propose that *The Secret Garden* uses a gothic register but only to subvert the gothic's usual political calling. Gothic romances are often heroic obituaries for the nineteenth-century aristocracy; in contrast, Burnett sets herself to the task of rescuing the great country house and the decrepit members of the elite class who own such properties. Her narrative structure performs this "socially symbolic act" by exploring the social value of a returning colonial elite, symbolically figured in Mary.

 —Jerry Phillips, "The Mem Sahib, the Worthy, the Rajah and His Minions: Some Reflections on the Class Politics of *The Secret Garden*," *The Lion and the Unicorn* 17 (1993): 171–73

ADRIAN GUNTHER

In my experience, children do *not* see Mary as displaced by Colin, and, until it is suggested to them, nor do most adult readers. My sense is that these readers believe she is *not* displaced but in fact remains the key figure throughout. In quest terms, she advances so much further along the path of self-discovery than does Colin that we cannot help but experience her as more important.

Add to this the fact that what Colin does achieve is predominantly a product of Mary's wisdom and effort rather than his own, and we begin to have a true picture of the impact of this book. In terms of the quest archetype, a key state in the journey is transcendence of ego, the kind of transcendence embodied in such an archetypal symbol as the phoenix where each new stage necessarily involves a burning down and shedding of the old self. Mary achieves this. Her behavior from very early on is characterized by a profound insight into others, an insight that in typical phoenix terms is a product of her own suffering and in fact would not have been possible without it, something Burnett stresses repeatedly. Thus her behavior in the last section of the book is characterized by an unselfish compassion and a total absence of egocentric concern. Colin, however, in true masculine mode, remains intrinsically self-centered up to the very last line. His development along the path of the quest is considerable, but he remains "blocked" in the real sense of the word, in that he cannot transcend the egocentricity that has characterized him from his very first appearance.

Some detailed analysis of the text will most certainly help here. First, although critics have variously seen Colin's predominance as over the latter half or the final third of the book, any examination in paginal terms indicates that Mary is present on at least an equal basis with Colin right up until the final scene. She remains the initiator in their relationship: it is her "inspiration" that provokes the opening up of the great house to the fun and laughter of their games, thus taking their healing energy into its most obscure corners. An examination reveals that in almost every case in this last section of the book, where Colin is referred to, she is also. The reader's attention is drawn to Mary's newfound beauty first by Mrs. Medlock ("She's begun to be downright pretty" [221]), and second in the penultimate chapter by Susan Sowerby's observations: "Tha'lt be like a blush-rose when tha grows up, my little lass, bless thee" (234). It should be noted that Susan Sowerby's comments and actions by this stage in the text carry great weight. When late in the narrative she says of Mary: "It was a good thing that little lass came to the Manor. It's been th' makin' o' her an' th' savin' o' him" (211), we take such a comment seriously, reasserting as it does Mary's predominance in the pattern of things. That Susan's final task is to call the lost father figure back into the garden, thus including him also in its healing power, in no way detracts from this impression. In the final scene, it is true, the males, both those egocentric and craven Cravens, do return to the great house to the "oohs" and "ahs" of the menials pulling forelocks, but surely the significant point here is that this leaves Mary in the domain that really holds the power and on which all other domains, including the patriarchal great house, depend, *the garden*. That these closing lines shift to the house is not sufficient, given the previous weighting against it, suddenly to empower this establishment and all it stands for. What is being asserted here, in the restoration to life of the great house, is actually the power of the garden—which can *even* transform this dead and imprisoning labyrinth, and which can *even* restore the self-pitying, self-absorbed males who belong to it. And of course at the heart of the garden and all it stands for is Mary.

—Adrian Gunther, "*The Secret Garden* Revisited," *Children's Literature in Education* 25, no. 3 (1994): 160–61

Bibliography

Dolly: A Love Story. 1877.
Pretty Polly Pemberton: A Love Story. 1877.
Surly Tim and Other Stories. 1877.
That Lass o' Lowries. 1877.
Theo: A Love Story. 1877.
A Quiet Life, and The Tide on the Moaning Bar. 1878.
Earlier Stories. 1878.
Earlier Stories (second series). 1878.
Kathleen: A Love Story. 1878.
Miss Crespigny: A Love Story. 1878.
Our Neighbor Opposite. 1878.
That Lass o' Lowries (adaptation with Julian Magnus). 1878.
Haworth's. 1879.
Jarl's Daughter and Other Stories. 1879.
Natalie and Other Stories. 1879.
Louisiana. 1880.
A Fair Barbarian. 1881.
Esmeralda (with William Gillette). 1881. Produced as *Young Folks' Ways*, 1883.
Through One Administration. 1883.
Little Lord Fauntleroy. 1886.
A Woman's Will; or, Miss Defarge. 1887.
The Fortunes of Philippa Fairfax. 1888.
The Real Little Lord Fauntleroy. 1888.
Sara Crewe: or, What Happened at Miss Minchin's. 1888.
Editha's Burglar. 1888.
Phyllis (adaptation of *The Fortunes of Philippa Fairfax*). 1889.
The Pretty Sister of José. 1889.

Editha's Burglar (adaptation with Stephen Townesend). 1890.
   Produced as *Nixie*, 1890.
Little Saint Elizabeth and Other Stories. 1890.
The Showman's Daughter (with Stephen Townesend). 1891.
Children I Have Known. 1892. Reprinted as *Giovanni and the Other: Children
   Who Have Made Stories*, 1892.
The Drury Lane Boys' Club. 1892.
The One I Knew Best of All: A Memory of the Mind of a Child. 1893.
The Captain's Youngest and Other Stories. 1894. Reprinted as *Piccino and
   Other Child Stories*, 1894.
The Little Pilgrims' Progress: A Story of the City Beautiful. 1895.
A Lady of Quality . . . 1896.
A Lady of Quality (adaptation with Stephen Townesend). 1897.
His Grace of Osmonde . . . 1897.
The First Gentleman of Europe (with Constance Fletcher). 1897.
In Connection with the De Willoughby Claim. 1899.
The Making of a Marchioness. 1901.
A Little Princess (adaption of *Sara Crewe*). Produced as *A Little Unfairy Princess*,
   1902; as *A Little Princess*, 1903.
The Methods of Lady Walderhurst. 1901.
That Man and I (adaptation of *In Connection with the De Willoughby Claim*). 1903.
The Pretty Sister of José (adaptation). 1903.
In the Closed Room. 1904.
A Little Princess, Being the Whole Story of Sara Crewe Now Told for the First Time. 1905.
The Dawn of a Tomorrow. 1906.
Racketty Packetty House. 1905.
The Troubles of Queen Silver-Bell. 1906.
The Cozy Lion, as Told by Queen Crosspatch. 1907.
The Shuttle. 1908.
The Spring Cleaning, as Told by Queen Crosspatch. 1908.
The Dawn of a Tomorrow (adaptation). 1909.
The Good Wolf. 1909.
Barty Crusoe and His Man Saturday. 1909.
The Land of the Blue Flower. 1909.
The Secret Garden. 1911.
My Robin. 1912.
Racketty Packetty House (adaptation). 1912.
T. Tembarom. 1913.
The Lost Prince. 1915.

The Way to the House of Santa Claus: A Christmas Story. 1916.
Little Hunchback Zia. 1916.
The White People. 1917.
The Head of the House of Coombe. 1922.
Robin. 1922.
In the Garden. 1925.

Louise Fitzhugh
1928 – 1974

LOUISE FITZHUGH was born on October, 5, 1928, into a marriage that lasted only a year. Her father, Millsaps Fitzhugh, came from a wealthy old southern family and, like his own father, went into law, becoming the U.S. district attorney in Memphis. Just after graduating from law school, he met and married Louise Perkins, a tapdancer aspiring to the New York City stage. The couple's divorce in 1930 led to a vicious fight over custody for Louise, a fight that Louise's father won. Shortly thereafter, her mother disappeared from Memphis, and Louise was later told that she was dead.

Louise grew up in her paternal grandparents' house, a huge mansion called Samarkand not far from and forever associated in her mind with the immense "Pink Palace" belonging to the founder of the Piggly-Wiggly food chain; in 1937, Samarkand burned down to the ground. Louise's closest bonds in childhood were with her black nurse and the black chauffeur. It was not until her mother, against the Fitzhughs' wishes, suddenly started to appear in places where Louise would be alone, that Louise learned that she was still alive. An arrangement for these visits must have been negotiated, for Louise began to see her mother periodically and would do so the rest of her childhood.

In 1932, Louise's father remarried, and she went to live with them until she left the South for good. She was sent to Miss Hutchinson's School for young ladies, which seems to have involved her in modeling clothes at the country club and other such society affairs. In defiance of her family's expectations and apparently to avoid becoming a debutante, Louise suddenly married a young man—although her parents quickly had the marriage annulled. In marrying, Louise may have been defending herself against the "scandalous" suggestion that she had been discovered with another girl from her school. Her family acted quickly to cover up the whole affair and had the other girl sent away from Miss Hutchinson's School.

Louise transferred three times before she decided to stay at Bard College in New York, where she studied literature and child psychology. A year into school, her paternal grandmother, the only relative to whom she felt at all close, died. Just two months short of graduating in 1951, Louise left college and moved to Greenwich Village to begin her life as a painter. It was here that Louise found a community open and welcoming of her lesbianism and her artistic talent. She studied painting for a time at Cooper Union and also entered into her 11-year commitment to her psychoanalysis.

Fitzhugh continued to develop her different talents, studying painting for a year in Italy, traveling in France, and showing her paintings in New York. Her first published effort was *Suzuki Beane* (1961), a book she illustrated in collaboration with Sandra Scoppettone, who wrote the text. But Fitzhugh's novel *Harriet the Spy*, which she both wrote and illustrated, distinguished her as a new and original voice in children's literature in 1964. The alienated autonomy of vision shared by her child protagonists suggests the kind of perspective Louise developed during her own difficult childhood. Her treatment of complicated material—described by critics as both satirical and realistic—would anger many critics but won her devoted readers.

A year after the publication of *Harriet the Spy*, Fitzhugh's father died, leaving her most of his estate. With this money, Louise could live comfortably for the rest of her life. She continued to write, however; her second novel, *The Long Secret* (1965), was a sequel to *Harriet*—as was her later *Sport* (1979)—but presented a shift in perspective. It was followed by another collaboration with Scoppettone, *Bang, Bang, You're Dead!* (1969), and by *Nobody's Family Is Going to Change* (1974).

Fitzhugh moved to Connecticut in 1969, where she continued to draw and write until her sudden death of an aneurysm on November 19, 1974.

Critical Extracts

SHEILA EGOFF

⟨Not⟩ all current writers contribute to the slice-of-life genre; there are a few who do not slavishly pursue verisimilitude but prefer to write on a more symbolic level. Significantly it is such authors—notably Louise Fitzhugh in *Harriet the Spy* (1964) and *The Long Secret* (1965) and Julia Cunningham in *Dorp Dead* (1965)—who are the most controversial. ⟨. . .⟩

In *Harriet the Spy* we gather first of all that Harriet's parents have not found the time to take a large part in her upbringing and have entrusted most of it to her nurse, Ole Golly. We are given a fairly detailed portrait of Ole Golly, though not of the other adults in the book. She comes from an impoverished and uninspiring background (the book begins with a visit to her grotesque, simple-minded mother), but she compensates for the dreariness of her youth with enormous intellectual pretensions. She has a fondness for inserting into a conversation dimly understood quotations from famous writers, no matter how irrelevant they may be. Undoubtedly it is Ole Golly who influenced Harriet to keep a diary as a prelude to her future writing career. Harriet's character is really quite consistent with the description we are given of Ole Golly's part in her upbringing. In a permissive atmosphere in which her ideas are taken seriously by her nurse, she has come to believe that all experience must be explored; at the same time she has been taught that she can and indeed must be objective in her observation of this experience:

> Miss Whitehead's feet look larger this year. Miss Whitehead has buck teeth, thin hair, feet like skis, and a very long hanging stomach. Ole Golly says description is good for the soul, and clears the brain like a laxative.

Harriet gets carried away and deliberately spies upon people to get the material she so accurately records in her diary. She comes to realize that 'some people are one way and some people are another and that's that.' In the book's denouement, which has horrified many adults, Harriet learns about human relations that 'Ole Golly was right. Sometimes you have to lie.'

The people she spies upon are her neighbours, her teachers, her parents, and her friends. None of them is 'real' in the sense that we could imagine such people existing in our own world. They are all exaggerations, even caricatures, yet they are real as symbols of the follies of contemporary society. Harriet's parents are presented far more realistically than most parents in modern children's books. At the beginning they ignore their parental responsibilities, but they do come to Harriet's aid when she is in trouble and so do her teachers. This runs counter to the current American trend of making adults ineffectual, which implies that children are in opposition to adults. ⟨. . .⟩

Opinions of *Harriet the Spy* have been sharply divided. It has been lauded for its 'realism' and condemned as being 'warped and unpleasant'. Both views misinterpret Miss Fitzhugh's approach to life, which, if it is to be pigeon-holed, should be described as 'naturalistic' rather than 'realistic'. She introduces into children's literature a mode of fictional writing that adults have learned how to deal with adequately in their own literature but that they do not quite know what to make of in a children's book. For example, an adult would not read Evelyn Waugh's *The Loved One* and think it was an accurate representation of American funerary practices, yet through its distortions the book tells us a great deal about life in southern California and indeed about contemporary life in general. But when Louise Fitzhugh in somewhat the same way brings a child to terms with adult life and in the process reveals its unpleasantness and dishonesty, she is criticized for her lack of fidelity. What is hampering judgement here is simply an old tradition of children's literature that life is fundamentally good and beautiful and that all the virtues will have their own reward.

—Sheila Egoff, "Precepts and Pleasures: Changing Emphases in the Writing and Criticism of Children's Literature," in *Only Connect: Readings from Children's Literature*, ed. Sheila Egoff, T. G. Stubbs, and L. F. Ashley (Toronto: Oxford University Press, 1969), 438–40

VIRGINIA WOLF

Harriet the Spy, by Louise Fitzhugh, illustrates beyond question that good realistic fiction is a viable possibility. The book operates on two levels. On the one hand, Harriet acts in a way that a child can immediately understand, and everything she does will fascinate him. With her spy route and continual note-taking, she is unique enough to provide adventure, and yet she is ordinary enough in her everyday habits to seem familiar. On another level, the reader undergoes the rare experience of being bombarded by a wealth of illuminating details. These continually expand and enrich the reader's perceptions and immerse him in the emotional context of Harriet's world.

As her notebook reveals, Harriet is above all else a completely and utterly honest child. Everything which attracts her attention, she evaluates and records. 〈. . .〉 What she thinks, she writes down without a thought about what anyone else would say. Anything that is not readily understandable is followed by appropriate notations or questions like: "Think about this. This might be important." or "What makes people poor or rich?" The notebooks are therefore an invaluable device for both revealing her actual reactions and portraying how her mind works. 〈. . .〉

In addition to the notebook and the spy route, which are so peculiarly appropriate to the characterization of Harriet, the author utilizes details about Harriet's family and home life. Harriet's obsession with order and routine reveals her need to establish that stability which her parents are not providing. The clean room with everything in its place, the carefully scheduled day, and the insistence upon a tomato sandwich for lunch are for this reason very relevant details.

After the departure of her lifelong nurse, Harriet has no one who can explain why her friends reject her after finding and reading her notebook. 〈. . .〉

All of this generates our sympathy for Harriet, but her problems and confusion never become overbearing. Mrs. Fitzhugh deftly maintains the novel's comic tone by keeping us within Harriet's perspective. Harriet always feels she is "ready for them," and the reader shares her optimism or innocence as she attempts to cope with each new discomfort. Never doubting that Harriet will triumph in the end, we can relax and enjoy the hilarity of her explosive reactions.

Harriet the Spy ⟨. . .⟩ portrays the whole child. There is ⟨. . .⟩ that unique
fusion, or double exposure, which creates the illusion of reality and affords us
the opportunity of assuming identity and experiencing a fictive world.
Without violating Harriet's perspective, Mrs. Fitzhugh provides all that we
need to know in order to understand and be convinced by her heroine's behavior. We participate because of the figure in the foreground (Harriet as she sees
herself and her world), but we understand because of all those details which
elicit the image in the background.

— Virginia Wolf, "The Root and Measure of Realism," *Wilson* Library *Bulletin* 44, no. 4
(December 1969): 414–15

VIRGINIA WOLF

Harriet the Spy is at its deepest level a celebration and an exploration of the
nature and the development of love. Ole Golly's quotation from Dostoievsky
is central to our understanding. In its portrait of Harriet, the novel allows us
to see that self-love is rooted in self-discovery; love of others, in self-love; and
knowledge of others, in love. Harriet's quest for self-discovery is the first stage.
This is transcended and the second stage begun when she fully comprehends
her need for understanding from others. Next comes her discovery that she
can maintain her own sense of the truth (her integrity) without being insensitive to others. This allows her to give, and having given, she moves on to the
final stage, a growing awareness of others. By the end of the novel, Harriet has
learned "THAT SOME PEOPLE ARE ONE WAY AND SOME PEOPLE ARE
ANOTHER AND THAT'S THAT" (p. 277). Less articulate than Dostoievsky,
this is nevertheless Harriet's restatement of the heart of Ole Golly's quotation:
"if you love everything, you will perceive the divine mystery in things" (p. 24).

We have not exhausted the novel's implications. These are rich and multiple. But this discussion suggests that the novel is more than the overt, simplistic social criticism of so many of the recent realistic novels for children.
Harriet the Spy is not a message book. It is first and foremost an experience. On
the primary level, we are immersed in Harriet and, by means of her, her world.
The fusion of Harriet and her world is the source of the novel's richness. This
structural device sets up a pattern of comparison and contrast which, on the
symbolic level, achieves theme. In T. S. Eliot's words, we are given an "objective correlative," in Ezra Pound's, a "vortex." We are confronted with vivid,
unforgettable images: that of a child looking into a series of rooms and those
of a series of rooms in which people play out their private dramas, virtually
unaware of the rest of the world. With the spy route superimposed on the spy,
we get a dialectic radiating throughout the novel with one image reflecting,
qualifying or opposing another.

Obviously, I believe that *Harriet the Spy* will survive. Harriet and her adventures are memorable. Like all good literature, the novel transcends the particular, evoking the inner spirit of a character and her world to explore eternal questions about love and happiness and truth. Significantly, the novel is not a fantasy like so many children's masterpieces. Perhaps this is revelatory of the mid-twentieth century. In any case, it is fortuitous for children's literature. Louise Fitzhugh has proven that contemporary, realistic fiction of psychological and philosophical depth is a viable possibility for children. *Harriet the Spy* is a milestone and a masterpiece of children's literature—perhaps *the* masterpiece of the mid-twentieth century.

—Virginia Wolf, "*Harriet the Spy*: Milestone, Masterpiece?" in *Reflections on Literature for Children*, ed. Francelia Butler and Richard Rotert (Hamden, CT: Library Professional Publications, 1984), 273–74

HAMIDA BOSMAJIAN

⟨Harriet⟩ takes in the world as if she were God's spy. Ole Golly reminds her of the godlikeness of spying when she encourages her to study the Greeks and Romans because "those gods spied on everybody all the time" (38).

The people on Harriet's spy route are literally framed by the apertures through which she observes them and thus become concentrated sets for problems that reflect her life. Subconsciously she *chooses* her objects of espionage. The Dei Santi grocery-story-family reveals to her that a large family does not necessarily share intimacy. They are stereotypical, and unreflective as they collide and reconcile, yet remain in their isolated eccentric patterns. She decides that she would not want to be part of them. The person she identifies with most is Harrison Withers, a recluse whose name aligns him with Harriet. He lives with twenty-six cats and makes wicker cages, but has no human contact. Harriet would "wither" if she were to imitate him. During the time that Harriet mourns her loss of Ole Golly, Withers is forced to relinquish his cats and goes into a deep depression, but, as Harriet is beginning to recover herself, he smuggles a tiny arrogant kitten into his apartment and once more absorbs himself blissfully in making his cages and caring for his pet. While Harriet likes him because he loves what he does (72), he is also an objective correlative for her tensions between freedom (cats) and confinement through routines (cages).

Another object lesson is the rich lady Amanda Plumber who, like Harriet, takes to her bed in order to escape the problems of being alive, but finally decides to engage herself in a whirl of social activities. The most negative image on her route is the Robinsons, a childless couple in love with things that they show off to their acquaintances. This solipsistic twosome purchase a large statue of a wooden baby, as an image of perfection of the child that is seen but never heard. Pathetic as they are, the Robinsons conclude that it is just perfect that they do not have any children (68).

Harriet refuses to be a wooden baby in her parents' life, though the reader gets the impression that they would not have been displeased had she been a pleasant object to be paraded on appropriate occasions. Both parents are very extroverted and image-conscious—he is in show business, she is his ornament for their many social occasions. In their house Harriet is less the secretive spy than the braggart tomboy and, in spite of her neat and tidy little room and her routines, she becomes the upsetter of their order as she forces them to become more involved parents. She is, however, unable to change them in any fundamental way, for, as is typical of this milieu, the parents do not become engaged in a growth process as parents but enlist "support systems"—Ole Golly, the psychiatrist, the school official—all of which are in a monetary relation to them.

At first glance Ole Golly seems the ideal nanny. Harriet is surprised when she learns that her name is Catherine, a formal name, whereas "Ole Golly" has comforting, humorous and nonsensical connotations. Yet Ole Golly is neither old nor is she a kind of "gee golly" person in her speech or actions. Her name signals her all-encompassing importance in Harriet's life, for "golly" is a diminutive substitute for God in oaths and exclamations. Though she always remains in the realistic mode, she has some of the mythic dimensions that adhere to the great nanny figures in children's literature, such as Mary Poppins. There are intimations of the "great mother" as she brings nurturance and order into Harriet's life, but she is also deeply troubled in her relation to her mentally deficient mother, as Harriet herself notices (19–20). That relation exemplifies the severe realization that we are often powerless to change people who are intimately related to us, and that the only things we can do then is change the direction of our lives.

—Hamida Bosmajian, "Louise Fitzhugh's *Harriet the Spy:* Nonsense and Sense," in *Touchstones: Reflections on the Best in Children's Literature*, vol. 1 (West Lafayette, IN: Children's Literature Association Publishers, 1985), 77–79

PERRY NODELMAN

In *The Long Secret*, Harriet fluctuates between being an agitating caricature—the person seen by others—and an interesting, sensitive person, seen by herself.

That fluctuation is central both to the shape and the meaning of *The Long Secret*. Harriet always thinks she understands everybody; in this second novel Fitzhugh continually points out that all she understands of others is all anybody ever understands—what we make of them. Not only do we find out that

Beth Ellen's idea of Harriet is different from Harriet's; we also learn that Beth Ellen's idea of Beth Ellen is different from Harriet's. Harriet's version of Beth Ellen as reported in *Harriet the Spy* turns out to have been based on incomplete information; here, and again in the later novel *Sport*, Fitzhugh returns to characters from an earlier novel we thought we knew completely, and reveals unexpected facets both of their lives and of their personalities.

Fitzhugh's insistence that we have the humility to acknowledge the limitations of our ideas about other people is expressed constantly in *The Long Secret*; characters repeatedly thwart our expectations of them.

The "long secret" of the title is that it is Beth Ellen, the mouse, who has been distributing anonymous notes to the townspeople. Her grandmother explains why: "shy people are angry people. . . . You're a very angry little girl." Beth Ellen's notes use familiar quotations, often biblical, to describe the "secret" desires that control other people. Since the notes create immediate recognition in everyone but the person who receives them, they comment on our willingness to ignore our failings. Ironically, a secret Beth Ellen, hidden even from Beth Ellen, has been telling other people where *they* live. Unlike Harriet's self-regarding notes to herself in her notebook, Beth Ellen's notes are an attempt to communicate.

Fitzhugh gets away with something tricky here; the person from whose point of view much of the story is told turns out to be the perpetrator of the mystery of the notes at the heart of the plot. She gets away with that because the double point of view allows her to switch off to Harriet whenever Beth Ellen might be thinking of leaving notes. In any case, the point of the book is that there is much Beth Ellen will not admit, even to herself. For a whole day, she is sick and lazy, and we learn all her thoughts but the important one—that, as she eventually tells Harriet, she is menstruating for the first time. Apparently she has been willing to think about that no more than she thinks about her secret note-leaving.

Symbolically speaking, the secrets we keep longest are the things at the heart of our being—what we really are. Beth Ellen's mother thinks such secrets are dangerous: "It's very hard to tell one fanatic from another these days. They look like ordinary people until you get to know them, and then you find out they're obsessed." But the real secret, which everyone else shares and Beth Ellen eventually learns, is that no one is "ordinary," and everyone is "obsessed." Beth Ellen says that more positively than her mother: "Everyone I know has something like this. Something to love. I need something to love." Fanaticism is merely knowing who you are, being positive about it, and being humble enough to accept the fanaticism of others. By the end of the novel, Beth Ellen is able to admit that, through her secret notes, she was always just as fanatical and just as definite as everybody else. She arrives at exactly the same balanced place Harriet reached, but from an opposite direction; Beth Ellen learns self-love, and Harriet charity.

The Long Secret is a subtle and energetic novel, as good in its own way as *Harriet the Spy*. Unfortunately, Fitzhugh's undeniably brave discussion of menstruation has attracted most of the attention that *The Long Secret* has received. But the interest excited by those few pages is not surprising; commenting on her first reading of the manuscript of this novel, Ursula Nordstrom says, "When I came to the page where the onset of Beth Ellen's first menstrual period occurred, and it was written so beautifully, to such perfection, I scrawled in the margin, 'Thank you, Louise Fitzhugh.' It was the first mention in junior books of this tremendous event in a girl's life."

—Perry Nodelman, "Louise Fitzhugh," in *American Writers for Children Since 1960: Fiction*, ed. Glenn E. Estes (Detroit: Gale Research Company, 1986), 138–39

J. D. STAHL

The satiric humor in Louise Fitzhugh's *Harriet the Spy* is of a much more blunt and sometimes brutal sort ⟨than is that in the works of Mark Twain and E. B. White⟩. Essentially, the satiric perspective of Fitzhugh's novel is a caustic attack on adults. Like Twain and White, Fitzhugh approximates the perspective of a child—in this case, a sophisticated, complex, precocious child—but her satire is much more radically grounded in the assumption of the child's interests. Harriet appropriates adult purposes through her use of grown-ups' forms of literacy, such as the diary, the gossip column, and the editorial. Adults are seen foreshortened, authentically distorted by the child's legitimate but limited point of view. Mrs. Plumber finds the true meaning of life in lying in bed all day long, until the doctor tells her she must lie in bed, when she changes to wishing to do anything but stay in bed. The Dei Santis act out their melodramatic but superficial emotions on a grand scale. And finally, the Robinsons satirically enact the absurdity—the infantilism—of obsession with material wealth, perfectly symbolized by the huge wooden doll baby holding a tiny adult woman in her palm. This art object satirizes the immaturity of such aesthetes, completely self-absorbed and vacuous. Whereas Twain attacks the contradictions of adult consciousness and White plays with the limitations of unimaginative adult realism, Fitzhugh combines and transforms these techniques of satire into something considerably more complex. She drastically forces her work towards the exclusion of the adult perspective through a variety of methods. She employs not only ridicule but also extrapolation, reversals, comic symmetries, and ultimately the subsumption of the adult's reality by the child.

Ridicule is obvious in the portrayal of the dance teacher who, writhing and flopping about on the floor, talks rapturously about the farmer preparing the field for plowing in a recital with obvious sexual double entendres. Sexuality and romance are represented as realms of experience that are not merely incomprehensible to Harriet but ridiculous, even grotesque. (Cf. Harriet's statement that Ole Golly's romance with Mr. Waldenstein has something to do with liking wurst, or Harriet's mother's absurd attempt to explain what falling in love was like by talking about Mr. Welsch throwing up at her feet.) It is clearly accurate to talk about the book as a form of social satire, as critics since Virginia L. Wolf have done.

By extrapolation, the dullness of adult conformity to upper-middle class behavior is criticized through the behavior of Marion Hawthorne, the "lady Hitler," and her friends, who play bridge and have tea parties just like their elders. Even in her painful isolation, Harriet is glad that she is not like those members of the spy-catchers' club. She knows she has individuality and a sense of purpose in life. Her "professions" of spying and writing are expressions of her adventuresome sense of discovery. They are also her heuristic means of self-discovery: of measuring by adult roles (mostly negative) what she could, but does not want to become, and, in the case of her notebooks, of keeping in touch with her perceptions and emotions. As Lissa Paul has argued, and as is shown by her rebellion against the conformities expected of her, such as dancing lessons (leading to debutante balls, acting properly with boys, etc.), Harriet is indeed a feminist writer.

Harriet's life is authentically hard. She experiences the existential crises of Ole Golly's leaving and of being ostracized by her peers after they read her notebook. But, hard as her life is, it is always real. Adults, on the other hand, are shown satirically to live unreal, inauthentic lives, lives of bad faith, to use Sartre's phrase. It is true that there are sympathetically portrayed adults, such as Ole Golly and Mr. Waldenstein, but even they have touches of inauthenticity: Ole Golly's tedious sententiousness, for example, and Mr. Waldenstein's fake compliments to Harriet. Adult rationality is shown to be absurd, while Harriet's myth-making is represented as truthful and meaningful. The adult who has the least falseness, Harrison Withers, is an alienated artist, very much like Harriet, and a kind of double reflecting Harriet's interests and identity.

Harriet, by choice, lives in a world of adults and of adult-like children, from her game of Town to her choice of friends who have professions such as chemistry or accounting, to her aspiration to publish in *The New Yorker*. But her point of view is adamantly a child's and Fitzhugh's narrator not only approximates but extrapolates her consciousness into the artistry of the adult creator by imitating Harriet's blunt descriptive style in the third-person narration.

Thus, in Fitzhugh's work, the adult reality is subsumed by the child's. Poulet's notion of interpenetration applies here: only the balance of forces can shift, as it does here, to allow the child, paradoxically, dominance over the adult.

    —J. D. Stahl, "Satire and the Evolution of Perspective in Children's Literature: Mark Twain,
    E. B. White, and Louise Fitzhugh," *Children's Literature Quarterly* 15, no. 3 (Fall 1990): 121–22

Bibliography

Suzuki Beane (with Sandra Scoppettone). 1961.

Harriet the Spy. 1964.

The Long Secret. 1965.

Bang, Bang, You're Dead! (with Sandra Scoppettone). 1969.

Nobody's Family Is Going to Change. 1974.

I Am Five. 1978.

Sport. 1979.

I Am Three. 1982.

I Am Four. 1982.

Kate Greenaway
1846 – 1901

KATE GREENAWAY was born in London on March 17, 1846, the second child of John and Elizabeth Greenaway. Kate's art and its vision of childhood would combine in her own original way her parents' vocations: her father was a draftsman and engraver; her mother, a milliner and seamstress. The remote, vaguely melancholy character of Kate Greenaway's images of children captures something of the self-contained, never-quite-realized life of its creator: Kate was solitary and shy as a child, taking comfort from the abandoned garden behind her mother's shop and from the gardens she imagined above the rooftops of London. Her illustrations would suggest the intensity of her attachment to the countryside in Nottinghamshire, where she often visited her cousins.

Kate had 12 years of formal training in drawing and painting, which culminated in an exhibit of her watercolors at the Dudley Gallery in 1868. Her work was admired by an editor of *People's* magazine, and she was commissioned to make illustrations for the publication. She also was commissioned by Marcus Ward to design cards for Christmas and St. Valentine's day and later was asked to illustrate an edition of *Madame D'Aulnoy's Fairy Tales*. She had her first exhibit at the Royal Academy in 1877.

Despite this gratifying—and financially crucial—work, Kate's true ambition was to illustrate and publish a book of her own verse. Her father took the illustrated manuscript of verses she had developed to a colleague, Edmund Evans, who was an innovator in color printing. Evans agreed to print the book, working with Routledge to edit and publish it in the autumn of 1879. Entitled *Under the Window*, the book was an immediate success, igniting the "Greenaway vogue" in aesthetics—and children's dress in particular—that spread beyond England into Europe, especially France.

The famed art critic John Ruskin so admired Greenaway's drawings for *Under the Window* that he wrote her a letter of extravagant praise in 1880. This letter initiated a 20-year relationship between Ruskin and Greenaway that proved to be the source of both intense happiness and terrible frustration and pain for the artist. Ruskin wrote often to praise, scold or lecture her for her work, in return for which Greenaway expressed her awe and love for the great man and showered him with watercolors and drawings. The relationship was especially trying for Greenaway because Ruskin was gradually losing his mind: she often mistook his sudden shifts of affection and mood or his capricious breaking of appointments and promises as reflections of his esteem. As an artist, however, Kate held her own, in spite of Ruskin's frequent attacks and his pressure upon her to change her style—in particular, to depict her little girls in less clothing.

In addition to the books she both wrote and illustrated—including *A Painting Book* (1884) and *Marigold Garden* (1885)—Greenaway illustrated more than 100 books written by others. By the mid-1880s, however, the craze for Greenaway's work was abating. At Ruskin's urging, she illustrated an edition of Robert Browning's "The Pied Piper of Hamelin" in 1888; although now considered one of her most interesting works, it received little attention and mixed reviews at the time.

Two years after the publication of *The Pied Piper of Hamelin*, Ruskin died. Greenaway went into deep mourning and in some way seems never to have fully recovered from the depth of the loss of a love she never really had—for Ruskin had loved not her, but her work. Despite her public's dulled appetite, she continued to draw and paint for herself, even as she fought breast cancer. Kate Greenaway died November 6, 1901. Only after her death did her talent once again win the recognition it deserved.

Critical Extracts

ANNE PARRISH

Waking or dreaming, ⟨Kate Greenaway⟩ remembered what she saw. When her illustrations for *Marigold Garden*, *The Language of Flowers* and *Little Ann* were exhibited in Paris, these "runaways from the nursery" "*vêtus à la mode bizarre et charmante qu'on appelle maintenant 'la Greenaway'*" enchanted the French with their freshness and innocence. They said her water-colors awakened memory.

"You can go into a beautiful new country if you stand under a large apple-tree and look up to the blue sky through the white flowers," she wrote when she was fifty. "I suppose I went to it very young before I could really remember and that is why I have such a wild delight in cowslips and apple-blossoms—they always give me the same strange feeling of trying *to remember*, as if I had known them in a former world."

She remembered going to her own country when she was two. She was sent to a farm in Nottinghamshire, where Ann the farmgirl was kind to the little London girl. The things Kate saw because of Ann glow through her work.

A cabbage-leaf of strawberries, a spray of harebell, are gifts to us from Ann as well as from Kate. When Ann took tea to the haymakers, she carried the child on one arm, and all her life Kate remembered the warm sun, the smell of steaming tea and new-mown hay, the meadow flowers, and her complete happiness.

She needed flowers. They made her happy, but the churchbells made her sad. She swung between gaiety and woe. Coming treats must be kept secret; her anticipation was too intense.

Lizzie, five years older, took care of Kate; the little sisters roamed the London streets, connoisseurs of shop-windows and Punch and Judy shows. Once a man dressed in skins, blowing a trumpet, cried that the end of the world was near. For months Kate was frantic with terror. She could read now, and she tried to find relief in stories. But her favorites were frightening or sad, and she was what she read. ⟨. . .⟩

When she was eleven, Kate's art schooling began, and continued for about eleven years. Overwork, and effort to follow the ideas of others, wrapped her in the quiet dullness of a cocoon.

But wings were growing, strong for flight in her own air.

Edmund Evans, master-craftsman of color-printing, longtime friend of Mr. Greenaway's, so believed in her that he printed a first edition of 20,000 copies of a book of pictures and verses. The edition sold before he could print another. With French and German editions, 100,000 copies were sold. The book was *Under the Window*, and Kate Greenaway was famous. ⟨. . .⟩

⟨Years later, when her vogue had ended, although frequently depressed, she said,⟩ "I go on liking things more and more, seeing them more and more beautiful." She tried to write a play; she tried to write her life. She planned a dressmaking business. She made other plans when the pain of acute muscular rheumatism let her think, in the restless resting between the nine takings of medicine, the eight beef teas. But her heart was in her painting. "Nothing I do pleases anyone else now . . . so I will please myself." She wanted to paint "a life-sized hedge" with all the hedgerow flowers and berries. She was sick of the words "little" and "dainty." She wanted to paint Night, with an angel rushing through a sky full of stars. "One day I shall."

She went on writing the verses that fill four thick manuscript volumes. Her verses for children are right with her pictures as the leaves are right with the rose. Her "love poems," written by a school-girl, would be silly and sweet. Written by a woman, they are wholly sad. Dreams without hope are cold shelter when night is near.

She was never the first, the belonging one. Welcomed, she came from outside for a little while to touch completenesses that loved her and were kind and did not need her.

But, like Hans Christian Andersen, Lewis Carroll, Edward Lear, like a blessed and valiant army of others, she found release from loneliness in her work for children.

—Anne Parrish, "Flowers for a Birthday: Kate Greenaway" (1846), reprinted in *A Horn Book Sampler on Children's Books and Reading*, ed. Norma R. Fryatt (Boston: The Horn Book, 1959), 41–43, 48–49

SELMA G. LANES

To Kate Greenaway, childhood was a metaphor for life at its richest and most bountiful. As an adult, she often recalled her early years with a nostalgia that bordered on pain:

> *October 1898:*
> How curiously days come back to you, or rather, live forever in your life—never go out of it, as if the impression was so great it could never go away again. I could tell you so many such. One is often present, I think I must tell that one now. Go and stand in a shady lane—at least, a wide country road—with high hedges, and wide grassy places at the sides. The hedges are all hawthorns blossoming; in the grass grow great patches of speedwell, stitchwort, and daisies. You look through gates into fields full of buttercups, and the whole of it is filled with sunlight. For I said it was shady only because the hedges were high. Now do you see my little picture, and me a little dark girl in a pink frock and hat, looking about at things a good deal, and thoughts filled up with such wonderful things—everything seeming wonderful, and life to go on for ever just as it was? What a beautiful long time a day was! Filled with time—

That shady lane with high hedges and wide grassy places—Miss Greenaway's Eden—recurs like an obsession in her illustrations. It is the locale of her world.

"What a beautiful long time a day was! Filled with time—" Her work is fraught with poignancy not because she strains or in any way reaches for it, but because this awareness of life's evanescence permeates her whole life view. ⟨. . .⟩

Something alive and breathing is at the heart of Miss Greenaway's world. When her "Little Maid" walks down the lane in *Mother Goose*, there is no question that she has a real destination in a real landscape and that we are merely privy to a passing moment. Children do not care "about children in an abstract way. That belongs to older people," Miss Greenaway once noted. Entirely devoid either of abstraction or condescension, Miss Greenaway's work appeals both to grownups and to children by virtue of its matter-of-fact naturalness. In her landscapes, children and adults alike are merely part of the architecture of her vision of English life. They have neither more nor less importance than roses or a blossoming apple tree.

> —Selma G. Lanes, *Down the Rabbit Hole: Adventures and Misadventures in the Realm of Children's Literature* (New York: Atheneum, 1971), 35–36

MICHAEL PATRICK HEARN

⟨Kate Greenaway⟩ could not merely hold up a mirror to the visible world; her realm in which Ruskin found refuge was the creation of her own fancy. She preferred to offer an idealized portrayal of childhood. "Children," she argued, "like to know about other things—or what other children did—but not about children in an abstract sort of way. That belongs to older people" ⟨M. H. Spielmann and G. S. Layard, *Kate Greenaway*, 1905, 124⟩. Ruskin insisted on her "exquisite feeling given to teach—not merely to amuse" ⟨letter to Greenaway, 15 June 1883⟩. Teach she did—not only in William Mavor's textbook *The English Spelling-Book* (1884) but also in the volumes she both wrote and illustrated. In each she offered examples of good behavior. Her world is free of conflict and everyday nuisances. Her delicate girls never tear their frocks while shinnying up trees; her roses rarely bear thorns. Her *Book of Games* (1889) avoids rough schoolyard sports; instead she selects word games and conundrums which require no strenuous participation. It is doubtful her two combatants in "F Fought for It" of *A Apple Pie* (1886) will ever come to blows; in *Little Ann* (1882), her dirty Jim is never so dirty and the little girl who beat her sister is never so vicious as the characters suggested by the verses of Ann and Jane Taylor. She could not bear such children. "I don't feel near strong enough for the strain of it," she wrote of painting children's portraits. "I know what the children are like—quite unaccustomed to sitting still. . . . I prefer the little girls and boys that live in that nice land, that come as you call them, fair or dark, in green ribbons or blue. I like making cowslip fields grow and apple trees bloom at a moment's notice. This is what it is . . . to have gone through life with an enchanted land ever beside you" ⟨Spielmann and Layard, 239-40⟩. In her "enchanted land," children act as they should and not as they do.

Perhaps she perfected her vision in *Marigold Garden* (1885), a companion volume to *Under the Window* but without the brown witch and other "mere ugly nonsense" which Ruskin had objected to in the earlier picture book. In the new volume of her own verses, her drawings were never prettier. When a child herself, she used to plan "out delightful places just close and unexpected" where her fancy might roam freely. "My bedroom window used to look out over red roofs and chimney-pots," she once wrote Ruskin, "and I made steps up to a lovely garden up there with nasturtiums growing and brilliant flowers so near to the sky. There were some old houses joined ours at the side, and I made a secret door into long lines of old rooms, all so delightful, leading into an old garden. I imagined it so often that I knew its look so well; it got to be very real" (Spielmann and Layard, 218). This private world is "Somewhere Town" of *Under the Window*, "Over the tiles and the chimney-pots . . . up in the morning early." Through her picture books this child-woman was able to take other children through that secret door to an enchanted marigold garden.

    —Michael Patrick Hearn, "Mr. Ruskin and Miss Greenaway," in *Reflections on Literature for Children*, ed. Francelia Butler and Richard Rotert (Hamden, CT: Library Professional Publications, 1984), 186

PATRICIA DOOLEY

⟨Although considered by many one of Greenaway's best works,⟩ *A Apple Pie* is not really representative of the whole body of the artist's work. There are disproportionately more interior scenes; not a single garden setting appears! Although Greenaway's gift for costume was almost equalled by her touch with flowers, there are no flowers to be found in this book. It is devoid of decorative marginalia—borders, flower sprays, wreaths, vases, etc.—apart from the apple-garland on the front boards. The colors are darker than Greenaway's characteristically delicate pastels. (This may be the fault of the printing: even Edmund Evans's careful reproduction sometimes failed to do justice to her very fine line and sensitive color.) There is also more continuity and structure to the illustrations. Not only does the picaresque pie appear in every episode, but some of its coterie also seem to recur. Of course, costume always provides a degree of continuity in a Greenaway book, but the participants in *A Apple Pie* are clearly dressed for the same occasion, not merely by the same hand. Identical accessories—elaborate hats, mob caps, coral necklaces, cameos, hair bows and shoe rosettes—and only slightly altered versions of the same frocks may be traced from page to page. (At the same time, to ensure against monotony Greenaway resorts to such devices as using five different models of a small stool supporting the pie.) Although Ruskin urged her to move away from the ornamental or decorative, opining that "her power should be concentrated in the direct illustration of connected story," most of her work remained "incidental." Even if the verses beneath it told a story, no more than a hint of narrative could enter the single-page picture, and some drawings, like those for *Kate Greenaway's Alphabet*, were purely decorative and not at all "illustrative." The major exception to this rule—and in the opinion of some, Kate Greenaway's masterpiece—was her work for *The Pied Piper of Hamelin*. (The magnificent frontispiece to this book contains practically every classic Greenway element: the thoroughly feminized figure of the Piper, the *locus amoenus*, the angelic children linked in a ring dance, the horizon obscured by a flowering tree, and so on.)

Naturally, *A Apple Pie* has the structure of an abcedarius, but in Greenaway's illustrations to the old rhyme, the alphabet is personified in the figures acting upon the pie. The elliptical verses sketch a terse narrative, and in Greenaway's pictures the pie's adventures are given a special importance as a focus of much earnest attention from the groups of children. The pie becomes the center of various rites: it is sacrificed, mourned for, and feeds a multitude. Its child-attendants and acolytes sing, and stand rapt in contemplation before it, dressed in their Sunday best. Eaten, it does not diminish; when not enthroned on its own table or stool it floats or hovers miraculously in air; it becomes a mystical object, a Holy Grail of pies. When "K knelt for it" and "L longed for it" they are shown with hands clasped prayerfully; "N nodded for it" inclines in a deep reverential bow. In illustrating *A Apple Pie*, Greenaway celebrates food as the center of children's existence, the impetus and the reward for their ceaseless activity. Depicting the pie as the focus of rituals engaged in entirely by children, Greenaway elevates the child's concerns and acknowledges the special, transcendent significance of certain traditional nursery dishes. In this celebration of child life in its own terms, apple pie achieves its apotheosis, far surpassing any utility it might have as an alphabet-teaching aid.

> —Patricia Dooley, "Kate Greenaway's *A Apple Pie*: An Atmosphere of Sober Joy," in *Touchstones: Reflections on the Best in Children's Literature*, vol. 3 (West Lafayette, IN: Children's Literature Association Publishers, 1989), 67–68

ALISON LURIE

It was during this period ⟨when John Ruskin was in turn rejecting and warmly embracing her⟩ that Kate Greenaway began to write a series of awkward and often unfinished but deeply felt love poems, of which only a few have ever been published. Her first biographers print several of these verses, while assuring the reader that they had nothing to do with Kate's life; rather it merely "pleased and soothed her to work out a poetic problem. . . . The case was not her own" ⟨Spielmann and Layard, 258⟩. Rodney Engen, who takes the opposite view, seems to be nearer to the truth. The poems do not suggest someone who is pleased and soothed:

> Nothing to do but part dear
> Oh love love love, my heart
> Is slowly breaking and coldness creeping
> Nearer into my every part. ⟨*Kate Greenaway*, 1981, 109⟩

During this same period of emotional turmoil Kate Greenaway produced her two most unusual books. The first one, *A Apple Pie*, published in the fall of

1886, was much larger in format than most of her work, and the figures were also larger and more active. Perhaps significantly, the drawings had never been submitted for Ruskin's approval, though she usually consulted him about all her major work. ⟨. . .⟩

It may not be too farfetched to view this large pie as John Ruskin, and the children as his various "pets" and admirers competing for a share of his attention as they so often did—and in the end literally eating him up. Whether or not Ruskin got the message, his reaction to A Apple Pie was very hostile. ⟨. . .⟩

The next uncharacteristic Greenaway project, The Pied Piper of Hamelin (1888), was undertaken with Ruskin's approval and under his supervision. He approved of her plan to illustrate Robert Browning's poem, adopting for the purpose a somewhat Pre-Raphaelite style and a palette dominated by rust, ocher, and olive tones instead of her usual pastels. He sent her copies of his favorite paintings as models, and also exercises in perspective which she carried out conscientiously but without noticeable result.

To illustrate any text is also to interpret it, and Kate Greenaway's The Pied Piper is an excellent example of this process. In Browning's poem the Piper is an eccentric trickster figure, "tall and thin, / With sharp blue eyes, each like a pin." Greenaway pictures him as a kind of romantic hero: pale, dignified, melancholy, and mysterious, with a resemblance to portraits of Ruskin that can hardly be accidental. ⟨. . .⟩

As Browning tells it, The Pied Piper is a moral fable. The burghers of Hamelin hire the Piper to charm away the rats that are plaguing the town, but once the rats have been drowned in the river they refuse to pay him. In revenge he plays a different tune, which draws all the children of Hamelin skipping and dancing after him. This enchanted procession (consisting, by my count, of 128 girls and only 46 boys) follows the Piper out of town and into a mountain crevice that supernaturally opens to receive them. Browning never reports what was inside the mountain. One child who was too lame to keep up with the rest says later that they were promised "a joyous land . . . Where waters gushed and fruit-trees grew, / And flowers put forth a fairer hue", but of course these promises may have been as illusory as the visions of tripe and pickles with which the Piper lured the rats to their doom. ⟨. . .⟩

Kate Greenaway's illustrations, however, make good on the Piper's promises. She added a final scene, reproduced as the frontispiece and cover of her book, which shows the Pied Piper sitting and playing in a springtime orchard while beautiful Greenaway children dance round a tree and others embrace him. Ruskin, who followed this project closely, "supervised her work on this one scene with unswerving dedication," and he later wrote, "Yes, that is just what it must be, the piper sitting in the garden playing. It perfects the whole story, while it changes it into a new one" ⟨Engen, 145⟩. He tried to get her to undress at least some of the children —"I think we might go the length of expecting the frocks to come off sometimes" ⟨Engen, 148⟩—but Kate, as usual, ignored this hint. She did, however, follow Ruskin's instructions in substituting flimsy white dresses and wreaths of flowers for the heavier, darker clothes in which the children had left Hamelin. So the "new story" was made to end with the Piper surrounded by beautiful girlies in what Ruskin called the "paradise scene" ⟨Engen, 145⟩ and said represented his idea of heaven. Kate, in this story, is nowhere—though perhaps we are to imagine her as the feminine-looking lame boy left outside the mountain.

—Alison Lurie, *Don't Tell the Grown-ups* (Boston: Little, Brown and Company, 1990), 62–65

Bibliography

Under the Window, with Coloured Pictures and Rhymes for Children. 1879.

Almanack for 1883. 1882.

Almanack for 1884. 1883.

A Painting Book. 1884.

Almanack for 1885. 1884.

Marigold Garden. 1885.

Kate Greenaway's Alphabet. 1885.

Almanack for 1886. 1885.

Almanack for 1887. 1886.

Almanack for 1888. 1887.

Kate Greenaway's Painting Book. 1888.

Almanack for 1889. 1888.

Kate Greenaway's Book of Games. 1889.

Almanack for 1890. 1889.

Kate Greenaway's Almanack 1891. 1890.

Kate Greenaway's Almanack 1892. 1891.

Kate Greenaway's Almanack 1893. 1892.

Kate Greenaway's Almanack 1894. 1893.

Kate Greenaway's Almanack 1895. 1894.

Kate Greenaway's Almanack and Diary for 1897. 1896.

Mother Goose or Old Nursery Rhymes; the complete Facsimile Sketchbooks from the Arents Collection, the New York Public Library. 1988.

Illustrations Only by Greenaway

Infant Amusements, or How to Make a Nursery Happy. 1867.
Aunt Louisa's Nursery Favourite: Diamonds and Toads. 1870.
My School Days in Paris. 1870.
Madame D'Aulnoy's Fairy Tales (9 vols). 1870.
A Child's Influence, or Kathleen and Her Great Uncle. 1872.
The Children of the Parsonage. 1873.
Fairy Gifts, or a Wallet of Wonders. 1874.
The Fairy Spinner. 1875.
A Cruise in the Acorn. 1875.
Turnaside Cottage. 1875.
Children's Songs With Pictures and Music. 1875.
Melcomb Manor: A Family Chronicle. 1875.
Puck and Blossoms, A Fairy Tale. 1875.
The Quiver of Love: A Collection of Valentines. 1876.
Two Little Cousins. 1876.
What Santa Claus Gave Me. 1876.
Tom Seven Years Old. 1876.
Starlight Stories Told to Bright Eyes and Listening Ears. 1876.
Pretty Stories for Tiny Folk. 1877.
Woodland Romances; or Fables and Fancies. 1877.
Poor Nelly. 1878.
Topo: A Tale about English Children in Italy. 1878.
Esther: A Story for Children. 1878.
Heartsease, or The Brother's Wife. 1879.
The Heir of Redclyffe. 1879.
Trot's Journey, With Pictures, Rhymes and Stories. 1879.
Toyland, Trot's Journey, and Other Poems and Stories. 1879.
The Little Folks Painting Book. 1879.
The Little Folks Nature Painting Book. 1879.
A Favourite Album of Fun and Fancy. 1879.
Christmas Snowflakes. 1879.
Three Brown Boys and Other Happy Children. 1879.
Art in the Nursery. 1879.
A Book for Every Little Jack and Gill. 1879.
Once Upon a Time: Play-Stories for Children. 1879.
The Two Gray Girls and Their Opposite Neighbors. 1880.
Kate Greenaway's Birthday Book for Children. 1880.
The Little Folks' Out and About Book. 1880.

The Illustrated Children's Birthday Book. 1880.
Freddie's Letter: Stories for Little People. 1880.
The Youngster. 1880.
Stevie's Visit. 1880.
The Purse of Gold. 1880.
The Lost Knife. 1880.
Little Sunbeam Stories. 1880.
Pleasant Hours and Golden Days. 1880.
Baby Dido; and Other Stories. 1880.
Dumpy. 1880.
The Easy Book for Children. 1880.
Five Mice in a Mousetrap. 1880.
Grandmamma's Surprise Baby. 1880.
London Lyrics. 1881.
A Day in a Child's Life. 1881.
Mother Goose, or The Old Nursery Rhymes. 1881.
Elise. 1881.
Hide and Seek Illustrated. 1881.
King Christmas. 1881.
Whose Fault Was It? 1881.
Some Little People. 1881.
Happy Little People. 1882.
Tales from the Edda. 1882.
Papa's Little Daughters. 1882.
Little Loving-Hearts Poem-Book. 1882.
Greenaway Pictures to Paint. 1882.
Little Ann and Other Poems. 1882.
Flowers and Fancy Valentines Ancient and Modern. 1882.
Jingles and Joys for Wee Girls and Boys. 1883.
Baby Chatterbox: Stories and Poems for Our Little Ones. 1883.
Fors Clavigera: Letters to the Workmen and Labourers of Great Britain. 1883.
Brothers of Pity and Other Tales of Beasts and Men. 1884.
The Language of Flowers. 1884.
A Summer at Aunt Helen's. 1884.
Baby's Birthday Book. 1884.
The English Spelling Book. 1884.
Chatterbox Hall. 1884.
The Children's Birthday Book. 1884.
Little Castles with Big Wings. 1884.
Songs for the Nursery. 1884.

Tick, Tick, Tick and Other Rhymes. 1885.
Mother Truth's Melodies: Common Sense for Children, A Kindergarten. 1885.
Little Patience Picture Book. 1885.
A Apple Pie. 1885.
The Queen of the Pirate Isle. 1886.
Rhymes for the Young Folk. 1886.
Bib and Tucker: With Pictures and Stories for Little People in the Nursery. 1886.
Christmas Dreams. 1886.
Queen Victoria's Jubilee Garland. 1887.
Lucy's Troubles and Other Stories. 1887.
Orient Line Guide: Chapters for Travellers by Sea and Land. 1888.
Around the House: Stories and Poems. 1888.
The Pied Piper of Hamelin. 1888.
The Old Farm Gate: Stories in Prose and Verse for Little People. 1888.
Miss Rosebud and Other Stories. 1888.
The Royal Progress of King Pepito. 1889.
Our Girls, Stories and Poems for Little Girls. 1890.
Songs of the Month. 1891.
Soap Bubble Stories for Children. 1892.
Doll's Tea Party, Merry Play Time. 1895.
Every Girl's Stories. 1896.
Stories Witty and Pictures Pretty. 1897.
To Pass the Time. 1897.
Little Folks' Speaker. 1898.
The April Baby's Book of Tunes, with the Story of How They Came to be Written. 1900.
London Afternoons. 1901.
Littledom Castle and Other Tales. 1903.
The Birthday Bouquet. 1903.
De Libris: Prose and Verse. 1908.

Ursula K. Le Guin
b. 1929

URSULA K. LE GUIN was born Ursula Kroeber on October 21, 1929, in Berkeley, California, the youngest of four children and the only daughter of Alfred and Theodora Kroeber. Her parents were intellectuals: Alfred was an anthropologist famed for his work with the indigenous American Indians of California; Theodora had her graduate degree in psychology but is better known for her biography of a North American Indian, *Ishi in Two Worlds* (1961). During the year, while Alfred taught at the University of California, the family stayed in their Berkeley house, but over the summers, they moved to their estate, Kishamish, in the Napa valley. Ursula remembers her childhood as relatively happy and recalls spending her time reading and listening to the family's interesting guests (including Robert Oppenheimer). Among her favorite reading matter growing up were collections of Greek and Norse mythologies, Frazer's *The Golden Bough*, and science fiction stories in *Thrilling Wonder Stories* and *Astounding*. She wrote her first fantasy at the age of nine, and at eleven she submitted a science fiction story to *Amazing Stories*.

After graduating from Radcliffe College in 1951, Ursula earned her master's degree in French and Italian Renaissance literature at Columbia University. Ursula won a Fulbright Fellowship to France to continue her doctoral work in 1953; on her ocean liner voyage to Europe, she met a history professor, Charles Le Guin, whom she married later that year in Paris and with whom she would have three children. She later chose to leave her graduate work and move with her husband to Portland, Oregon, where he was to teach at the university. Her father in the meantime had died in Paris.

Although she was busy raising her children, Le Guin continued to write when she could. Her first work to be accepted was "An Die Musik" in *Western Humanities Review* in 1961; a year later, a story, "April in Paris," was published in *Fantastic*. After these first publications, Le Guin's career as a writer accelerated: she published several volumes of poetry and numerous short stories in magazines, and, on the suggestion of a publisher at the Parnassus Press, Le Guin first considered writing fiction for young adults.

Out of this suggestion came Le Guin's award-winning Earthsea series, beginning with *A Wizard of Earthsea* in 1968. She would become most famous as an original writer of science fiction, but her first great success as a published writer was this young-adult fantasy novel.

Le Guin compares her fictive power of creating credible and coherent other worlds to her father's and mother's studies of the "other worlds" of different peoples.

A Wizard's sequel, The Tombs of Atuan, came out three years later and was named a Newbery Honor Book. Within a year, Le Guin had published The Farthest Shore (1972), the third book of the series, and had won the National Book Award for Children's Literature. In 1990—to the surprise of her readers, who had thought the Earthsea saga complete—Le Guin published the last of the Earthsea books, Tehanu. In the interval, she had written many essays, book reviews, adult science fiction novels, and several other young adult novels, including Very Far Away from Anywhere Else (1976) and The Beginning Place (1980).

Le Guin continues to write poetry, fiction, short stories, criticism, children's books, and screenplays, and she has edited anthologies and published more than 60 stories in various magazines, including The New Yorker, The Kenyon Review, Playboy, Playgirl, Omni, and the Triquarterly.

Critical Extracts

URSULA K. LE GUIN

⟨When asked to write a book for young readers,⟩ for some weeks or months I let my imagination go groping around in search of what was wanted, in the dark. It stumbled over the Islands, and the magic employed there. Serious consideration of magic, and of writing for kids, combined to make me wonder about wizards. Wizards are usually elderly or ageless Gandalfs, quite rightly and archetypically. But what were they before they had white beards? How did they learn what is obviously an erudite and dangerous art? Are there colleges for young wizards? And so on.

The story of the book is essentially a voyage, a pattern in the form of a long spiral. I began to see the places where the young wizard would go. Eventually I drew a map. Now that I knew where everything was, now was the time for cartography. Of course a great deal of it only appeared above water, as it were, in drawing the map.

Three small islands are named for my children, their babynames; one gets a little jovial and irresponsible, given the freedom to create a world out of nothing at all. (Power corrupts.) None of the other names "means" anything that I know of, though their sound is more or less meaningful to me.

People often ask how I think of names in fantasies, and again I have to answer that I find them, that I hear them. This is an important subject in this context. From that first story on, *naming* has been the essence of the art-magic as practiced in Earthsea. For me, as for the wizards, to know the name of an island or a character is to know the island or the person. Usually the name comes of itself, but sometimes one must be very careful: as I was with the protagonist, whose true name is Ged. I worked (in collaboration with a wizard named Ogion) for a long time trying to "listen for" his name, and making certain it really was his name. This all sounds very mystical and indeed there are aspects of it I do not understand, but it is a pragmatic business too, since if the name had been wrong the character would have been wrong—misbegotten, misunderstood. ⟨. . .⟩

I said that to know the true name is to know the thing, for me, and for the wizards. This implies a good deal about the "meaning" of the trilogy, and about me. The trilogy is, in one aspect, about the artist. The artist as magician. The Trickster. Prospero. That is the only truly allegorical aspect it has of which I am conscious. If there are other allegories in it please don't tell me; I hate allegories. A is "really" B, and a hawk is "really" a handsaw—bah. Humbug. Any creation, primary or secondary, with any vitality to it, can "really" be a dozen mutually exclusive things at once, before breakfast.

Wizardry is artistry. The trilogy is then, in this sense, about art, the creative experience, the creative process. There is always this circularity in fantasy. The snake devours its tail. Dreams must explain themselves.

—Ursula K. Le Guin, "Dreams Must Explain Themselves" (1973), in *The Language of the Night: Essays on Fantasy and Science Fiction* by Ursula K. Le Guin, ed. Susan Wood; rev. ed. (New York: HarperCollins Publishers, 1992), 46–48

Robert Scholes

⟨Like C. S. Lewis,⟩ Ursula Le Guin, in the Earthsea trilogy, relies on the mythic patterns of sin and redemption, quest and discovery, too, but she places them in the service of a metaphysic which is entirely responsible to modern conditions of being because its perspective is broader than the Christian perspective—because finally it takes the world more seriously than the Judeo-Christian tradition has ever allowed it to be taken.

What Earthsea represents, through its world of islands and waterways, is the universe as a dynamic, balanced system, not subject to the capricious miracles of any deity, but only to the natural laws of its own working, which include a role for magic and for powers other than human, but only as aspects of the great Balance or Equilibrium, which is the order of this cosmos. Where C. S. Lewis worked out a specifically Christian set of values, Ursula Le Guin works not with a theology but with an ecology, a cosmology, a reverence for the universe as a self-regulating structure. This seems to me more relevant to our needs than Lewis, but not simply because it is a more modern view— rather because it is a deeper view, closer to the great pre-Christian mythologies of this world and also closer to what three centuries of science have been able to discover about the nature of the universe. No one, in fact, has ever made magic seem to function so much like science as Ursula Le Guin—which is perhaps why it is no gross error to call her work science fiction, and also why the term *science fiction* seems finally inadequate to much of the material it presently designates in our bookstores and other rough and ready categorizations.

A Wizard of Earthsea is the story of the making of a mage, the education and testing of a young man born with the power to work wonders but lacking the knowledge to bring this power to fruition and to control its destructive potential. ⟨. . .⟩

⟨. . . But⟩ the greater knowledge, the greater the limitations—a view which is voiced by the Master Summoner after Ged has abused his youthful powers and unleashed a shadow of terror into the world:

> You thought, as a boy, that a mage is one who can do anything. So I
> thought, once. So did we all. And the truth is that as a man's real
> power grows and his knowledge widens, ever the way he can follow
> grows narrower: until at last he chooses nothing, but does only and
> wholly what he *must do.* . . .

Ged's quest, after his recovery (for the shadow wounded him gravely), is to find the shadow and subdue it, to restore the Balance that he has upset by working his power in a way beyond his knowledge. His quest is both an adventure story and an allegory which clearly raises the parallel to Lewis's Narnian allegory. For Ged must try to redeem his world, too. He must struggle with an evil power and suffer in the process. The difference is that Ged himself is the sinner who has made this redemption necessary. ⟨. . .⟩

⟨. . .⟩ The shadow was himself, his own capacity for evil, summoned up by his own power. To become whole, he had to face it, name it with his own name, and accept it as a part of himself. Thus by restoring the balance in himself, he helped to restore the balance of his world. The poetry of this balance shines through Ged's words, which are Ursula Le Guin's, as he explains the sources of power to a little girl.

> It is no secret. All power is one in source and end, I think. Years and
> distances, stars and candles, water and wind and wizardry, the craft in
> a man's hand and the wisdom in a tree's root: they all arise together.

My name and yours, and the true name of the sun, or a spring of
water, or an unborn child, all are syllables of the great word that is
very slowly spoken by the shining of the stars. There is no other
power. No other name.

Is this magic? Religion? Science? The great gift of Ursula Le Guin is to
offer us a perspective in which these all merge, in which realism and fantasy
are not opposed, because the supernatural is naturalized—not merely postu-
lated but regulated, systematized, made part of the Great Equilibrium itself.
And of course, this is also art, in which the sounds of individual sentences are
so cunningly balanced as the whole design, in which a great allegory of the
destructive power of science unleashed, and a little allegory of an individual
seeking to conquer his own chaotic impulses, come together as neatly as the
parts of a dove's tail. If Ursula Le Guin had written nothing but her three
books for young people, her achievement would be secure ⟨. . . .⟩
    —Robert Scholes, "The Good Witch of the West" (University of Notre Dame Press, 1975),
    reprinted in *Ursula K. Le Guin*, ed. Harold Bloom (New York: Chelsea House Publishers,
    1986), 36–39

T. A. SHIPPEY

We are on our own; living is a process not a state; reality is to be endured not
changed: precepts of this nature underlie the *Earthsea* trilogy. Of course it is not
the business of literature to hutch such moral nuggets, nor of criticism to dig
for them, and especially not when dealing with books as full of the sense of
place and individuality and difference as Mrs. Le Guin's. Nevertheless it has to
be said that these three books clearly aim at having some of the qualities of
parable as well as of narrative, and that the parables are repeatedly summed up
by statements within the books themselves. Mages appear to think in contrasts. "To light a candle is to cast a shadow," says one; "to speak, one must be
silent," says another; "There must be darkness to see the stars," says Ged, "the
dance is always danced . . . above the terrible abyss." In their gnomic and
metaphorical quality such remarks are alien to modern speech; and yet they
turn out to be distinctively modern when properly understood, the last one for
example relying strongly on our rediscovery of the importance of social ritual
(the dance), and our new awareness of the extent of time and space (the
abyss). A reader may start on *A Wizard of Earthsea* for its spells and dragons and
medieval, or rather pre-medieval trappings; he would be imperceptive, however, if he failed to realise before long—however dim the realisation—that he
was reading not just a parable, but a parable for our times.
    It is tempting to lead on and declare that Mrs. Le Guin is a "mythopoeic"
writer (an adjective many critics find easy to apply to fantasy in general). The

truth, though, seems to be that she is at least as much of an iconoclast, a myth-breaker not a myth-maker. She rejects resurrection and eternal life; she refutes "cathartic" and "intellectualist" versions of anthropology alike; her relationship with Sir James Frazer in particular is one of correction too grave for parody, and extending to "The Perils of the Soul" and "The Magic Art" and even "The Evolution of Kings," his sub-titles all alike. As was said at the start, she demands of us that we reconsider even our basic vocabulary, with insistent redefinitions of "magic," "soul," "name," "alive," and many other semantic fields and lexical items. One might end by remarking that novelty is blended with familiarity even in the myth which underlies the history of Earthsea itself, the oldest song of *The Creation of Éa* which is sung by Ged's companions in at least two critical moments. "Only in silence the word," it goes, "only in dark the light. . . ." By the end of the trilogy we realise that this is more than just a rephrasing of our own "Genesis" as given by St. John. Mrs. Le Guin takes "In the beginning was the Word" more seriously and more literally than do many modern theologians; but her respect for ancient texts includes no great regard for the mythic structures that have been built on them.

—T. A. Shippey, "The Magic Art and the Evolution of Words: 'The Earthsea Trilogy'" (University of Manitoba Press, 1977), reprinted in *Ursula K. Le Guin*, ed. Harold Bloom (New York: Chelsea House Publishers, 1986), 116–17

EDGAR C. BAILEY JR.

Because ⟨Ursula Le Guin⟩ is a highly self-aware writer, it is probably not surprising that the most sensitive examination so far of the Earthsea trilogy has been her own. It appears in an essay entitled "The Child and the Shadow," originally delivered at a Library of Congress symposium. Interestingly, in it she never once mentions her own works, focusing instead on such masters of fantasy as J. R. R. Tolkien and C. S. Lewis and leaving the reader to apply her theories to her own writings.

As the title suggests, Le Guin's subject is the role of shadow symbolism in fantasy; most of her analysis is based on the psychological concept of the shadow formulated by Carl Jung. After noting the difficulty of strictly defining any Jungian term without doing violence to its subtle complexity, she devotes much of the essay to an attempt to explain what Jung means by the shadow. Although simplified and adapted somewhat to her own purposes, the definition is generally accurate: "It is all we don't want to, can't, admit into our conscious self, all the qualities and tendencies within us which have been repressed, denied, or not used" ⟨"The Child and the Shadow," 1975, 143⟩. ⟨. . .⟩

As Le Guin points out, Jung was primarily interested in studying the confrontation with the shadow which occurs in middle age. For Le Guin, however, the most significant confrontation often comes during adolescence, at a time when the shadow may appear suddenly, seemingly even blacker than it really is. In order not to be overwhelmed by this previously unsuspected part of the psyche, a young person must face and accept it "warts and fangs and pimples and claws and all. . . ." It is Le Guin's contention that this confrontation, involving the same "moral effort" and possessing "the meaning of a suffering and passion," is the basic theme of most great fantasies. It is usually symbolically presented as a journey in which, paradoxically, the dreaded shadow, whose existence cannot at first even be admitted, actually serves as a guide into the depths of the psyche. The journey, if survived, brings psychological wholeness and maturity. Although she uses Tolkien's *The Lord of the Rings* as her primary example, it is quite clear that Le Guin intended the first volume of her own trilogy, *A Wizard of Earthsea*, as a portrayal of the same hazardous but necessary journey to maturity. ⟨. . .⟩

⟨In the book⟩ Le Guin introduces the young boy Ged, destined to become the greatest mage of all. *A Wizard of Earthsea* describes his confrontation with the shadow which he must recognize and assimilate. Reinforcing this main theme, shadows of all types crop up throughout the story. ⟨. . .⟩

Ged's final confrontation with the shadow—the climax of the book— occurs in the company of another wizard, Vetch, who had been Ged's only friend at Roke and who now agrees to accompany him on his quest. The episode is so important that Le Guin apparently wanted an external observer to provide the reader an objective description of the incredible events symbolizing Ged's unexpected victory. The encounter takes place in the open sea at a spot where, to Vetch's astonishment, the boat literally runs aground, the water abruptly disappearing to be replaced by a vast empty expanse of sand. The meeting—not, as had been expected, a battle—is described by Le Guin in explicitly Jungian terms:

> . . . aloud and clearly, breaking that old silence, Ged spoke the
> shadow's name, and in the same moment, the shadow spoke without
> lips or tongue, saying the same word: "GED." And the two voices
> were one voice.
>   Ged reached out his hands, dropping his staff, and took hold of
> the shadow, of the black self that reached out to him. Light and dark-
> ness met, and joined, and were one. (p. 201)

Vetch, watching this merging, and thinking his friend lost, leaps from the grounded boat and rushes to assist him. Almost immediately the sand turns back to water and both friends are left floundering in the sea. When they have struggled back to the boat, Ged announces, "It is over. . . . I am healed" (p. 202). Finally, and perhaps a bit too obviously, Le Guin summarizes her message so that even her younger readers will not miss it: "Ged had neither lost nor won but, naming the shadow of his death with his own name, had made himself whole: a man who, knowing his whole true self, cannot be used or possessed by any other power than himself . . ." (p. 203).

Lifted out of context as they are here, these quotations may seem rather too bald explanations of symbolic events perfectly capable of expressing their own significance. In fact, it is certainly here, if anywhere, that Le Guin lapses into didacticism; the ideas are not, as she claimed in her comments on the book, "totally incarnated." It is also true, however, that the climactic scene of the book is so dramatically and vividly realized that even such explicitly obvi-ous glosses are by no means as obtrusive as they may seem out of context. In fact, considering how consistently Le Guin kept her symbolic message in mind as she wrote, it is surely a tribute to her skill that one cannot help but read the book first as a captivating adventure story. This dual accomplishment places her work very nearly in that category of "great fantasy" which she describes so insightfully and praises so highly in the essay which furnishes the key to understanding her efforts.

—Edgar C. Bailey Jr., "Shadows in Earthsea: Le Guin's Use of a Jungian Archetype," *Extrapolation* 21, no. 3 (Fall 1980): 254–56, 260–61

Brian Attebery

Most writers of fantasy reach a point where they start to defend what they have written against charges of irrelevance or meaninglessness. There are essays by George MacDonald, J. R. R. Tolkien, C. S. Lewis, and many other fantasists that say, "This is real. It matters. My stories are born from and reflect back upon the outside world of perception and action." The impulse is under-standable: many readers and, unfortunately, a few writers mistake fantasy's alteration of reality for an evasion of reality. Such readers fail to note how carefully the best fantasists order their creations—how they limit the magical possibilities and bind them to a stringent moral order. Ursula K. Le Guin, in one of these defenses of fantasy, says that "fantasy is true, of course. It isn't fac-tual, but it is true. Children know that. Adults know it too, and that is precisely why many of them are afraid of fantasy. They know that its truth challenges, even threatens, all that is false, all that is phony, unnecessary, and trivial in the life they have let themselves be forced into living."

Le Guin's best known fantasy is the Earthsea trilogy: three tales of wiz-ardry and self-discovery set in a world of islands inhabited by men, dragons, and lesser beings. The high quality of these stories has been recognized in a number of critical essays, in major awards—a *Boston Globe-Horn Book* Award for *A Wizard of Earthsea*, a Newbery Honor Medal for *The Tombs of Atuan*, and a National Book Award for *The Farthest Shore*—and in the response of the children and adults who read them. What kind of response? The same kind that Le Guin, in another essay, tells of having arisen in her upon reading, at age ten, a fairy tale by Hans Christian Andersen: ". . . It was to that, to the unknown depths in me, that the story spoke; and it was the depths which responded to it and, nonverbally, irrationally, understood it, and learned from it."

But having located the truth of fantasy in the unconscious, how can we act consciously in accordance with it: what is the use of a dream upon awakening? That is a question that Le Guin and her predecessors have skirted in their essays. However, Le Guin's most recent fantasy novel, *The Beginning Place*, is largely about the relationship between fantasy and ordinary, daylight reality. It tells, in a sense, what happens when we close the book and drift back from Middle Earth or Narnia or Earthsea. Le Guin explores this relationship by establishing not one but two fictional realms, one fantastic and one modeled on the world we live in. Her protagonists, Irene Pannis and Hugh Rogers, cross from one world to the other, like fictional representatives of the reader as he picks up a work of fantasy and puts it down, adjusting his eyes and his expectations each time to a new order of being. In their actions and reactions Le Guin embodies her notion of the ways fantasy can be used either to evade or to achieve psychological growth. ⟨. . .⟩

The Beginning Place works better as metafantasy, or commentary on fantasy, than as a fantasy tale. In showing how to emerge from the world of the unconscious, how to, as it were, wake up again, Le Guin is obliged rather to slight the dream. It is a frustrating book to read because Irene and Hugh's story only touches briefly on the story, or history, of the fantasy world. If they truly belonged to the twilight world and were actually, as they seem briefly to be, its culture heroes, its saviors, then we would learn the fate of that world in learning of their adventures. That is the way it is with Frodo and Middle Earth or Ged and Earthsea. In this case, however, the individual drama, the coming of age of Hugh and Irene, is worked out without any corresponding solution of the problems of Tembreabrezi and its countryside. We are left asking questions: What happens to Horn, Sark, Allia? Where is the City and what is it like? Is the twilight a perpetual state or does it mark a long-delayed transition to dawn or utter night? Why are there no birds, no flowers, no songs? Hugh and Irene do not need to know, having reached their goal, but the reader would like to. We are too accustomed to grand finales and happily-ever-afters; like children greedy for more bedtime story we want to know "what happened after that?" We accept Irene and Hugh's return to reality and the implied message about times to dream and times to wake up, but we do so grudgingly, with many a backward glance.

Perhaps Le Guin will return to the beginning place, as she did to Earthsea, and take up the loose threads of its tapestry. Until then, *The Beginning Place* is most satisfyingly read, first, as a tale of two striking characters and their inward growth, and, second, as a fantasy about fantasy, just as *The Lathe of Heaven* is her science fiction novel about science fiction. *The Beginning Place* can tell us much about the richer world of Earthsea and how, like all fully developed fantasy worlds, it may properly be used not as an escape from, but as a means of reimagining, of reseeing the world we live in.

—Brian Attebery, "'The Beginning Place': Le Guin's Metafantasy" (*Children's Literature* 10 [1982]), reprinted in *Ursula K. Le Guin*, ed. Harold Bloom (New York: Chelsea House Publishers, 1986), 235–36, 242

M. TERESA TAVORMINA

Le Guin transmutes a specific passage from the *Aeneid* into an image whose meaning is unmistakably her own. The passage I have in mind occurs at the end of *Aeneid* 6, when Aeneas leaves Hell by its back door, the Gates of Sleep:

> There are two gates of Sleep: the one is said / to be of horn, through it an easy exit / is given to true Shades; the other is made / of polished ivory, perfect, glittering, / but through that way the Spirits send false dreams / into the world above. And here Anchises, / when he is done with words, accompanies / the Sibyl and his son together; and / he sends them through the gate of ivory. (*Aen.* 6.893–98)

In linking true and false dreams with twin gates of horn and ivory respectively, Virgil follows a long-standing classical tradition which can be traced back to the *Odyssey*, where Penelope describes the "double . . . portals of flickering dreams" in similar terms (*Odys.* 19.562). Classical, medieval, and Renaissance commentators on the *Aeneid* regularly explained the truthfulness of the gate of horn in terms of the translucence of horn and of its etymological connection with the eye (*cornu, cornea*); the falsity of dreams from the ivory gate was explicated in terms of ivory's opacity and its connection with teeth, the mouth, and thus with lying words. What can be seen is true; what is reported may be false. ⟨. . .⟩

Like Virgil and Homer in their epics of journey and self-discovery, Le Guin erects a gateway of horn and ivory at a crucial threshold in the Earthsea trilogy. When the young would-be-mage Ged first arrives at the School of Magery on Roke Island, he must pass through what appears to be "a mean little door of wood"—though only after telling his true name to the Master Doorkeeper. Once inside, he looks back at the doorway, and sees that it is "not plain wood as he had thought, but ivory without joint or seam: it was cut, as he knew later, from a tooth of the Great Dragon. The door that the old man closed behind him was of polished horn, through which the daylight shone dimly, and on its inner face was carved the Thousand-Leaved Tree" (*Wizard* 46–47). We learn later that this "door of horn and ivory" is "the back door of the Great House" (*Wizard* 89) and yet again, in *The Farthest Shore*, that it is the "eastern door, carven of horn and dragon's tooth" (31).

Like Virgil, and in this respect unlike Homer, Le Guin has her protagonist pass through this liminal structure, though it must be noted that Le Guin's protagonist, as a mage-to-be rather than a future king, is more analogous to the Sybil than to Aeneas. If the Earthsea trilogy has an Aeneas, it is young Prince Arren, who will "[cross] the dark land living," and eventually unite all Earthsea under his rule; nonetheless, the trilogy is primarily Ged's story, and it is Ged's passages through the horn and ivory door that we see as challenging tests. Arren gives his name and passes through the door easily enough, not only when he first arrives on Roke but also on the equinoctial morning when he runs down to the harbor to begin the journey that will take him through death to the "far shores of the day" (*Farthest Shore* 17, 20, 31). *Facilis descensus Auerno* (*Aen.* 6.126).

But Le Guin's doorway is no longer a twin gate of horn and ivory, nor does it open directly onto or out of the kingdom of the dead. Instead, she gives us a single gate, its frame cut from the One of a single dragon's tooth, its door made of dimly translucent horn on which is depicted the living Many of the World-Tree. Since dragons are the only creatures in Earthsea who can lie in the Old Speech, it seems possible that the ivory of Le Guin's doorframe owes something to the traditional association of the classical ivory gate with teeth, mouth, and lies. Likewise, the fact that light shines dimly through the door proper suggests that Le Guin is fully aware of the traditional explanation for true dreams leaving the underworld by way of the gate of horn.

It bears repeating: Le Guin's gate of horn and ivory is one, not two. If we allow ⟨. . .⟩ that the back door of the Great House is still in some sense a gate of dreams, then it must be acknowledged that those dreams cannot be readily dichotomized as true or false—at least not by the simple expedient of seeing which door they enter our consciousness by. Fortunately, such an acknowledgment will be relatively easy for readers of Le Guin, thanks to her clear commitment to the integration rather than the separation of complements. If "Light is the left hand of darkness / and darkness the right hand of light," then "true" dreams and "false" dreams may also be inseparable ⟨. . . .⟩

—M. Teresa Tavormina, "A Gate of Horn and Ivory: Dreaming True and False in Earthsea," *Extrapolation* 29, no. 4 (Winter 1988): 339–41

W. A. SENIOR

At the center of fantasy lies the concern for order, for things in their rightful places in a systematic and comprehensible world. In the case of Le Guin's Earthsea novels, many types of exchanges take place to help us understand the

cultural patterning of this cosmos: bargains, barters, deals, sales, thefts (negative exchanges), and trades, but primarily gifts. There is a pervasive pattern of
gifts and returns in various forms: from physical objects, to names, to magical
spells, to abstractions such as friendship and sacrifice. In all these cases, the
gifts given and received comply with Marcel Mauss's observation that in
archaic societies all gifts carry a spiritual import or content and entail the giver
offering a piece of himself and that gifts underpin and represent a universal
need for reciprocity ⟨The Gift, 1990, chapter one⟩. Gifts play especially en-
lightening roles in two facets of Earthsea: in encapsulating the macrocosmic
system of the Balance that governs and stabilizes Earthsea and in charting
Ged's development, moral growth, and integration into the world about him.

These two facets, however, are also mutually supportive, and in an essay
entitled "Gifts" the holistic philosopher Ralph Waldo Emerson used a
metaphor that is particularly appropriate for Le Guin's fiction: "The gift, to be
true, must be the flowing of the giver unto me, correspondent to my flowing
unto him. When the waters are at level, then my goods pass to him, and his to
me" ⟨Emerson's Essays, 1883, 156–57⟩. Captured in this ecological metaphor is
the view that gifts have both a metaphysical and a physical dimension, that
the gift becomes part of both giver and receiver, just as it maintains a connection to the world as a whole. The exchange of gifts, and the onus that comes
with an exchange, reflects and foregrounds the very nature of the Balance, and
thus the ontology of Earthsea itself. As Robert Scholes explains, the ontology
of Earthsea reflects a view of the universe as "a dynamic balanced system, not
subject to capricious miracles of any deity, but only to the natural laws of its
own working, which include a role for magic and for powers other than
human, but only as aspects of the great Balance or Equilibrium, which is the
order of this cosmos" ⟨"The Good Witch of the West," (1975) 1986, 36–37⟩. Framed
in its broadest parameters, Earthsea's Equilibrium or Balance consists of a system of exchanges, a system which implies obligations and responsibilities for
those involved because of the reactions and fluxions that any earlier action
generates. A young Ged grumbles at Ogion's lack of magic as they are being
drenched in a downpour, yet later an older Ged explains to Arren that a wizard must understand that causing rain one place might well cause drought in
another, a drought for which he would then be responsible.

Gift exchanges are tied to the same exigencies, in keeping with Le Guin's
insistence that "all things—organic and inorganic, material and spiritual,
object, and force—shape and are shaped by each other" ⟨Elizabeth Cummins,
Understanding Ursula K. Le Guin, 1990, 10⟩. Each "present" and/or "presentation"
conforms and responds to a need on both the macrocosmic and the micro-
cosmic scales. ⟨. . .⟩

As Kathryn Hume states in her study of fantasy, "Meaning for the individual comes from imitating mythic patterns; meaning for the reader or listener comes from seeing these patterns imitated in the story" ⟨*Fantasy and Mimesis*, 1984, 33⟩. Le Guin's uses of archetypal myths and traditional narrative patterns—the development of the hero, the voyage of discovery, the descent into death, the falling world—have been well documented, but her true genius lies in the specific details of worldbuilding that tie her fictional worlds to ours. Gift-giving, as a result of its relationship to the Equilibrium and because of the way it functions in the everyday life of the characters, achieves mythic status by asserting values as both part of a pattern and as a pattern in its own right. The philosophy of exchange "is total—religious, moral, sentimental" ⟨H. R. Hays, *From Ape to Angel*, 1971, 392⟩, and in this way the gift itself reveals the heart of the world. Exchange is the dynamic which permits community, individual and corporate prosperity, relations between strangers, stability, and even salvation.

—W. A. Senior, "Cultural Anthropology and Rituals of Exchange in Ursula K. Le Guin's 'Earthsea,'" *Mosaic* 29, no. 4 (December 1996): 103–4, 112

Bibliography

(limited to works in English)

Planet of Exile. 1966.
Rocannon's World. 1966.
City of Illusions. 1967.
A Wizard of Earthsea. 1968.
The Left Hand of Darkness. 1969.
The Lathe of Heaven. 1971.
The Tombs of Atuan. 1971.
The Farthest Shore. 1972.
The Word for World Is Forest. 1972.
From Elfland to Poughkeepsie. 1973.
The Dispossessed. 1974.
Dreams Must Explain Themselves. 1975.
The Eye of the Heron. 1975.
Wild Angels. 1975.
The Wind's Twelve Quarters: Short Stories. 1975.

Orsinian Tales. 1976.
Very Far Away from Anywhere Else. 1976.
The Water Is Wide. 1976.
The Language of the Night: Essays on Fantasy and Science Fiction. 1979;
    rev. ed., 1992.
Leese Webster. 1979.
Malafrena. 1979.
The Beginning Place. 1980.
Tillai and Tylissos. 1980.
Gwilan's Harp. 1981.
Hardwords and Other Poems. 1981.
The Adventure of Cobbler's Rune. 1982.
*The Art of Bunditsu: How to Arrange Your Bonzo—A Form of Japanese
    Tabbist Meditation.* 1982.
The Compass Rose: Short Stories. 1982.
In the Red Zone. 1983.
Solomon Leviathan's Nine Hundred and Thirty-First Trip Around the World. 1983.
The Visionary: The Life Story of Flicker of the Serpentine of Telina-Na. 1984.
Always Coming Home. 1985.
Five Complete Novels. 1985.
King Dog: A Screenplay. 1985.
Buffalo Gals and Other Animal Presences. 1987.
Catwings. 1988.
A Visit from Dr. Katz. 1988.
Wild Oats and Fire Weeds: New Poems. 1988.
Catwings Return. 1989.
Dancing at the Edge of the World: Thoughts on Words, Women, Places. 1989.
Fire and Stone. 1989.
Napa: The Roots and Springs of the Valley. 1989.
The New Atlantis. 1989.
Way of Water's Going: Images of Northern California Coastal Range. 1989.
Tehanu: The Last Book of Earthsea. 1990.
No Boats. 1991.
Searoad: Chronicles of Klantsand. 1991.
Fish Soup. 1992.
A Ride on the Red Mare's Back. 1992.
Blue Moon over Thurman Street. 1993.
Earthsea Revisited. 1993.
The Ones Who Walk Away from Omelas. 1993.

Buffalo Gals, Won't You Come Out Tonight? 1994.
A Fisherman of the Inland Sea. 1994.
Going Out with Peacocks and Other Poems. 1994.
Four Ways to Forgiveness. 1995.
She's Fantastical. 1995.
Wonderful Alexander and the Catwings. 1994.
Unlocking the Air and Other Stories. 1996.
Worlds of Exile and Illusion. 1996.
Tao Teh Ching (translator, with J. P. Seton). 1997.

Madeleine L'Engle
b. 1918

MADELEINE L'ENGLE CAMP was born shortly after the end of World War I, on November 29, 1918, in New York City. Her father, Charles Wadsworth Camp, was a foreign correspondent and writer who had been gassed during the war; L'Engle recalls subsequently "watching [her] father dying for eighteen years." Her mother, Madeleine Barnett Camp, was a talented pianist who chose not to pursue her potential career as a concert pianist. Madeleine's parents raised her in the British fashion, with a nanny and a governess, so, when her brother died in his infancy, much of her childhood was isolated. She spent her time writing stories, drawing, learning to play the piano, and reading. The books she prized most were those of George MacDonald, Lucy Maud Montgomery, and Edith Nesbit.

Because Charles Camp was susceptible to pneumonia, the family moved to Switzerland, where the air would be less irritating to his lungs. L'Engle recalls enjoying her life in the chateau the Camps rented, but her recollection of the Swiss boarding school she attended is less idyllic, for she was mocked for being lame and was mistakenly considered dull-witted by her teachers. Once she entered a poetry contest at the school and won the competition, but when her teachers discovered that she had won, they questioned the authenticity of her poem. In Madeleine's defense, her mother showed her teacher "the mass of poems, novels and stories" she had written, and it was conceded that Madeleine could indeed have written the prize poem.

At 14, Madeleine was sent to live with her maternal grandmother in Florida because both her parents were unwell. L'Engle's sense of alienation from the Floridean culture made her subsequent life in a Charleston, South Carolina, girls' boarding school a relief in contrast. Her last year at school seems to have been a happy one: she was busy acting in the school's plays and writing for and editing the literary magazine. That same year, however, her father died.

L'Engle graduated from Smith College in 1941, and, rather than return to the South to join her ailing mother, she moved to New York City to enter the theater. For the next five years, she was busy acting and writing; her first book of fiction, *The Small Rain*, was published in 1945. During a rehearsal for Chekhov's *The Cherry Orchard*, Madeleine met the actor Hugh Franklin, whom she married in January of 1946.

The couple left the theater and moved to Goshen, Connecticut, where they ran the local general store and raised three children. Even thus preoccupied with her family and their business, L'Engle continued to write and publish her fiction into the early 1960s. These were not altogether easy times for her as a writer, however: beyond her own personal conflicts about finding the time to write, she was immensely frustrated by publishers' rejections of three of her novels. Her science fiction/fantasy novel for young adults, *A Wrinkle in Time*, was one of those rejected; 20 times the novel was refused by publishers as being too sophisticated for children. Finally, in 1962, Farrar, Straus and Giroux published the novel, which within a year had won the Newbery Medal. One of the two sequel novels, *A Swiftly Tilting Planet* (1978), was also honored, receiving the American Book Award for Best Children's Paperback in 1980. L'Engle's more directly Christian work, *A Ring of Endless Light* (1980), was named a Newbery Honor book that same year.

In addition to her work as a librarian at the Cathedral of St. John the Divine in New York City and her various appointments as a visiting writer at colleges and universities, L'Engle continues to write essays and fiction for adults and children.

Critical Extracts

MADELEINE L'ENGLE

The lines between science fiction, fantasy, myth, and fairy tale are very fine, and children, unlike many adults, do not need to have their stories pigeonholed. Science fiction usually takes a contemporary scientific idea and then extrapolates: "Yes, but what if . . .?" In the days before astronauts had landed on the moon, no one was certain just what the surface of the moon would be. We knew that there would be little gravity, but we did not know whether the surface would be hard rock or rock covered with sand and silt. So one science fiction writer described a spaceship landing on the moon. The landing shifted the great layer of fine sand which had built up over the millennia and all the familiar mares and mountains vanished. The speculation of the science fiction writer is not always prophetic, but it always stirs the imagination. We are so accustomed to Jules Verne that we forget that he did, in fact, prophesy many things considered improbable in his day—flying, for example.

Fairy tales usually deal with magic, and magic has power. E. Nesbit used magic to help her protagonists journey into both the past and the future. Although her stories may seem pure fantasy, they touch science fiction, for scientists today conceive of time as nonlinear and suggest that one day it may be possible for us to move along different branches of the tree of time. Ursula Le Guin, in her children's fantasies and in her adult science fiction, touches on myth as well as fantasy and science fiction. In a similar fashion, Susan Cooper's fantasies are deeply rooted in British mythology.

Any story, whether myth, fantasy, fairy tale, or science fiction, explores and moves beyond daily concerns to wonder. A story, instead of taking a child away from real life, prepares him to live in real life with courage and expectancy. A child denied imaginative literature is likely to have more difficulty understanding cellular biology or post-Newtonian physics than the child whose imagination has been stretched by fantasy and science fiction. ⟨. . .⟩

Most writers of fantasy for children do not write for children; they write for themselves. "To write for children" is usually synonymous with writing down and is an insult to children. I have said that children are better believers than grown-ups. They are aware of what most adults have forgotten: that the daily, time-bound world of fact is the secondary world, and that literature, art, and music, though they are not themselves the primary world, give us glimpses of the wider world of our whole self—the self which is real enough to accept its darkness as well as its light.

There is something of the fantasy or science fiction monster in all of us, but mostly we are afraid to admit it. Chewbacca, the large woolly creature in *Star Wars*, is so appealing because we are free to recognize ourselves in him as well as in the white-clad hero and heroine. Rainer Maria Rilke writes, "How should we be able to forget those ancient myths that are at the beginning of all peoples, the myths about dragons that at the last moment turn into princesses; perhaps all the dragons of our lives are princesses who are only waiting to see us once beautiful and brave. Perhaps everything terrible is in its deepest being something helpless that wants help from us" ⟨*Letters to a Young Poet*, 1934, 69–70⟩. Stories which appeal to our imaginations enable us to recognize this helplessness and give us the courage to help.

    —Madeleine L'Engle, "Childlike Wonder and the Truths of Science Fiction," *Children's Literature* 10 (1982): 104–5, 110

NANCY-LOU PATTERSON

Each of Madeleine L'Engle's three fantasies begins with the irruption into the ordinary world of a supernatural being. Meg and Charles Wallace Murray may not be ordinary children, but their world includes rain boots and hot cocoa, the paraphernalia of life as understood by many North American readers. In each fantasy the visitor has come to escort the children into an otherworld of conflict, where they achieve victory over evil. A being "who leads the way to the other world" is a psychopomp, a role generally played by an angel in Christian thought. Works like L'Engle's are part of what has been called "ethical fantasy," characterized by a battle between good and evil: "the Psychomachia, the *bellum intestinum*, the Holy War." Their major action occurs in a place beneath the level of consciousness, to which the ego must travel with the aid of a spiritual guide. ⟨. . .⟩

In keeping with Christian thought, these figures of spiritual guidance ⟨Mrs. Whatsit and her friends; the cherubim; and the unicorn⟩ are fully manifested and even multimorphic, while the evil spirits are insubstantial and empty—mere airs and noises—howls, smokes, chills, stinks, and shadows of negation. Because the spirit escorts are such intensely compelling realizations, endlessly delightful and unexpected, the evil beings sometimes approach monotony and predictability. One reads through their affairs with impatience to return to the presence of the good.

To put the matter fairly: does this presentation of the good as characters "altogether lovely" (*The Song of Solomon*, 5:16), and the evil characters as inevitably overcome by Love, make for an imbalance in the narrative structure? Does it weaken the suspense and hence the narrative thrust? Perhaps L'Engle's plots are so complexly constructed just in order to counter this possibility: victory is not in doubt, but the manner of its achievement may be. This is not to say that there is no narrative tension in her works. Far from it. Indeed, the outcome of the eucatastrophic structure (to use J. R. R. Tolkien's coinage) is not more inevitable than that of its tragic counterpart. And there *is* an implicit imbalance in the Christian world view: a moral universe with perfect balance would be a dualist universe, and its equal antagonists would render it static.

In L'Engle's works, as in the works of other Christian fantasists, the narrative gains its dynamism from the creative and attractive powers of the good characters. There is a dialectic in Christian literature in which the meeting of good and evil results in more and better good. The plot is always precisely this, that the corruption of the good created world by the forces of antibeing proves to be a *felix culpa*, a happy fault, whereby the action of God brings a new good, a new creation, even out of evil. In the central eucatastrophe, Christ dies and is resurrected; death and evil do their worst and are bested. Dorothy L. Sayers once wrote that if this plot were boring, she did not know what could be interesting.

The central title suggests that this set of works could be called "The Wind Trilogy." Throughout the series, the symbol of wind appears as the operative spirit image, and the association of wind with each of the psychopomp figures makes clear that they are all images of spirit; indeed, the three novels may be read as meditations upon the Spirit, the divine wind or breath of the Holy

Spirit in action in the world, expressed as trifold feminine wisdom, as masculine power, as angelic knowledge, and as the unifying unicorn. With guides
like these, Madeleine L'Engle's child characters win their wars within.
    —Nancy-Lou Patterson, "Angel and Psychopomp in Madeleine L'Engle's 'Wind' Trilogy,"
    Children's Literature in Education 14, no. 4 (1983): 195, 201–2

WILLIAM BLACKBURN

Because of its complexity of plot, character, and theme, *A Wrinkle in Time* mer-
its the attention it has received. Meg's quest is perfectly suited to her character, and the novel artfully uses the traditional journey-to-the-Otherworld of
fantasy to enrich its equally-traditional motif of the child's quest for the lost
parent, a fruitful theme in children's literature since Telemachus' search for his
lost father at the opening of *The Odyssey. A Wrinkle in Time* is, in short, a remarkably ambitious novel, a novel which attempts to achieve at least three things,
and which, in the opinion of many of its readers, achieves them very well.

    First of all, it is a novel about self-discovery, a novel about an alienated
teen-ager who finds within herself the resources to overcome that alienation.
Those familiar with the contemporary adolescent novel will recognize this, or
some trivial variation thereon, as the creaking mainstay of that genre. Suffice
it to say that *A Wrinkle in Time* is superior to most of its plethora of imitators in
its handling of this subject.

    Second, the novel is a story of time travel and of journeys to other worlds;
the flexibility of space and time provide circumstances in which Meg's growth
can be accentuated and clearly understood; character and situation are mutually illuminating.

    Finally, the novel attempts an anatomy of evil; in rescuing her father and
Charles Wallace, Meg faces an evil power which not only threatens her per-
sonally, but is also presented as a power cosmic in its ambitions and opera-
tions. (Meg watches as a mysterious black shadow absorbs a star, and later sees
it ravening for our own planet, which it encircles). It is in the matter of the
presentation of evil that *A Wrinkle in Time* shows its greatest ambition—and its
greatest weakness. In this, for all its virtues, it amply demonstrates the wisdom
of another student of human misery, Lao-Tse, who once observed that "It is
difficult to use the Master Carpenter's tools without cutting one's fingers." ⟨. . .⟩

    ⟨. . . D⟩espite its use of a brain as a figure for evil, *A Wrinkle in Time* insists
on seeing evil as something external to the human psyche. (Hawthorne might
well have used the same symbol; he would never have made the same mistake.)
Meg always speaks of Charles Wallace as having been "taken" by IT: "'That
isn't Charles! Charles is gone'" and "Charles Wallace was gone that . . . little

boy in his place was only a copy of Charles Wallace, only a doll." When Charles argues in support of IT, Meg tells her father "that isn't Charles . . . Charles isn't like that. IT has him." Despite the occasional hint that evil may be internal as well as external, prompting from within as well as attacking from without (as when we are told of Meg that "disappointment was as dark and corrosive in her as the Black Thing"), the novel as a whole insists on depicting evil as foreign to human nature. ⟨. . .⟩

One is prepared to concede a certain subjective validity to this character-ization of evil. Evil often appears external to the conscious self, the ego. And there are also theological reasons for this characterization, for man was not originally created evil. (This is why the White Witch, the incarnation of evil in Lewis' *The Lion, The Witch, and The Wardrobe*, is not human.) But, as C. G. Jung and others have noted "the ego knows only ⟨its⟩ own contents, not the uncon-scious and its contents" ⟨*The Undiscovered Self*, 1959, 15⟩. And what meets the requirements of the theologian will not always satisfy those of the psycholo-gist—particularly in a book which is all about the quest for identity. Fighting an external force, no matter how powerful the opponent or how painful the experience, is significantly different from confronting an evil power which originates in oneself. ⟨. . .⟩

And so, for all its strengths, *A Wrinkle in Time* shrinks from holding the mir-ror up to human nature; it shirks the task of providing the looking-glass we seek so fearfully, and so tenaciously. For despite our fears, we must see before we can understand, and we cannot hope to deal with evil until we come to terms with its presence within ourselves. Since it strenuously denies that pres-ence, *A Wrinkle in Time* also denies us that hope; denying us a full 'imagination in evil,' it also denies us literature's power to lead us to the painful conscious-ness of our own full humanity, the true and piercing awareness of all we are and of all we might become.

—William Blackburn, "Madeleine L'Engle's *A Wrinkle in Time*: Seeking the Original Face," *Touchstones: Reflections on the Best in Children's Literature*, vol. 1 (West Lafayette, IN: Children's Literature Association Publishers, 1985), 124–25, 129–31

VIRGINIA L. WOLF

I was teaching Louise Fitzhugh's *Harriet the Spy* and Madeleine L'Engle's *A Wrinkle in Time*, ⟨. . .⟩ when I noticed for the first time, after studying these nov-els for years, that both Harriet and Meg have read *Alice*. The evidence in L'Engle's novel is that Mrs. Who's slow disappearance, her glasses fading last, reminds Meg of the Cheshire Cat and that she thinks the man rushing out of a building on Camazotz is like the White Rabbit. In Fitzhugh's novel, Harriet chants "The Walrus and the Carpenter" with Ole Golly on the night that the nurse decides to leave her position with the Welsches. Certainly, one could easily overlook these brief allusions to *Alice*.

In any case, it would never have occurred to me to compare these two characters or books, or to compare the two books with Alice, until I saw the evidence that Harriet and Meg are readers of *Alice*, and until I had read Hamida Bosmajian's *Harriet the Spy*: Nonsense and Sense." Then I realized that the structure of *Harriet the Spy* and *A Wrinkle in Time* is very like that of the *Alice* books. Both books confront their heroines with worlds that make no sense to them. Both girls are, in other words, alienated—alone and unhappy, often among confusing, inadequate, unsympathetic strangers. Indeed, *Harriet the Spy* and *A Wrinkle in Time* are both about their heroines' journeys among characters and through places very much like those found in Wonderland or through the Looking Glass, and each ends, like the *Alice* books, with the heroine's assertion of her own individuality.

There are, in fact, many surprising similarities between L'Engle's and Fitzhugh's novels. Both of their protagonists like tomatoes on their sand-wiches. Each has a room at the top of the house. Like Mrs. Who, Ole Golly quotes all the time, and their quotations are important to an understanding of the novels. Both books include one atypical boy, who in each case is the boyfriend, but who does not rescue the heroine. And, most importantly, both girls learn that love is the solution to their alienation. Harriet begins to learn to empathize with her friends and to use writing to put love in the world. Meg learns that her love for Charles Wallace makes her different from It and allows her to rescue her baby brother from It's evil hold over him. What's more, they both learn the importance of love on their own without the help of their respective families or boyfriends. Both have as guidance only the advice of wise women, very like the mythological figures, the fairy godmothers or god-desses of folklore, who often assist young initiates through their passage to adulthood. Harriet has Ole Golly; Meg has Mrs. Whatsit, Mrs. Who, Mrs. Which, and Auntie Beast. Finally, both novels are *bildungromans*. They are growing up stories, focused on the critical point of transition into adulthood—that point at which each girl willingly takes responsibility for her own actions and renounces her expectation that someone else will and should take care of her. ⟨. . .⟩

⟨. . .⟩ *Harriet the Spy* and *A Wrinkle in Time* suggest that the perception of real-ity as nonsense may result from being trapped in one's own egocentricity. Certainly, both girls' allusions to *Alice* occur at moments when they are blind to their self-centered illusions. When Ole Golly leaves, Harriet believes her-self totally independent, as Meg believes herself totally dependent when she finds herself on Camazotz without Mrs. Who. Moreover, both novels finally suggest that replacing the desire for control with love brings understanding.

Sense replaces nonsense. In the words of Dostoievsky, as quoted by Ole Golly to Harriet, "If you love everything, you will perceive the divine mystery in things. Once you perceive it, you will begin to comprehend it better every day. And you will come at last to love the whole world with an all-embracing love" (24). In the words of the Bible, as quoted by Mrs. Who to Meg, "God hath chosen the foolish things of the world to confound the wise; and God hath chosen the weak things of the world to confound the things which are mighty" (201–202). Love is, of course, both foolish and weak, but, paradoxically, it makes life meaningful despite the certainty of suffering, failure, and death. It makes sense out of nonsense.

 —Virginia L. Wolf, "Readers of *Alice*: My Children, Meg Murry, and Harriet M. Welsch," *Children's Literature Association Quarterly* 13, no. 3 (Fall 1988): 135, 137

LEONA W. FISHER

There is a genre of children's literature that transcends the radical subjectivity of these other forms by grafting children's natural companionability onto the root of visionary writing. This genre of "mystical fantasy" connects private insight and public communication by breaking down the apparent opposition between mystical tradition and literary fantasy (as well as between silence and speech, grace and nature, the individual and the community), thereby expanding and enriching our sense of both traditions. In this form of fantasy, the *silence* of mystical writing is retained, as both technique and theme, but it is joined to collaborative or *communal* experience, which verifies the mystical moments by allowing several protagonists to share them. This form typically includes a concrete Secondary World 〈J. R. R. Tolkien, "On Fairy-Stories," 1983, 132ff.〉, a supernatural device or being who transports the child protagonists to that world, a strong (adult) narrative voice which both identifies with the protagonists and mediates for us, and most importantly, a community of friends who share (equally, or as supporters of a central character) the mystical insights and developing moral perspective. The result of all these elements working together is the establishment of a "realistic" fantasy world in which the child-reader participates as a believing contributor. As a structure, of course, this is an ideal, with the elements occurring to different degrees in each actual text. 〈. . .〉

 George MacDonald's *At the Back of the North Wind* (1870–1871), Kenneth Grahame's *The Wind in the Willows* (1908), C. S. Lewis's *The Lion, the Witch and the Wardrobe* (1950) and *The Last Battle* (1956), and Madeleine L'Engle's *A Wrinkle in Time* (1962) will serve as my examples of a developing tradition in this form. 〈. . .〉 〈T〉hese mystical fantasies can teach us about the power of inexpressibility and communal silence in the face of transcendent "truth." 〈. . .〉

In the tradition of mystical fantasy, Madeleine L'Engle's *A Wrinkle in Time* also presents a collective journey toward visionary insight and self-discovery, although it does so in less conventionally religious and apocalyptic ways than the previous texts. Relying on science fiction, psychology, and totalitarian political movements to provide its plot and themes, this modern, experimental text focuses not on the vision of external moral good that we have seen in the other books, but on the mystical confrontation with evil in the form of the dehumanized "IT." Instead of North Wind or Pan or Aslan, we are presented with a variety of good figures, both human and trans-human: from the three stars who have become women (Mrs. Whatsit, Mrs. Which, and Mrs. Who) to the maternal Aunt Beast who nurses the central protagonist Meg back to health after a terrifying confrontation with the Dark Thing. Eerily domestic, these supernatural figures can help the children in their quest to free Meg's father from the evil planet Camazotz, but the spirit of goodness which they represent is not external to the children; it is the maternal figures' function to enable the children to find their immanent moral powers—within themselves. Because of its extended community, the absence of a deity figure, and the increased emphasis on the individual strength of the human protagonists, this book accentuates the apparent contradiction between silence and community that this genre consistently dissolves. Retaining the themes of its predecessors, *A Wrinkle in Time* complicates the relationship by emphasizing independent moral action, albeit undertaken with the necessary support of others.

—Leona W. Fisher, "Mystical Fantasy for Children: Silence and Community," *The Lion and the Unicorn* 14 (1990): 38–39, 49

KATHERINE SCHNEEBAUM

When it was first published in 1962, Madeleine L'Engle's *A Wrinkle in Time* presented a view of women which was ahead of its time. The now classic fantasy novel features a female protagonist, Meg, who is a math and science whiz with a sharp and unabashed tongue, and her mother, Mrs. Murry, who is herself a whiz at juggling the roles of mother, faithful wife, and brilliant chemist. In the early 1960s, such success in the male sphere of science was the stuff of fantasy for most young women. L'Engle's portrayal of women was truly progressive for the era ⟨. . . .⟩

⟨. . .⟩ Today, a rereading of *A Wrinkle in Time* is a lesson in the power of hindsight; trumpeting the breakthrough ideals of feminism in the 1960s, L'Engle could not see the dangers inherent in the realization of the seemingly simple dream.

Meg Murry, the central character in *A Wrinkle in Time*, is constantly being told that she must learn something or change something about herself; this message comes from her mother, her brothers, and herself. The particular way in which she must change seems clear early on, when both Mrs. Murry and Meg's brothers, Sandy and Denys, tell her she needs to seek "a happy medium." In its traditional idiomatic sense, this would imply that Meg must learn to compromise and to be more moderate in her actions and emotions. However, the traditional interpretation of the phrase is not the only possible one, and as the story progresses, its more obvious meanings are belied by the course of events. This gradual refutation of the goals implied by the phrase seems, on the surface, to suggest that those who admonished Meg were wrong, and she need not change. However, a closer examination of the course of events points to another reading of the phrase "happy medium": Meg's real problem has been not a fundamental personality flaw, but a failure to direct her efforts in the manner most suitable to the female role. The "happy medium" she needed to find, and does find, is the "most fortuitous sphere" in which she, as a woman, can function. In keeping with age-old gender-role stereotypes, that sphere is one of morally redemptive love. ⟨. . .⟩

⟨Near the end of the novel,⟩ Meg says that she is "the only one" who can save Charles Wallace, yet Calvin has come very close earlier in the book, and only failed due to the interference of It. Mrs. Whatsit says to Calvin: "You will not be permitted to throw yourself in with him, for that, you must realize, is what would happen" (194). It is not clear to the reader as it is to Mrs. Whatsit why this should be the case; in the past, Calvin and Mr. Murry have been extraordinarily good at holding out against It, while Meg was nearly lost. Somehow, then, they all sense that the methods must be different this time; Charles Wallace must be saved not through the mind, but through the heart. Even if love is considered the key, though, it is not as clear as Meg would have it that she is the only one who can do the job; Mr. Murry, despite his prolonged absence, is still Charles's father, and loves him although he may not really know him. The criterion by which Meg and the others choose her as the savior is gender. Meg's strong emotions, misguided until now into masculine behavior, will be most effective in their intended mode: powerful, redeeming love. Love is indeed powerful, and it does save Charles Wallace. It is, however, a passive power; Meg "could stand there . . ." (208) and still save Charles with love.

Meg's deed is highly praised by all, and it is truly a noble one. However, after two hundred pages in which she was criticized much of the time for her lack of femininity, this praise smacks disturbingly of a vindication. Meg is portrayed as in her element, her "happiest medium" as it were, when she is operating in the traditionally feminine sphere of maternal love as redeeming force. The final message is that a girl becomes a woman only when she voluntarily takes on the role of moral leader and keeper of love, subordinating her other

interests and capabilities to this one. The seeming inevitability of Meg's transformation and its quality of revelation imply a lack of freedom for a young
woman like Meg to choose her own path; it is simply woman's destiny and
duty to care for the moral health of others.

    —Katherine Schneebaum, "Finding a Happy Medium: The Design for Womanhood in
    A Wrinkle in Time," The Lion and the Unicorn 14 (1990): 30–31, 36

ℬ i b l i o g r a p h y

(limited to works in English)

18 Washington Square, South. 1944.
The Small Rain. 1945.
Ilsa. 1946.
And Both Were Young. 1949.
Camilla Dickinson. 1951.
A Winter's Love. 1957.
Meet the Austins. 1960.
A Wrinkle in Time. 1962.
The Moon by Night. 1963.
The Twenty-Four Days Before Christmas. 1964.
The Arm of the Starfish. 1965.
The Love Letters. 1966.
The Journey with Jonah. 1967.
The Young Unicorns. 1968.
Dance in the Desert. 1969.
Prelude. 1969.
Lines Scribbled on an Envelope, and Other Poems. 1969.
The Other Side of the Sun. 1971.
A Circle of Quiet. 1972.
A Wind in the Door. 1973.
The Summer of the Great-Grandmother. 1974.
Prayers for Sunday. 1974.
Everyday Prayers. 1974.
Dragons in the Waters. 1976.
Spirit and Light: Essays in Historical Theology. 1976.
The Irrational Season. 1977.

A Swiftly Tilting Planet. 1978.
The Weather of the Heart. 1978.
Ladder of Angels. 1979.
A Ring of Endless Light. 1980.
The Anti-Muffins. 1980.
Walking on Water. 1980.
A Severed Wasp. 1982.
The Sphinx at Dawn. 1983.
And Both Were Young. 1983.
And It Was Good: Reflections on Beginnings. 1983.
Dare to Be Creative. 1984.
A House Like a Lotus. 1984.
The Twenty-Four Days of Christmas. 1984.
Trailing Clouds of Glory: Spiritual Values in Children's Books. 1985.
A Stone for a Pillow. 1986.
Many Waters. 1986.
A Cry Like a Bell. 1987.
Two-Part Invention: The Story of a Marriage. 1988.
An Acceptable Time. 1989.
Sold into Egypt: Joseph's Journey into Human Being. 1989.
The Glorious Impossible. 1990.
Certain Women. 1992.
Mothers and Daughters (with Maria Rooney). 1992.
The Rock That Is Higher: Story as Truth. 1993.
Anytime Prayers. 1994.
Troubling a Star. 1994.
Glimpses of Grace: Daily Thoughts and Reflections (with Carole F. Chase). 1996.
A Live Coal in the Sea. 1996.
Penguins and Golden Calves: Icons and Idols. 1996.
Wintersong: Christmas Readings (with Luci Shaw). 1996.
Friends for the Journey (with Luci Shaw). 1997.

Lucy Maud Montgomery
1874 – 1940

LUCY MAUD MONTGOMERY was an orphan raised on the small seaside settlement of Cavendish on Prince Edward Island: less than two years after her birth on November 30, 1874, her mother, Clara MacNeill Montgomery, died of tuberculosis; her father, a shopkeeper, left his only child in the care of her maternal grandparents and went west. Lucy and Alexander MacNeill were of old Scotts stock, severe in their Presbyterian beliefs, and Lucy Maud's sensitive, artistic temperament was antithetical to the ethos of her grandparents and their farming community. The natural beauty that surrounded her, however, and her pleasure in keeping a journal provided solace in her otherwise isolated childhood.

In 1890, Lucy Maud's father sent for her to join him, his new wife, and their two children in Saskatchewan. Despite her pleasure in being reunited with her father, her stay lasted only a year, for her stepmother exploited her as a wageless housekeeper and nanny. The publication of a poem and an article on the beauties of Saskatchewan in various newspapers during this time somewhat alleviated her frustration and her homesickness for the beauty of her island home.

Upon returning to Cavendish, Lucy Maud entered the Prince of Wales College, where she earned her teaching license. She taught for a year in Bideford and used her earnings to return to school, this time in Halifax at Dalhousie College. Shortly thereafter, she fell in love with a farmer, but, despite the intensity of her sexual attraction to him, she felt that their class difference was too great to overcome. News of her grandfather's death gave her an escape from this dilemma, and she returned to Cavendish to care for her grandmother.

From 1901 to 1911, Lucy Maud lived with her grandmother, leaving only briefly to work as a columnist and editor at the Halifax *Daily Echo* and to build her career as a writer. In 1906 she became engaged to Ewan MacDonald, a minister at the Cavendish Presbyterian church, despite her distaste for the life of a minister's wife and her lack of passion for Ewan; she convinced him to postpone the wedding until after her grandmother's death. In the intervening five years, Lucy Maud wrote and published her first and most popular novel, *Anne of Green Gables* (1908), and three sequels.

When her grandmother died, in 1911, Lucy Maud and Ewan were married and moved to Leaksdale, Ontario; a year later, their first son was born. Lucy Maud's dislike of the role of the minister's wife did not interfere with her performance of it, though to her journals she confided her boredom and her embarrassment over the artifice the role required. Compounded with the compromise she had made in marrying was the aesthetic compromise she felt she made in writing her "Anne" novels: she regarded herself as a frustrated poet and adult novelist. These frustrations no doubt contributed to her recurring periods of depression, headaches, and nervousness.

The year World War I started, Lucy Maud began her long struggle to conceal from the public her husband's attacks of mental illness. Ewan was diagnosed as a victim of "religious melancholia," which was believed to be serious but "unlikely to develop into violent insanity." Despite the strain of her private life, over the next 10 years at Leaksdale, Lucy Maud wrote and published 15 books and wrote continuously for various periodicals. In 1923, her fame as a writer was such that she became the first woman of Canada to be named a fellow of the Royal Society of Arts of Great Britain.

The family moved to Norval, Ontario, in 1925, and here Lucy Maud did not let her role as the minister's wife keep her from directing plays at the Young People's Guild or from writing six more novels. Privately, however, her life was terribly strained by the increasing intensity of her husband's attacks, which reached such a pitch that in 1934 he spent four months in a sanatorium—and she herself endured a nervous breakdown. Ewan retired soon after, and the couple moved to Toronto, where their two sons were studying medicine and law. Montgomery periodically visited Prince Edward Island, as she had throughout her married life, and found that a theme park had been built celebrating the Anne of her novels. Although appalled, she was relieved to discover that the park had actually preserved much of the land from more destructive forms of commercial development.

The coming of World War II and her husband's persistent and severe attacks led to Montgomery's suffering another nervous breakdown that interfered with her ability to read or write. In April of 1940, Lucy Maud Montgomery died and was buried beside the grave of her mother.

Critical Extracts

THOMAS E. TAUSKY

The biographical research of the past decade has revealed a new dimension of Lucy Maud Montgomery's character. Mollie Gillen's biography, *The wheel of things*, takes for its title a phrase from Kipling which Gillen sees as epitomizing the destructive surrender to convention Montgomery felt compelled to make, both as an author and as a minister's wife. Montgomery's intimate letters to G.B. MacMillan ⟨*My Dear Mr. M.*, 1980⟩ confirm this interpretation. Montgomery portrays herself as a victim of severe depression throughout her life. She seems to regard the writing of the *Anne of Green Gables* sequels as unwelcome drudgery, and is increasingly oppressed by family difficulties. Montgomery's final letters to MacMillan pour out the agony that can no longer be restrained. The following passage (the complete text of a postcard) is representative:

> Am no better dear friend & never will be. You do not know the blows
> that have fallen on my life for years. I tried to hide them from my
> friends. I feel my mind is going. ⟨15 September 1941⟩

Emily of New Moon (1923), *Emily climbs* (1925), and *Emily's quest* (1927)—can be read as the fictionalized confession of a troubled personality alternating between confidence in creativity and despairing self-doubt. Before the first of these novels was completed, Montgomery confided to a friend that Emily was an autobiographical character:

> "Emily" will be, in a sense, more autobiographical than any of my
> other books. People were never right in saying I was "Anne" but, *in
> some respects*, they will be right if they write me down as Emily.
> ⟨19 October 1921⟩ ⟨. . .⟩

The *Emily* novels are intensely Romantic works. Especially in *Emily of New Moon*, the protagonist's delight in Nature (which extends to symbolic identification: she is called a star, a skylark, a young eagle and a wild cherry tree) and joy in the "flash" define her being. In one extended and passionate scene, the narrator uses the Romantic vocabulary of Nature-worship as religion and poet as priest to describe Emily's emotions upon gazing at the Northern lights: "She was a high priestess of loveliness assisting at the divine rites of her worship" (*EC*, 170).

When Romantic visions fade, however, there are also specifically Romantic forms of depression. In a passage which in its entirety alludes to both the "Intimations Ode" and "Tintern Abbey," Emily wonders whether she might lose "the flash": "Will I lose it altogether as I grow old? Will nothing but 'the light of common day' be mine then?" (*EQ*, 182). In sympathy with Shelley's lament that "the mind in creation is as a fading coal," Emily regrets that *"Nothing* ever seems . . . as beautiful and grand . . . when it is written out, as it does when you are thinking or feeling about it" (*EC*, 9). In the account of Emily's "great and awful weariness" of the soul, already quoted, one can find a parallel with the "grief without a pang" of Coleridge's "Dejection: An Ode," particularly since Emily, like Coleridge, attributes tragic utterances to the wind (*EQ*, 181).

If Romantic poets fear the loss of visionary power, women novelists (or fictional women novelists) may have cause to fear the harmful consequences of divided interests. As Patricia Meyer Spacks has said, "the conflict between the yearning for artistic expression and the desire for relationship is not peculiar ⟨to⟩ women, but women are likely to experience it with special intensity" ⟨*The Female Imagination*, 1976, 213⟩. At the conscious level Emily experiences little of this conflict, since Teddy is himself an artist, and interests himself in her work. Yet ⟨. . .⟩ love for Teddy gets in the way of Emily's devotion to her art; even more fundamentally, Emily's feeling for Teddy is directly contrary to the state of mind which best suits her Romantic art. As an artist, Emily needs to walk by her wild lone; as a lover, Emily literally comes to Teddy's whistle, feeling "in the mad ecstasy of the moment" (*EQ*, 120) that she is "helpless— dominated" (*EQ*, 121) and reveling in her abasement.

Yet, if in this episode Emily's conduct seems to recall the behaviour of the Victorian heroine, she also may be linked with the women novelists who were contemporary with her creator. In her influential book, *A literature of their own*, Elaine Showalter suggests that women novelists of the 1920s "found themselves pulled apart by the conflicting claims of love and art" ⟨1977, 244⟩. Consequently, novels of Montgomery's own time portray heroines subject to the kind of distress from which Emily suffers in much of *Emily's quest*. As Showalter puts it: "The female *Künstlerroman* of this period is a saga of defeat ⟨. . . .⟩ There is indeed a new interest in the psychology of women, but it is full of self-recrimination." Like her creator, Emily seems half-Victorian, half-modern; half-submissive, half self-sufficient; half the socially acceptable public mask, half the intensely private creative personality. The conventional ending of *Emily's quest* does not really unify these divided selves.

—Thomas E. Tausky, "L. M. Montgomery and 'The Alpine Path, So Hard, So Steep,'" *Canadian Children's Literature* 30 (1983): 5, 17–18

ELIZABETH R. EPPERLY

To L. M. Montgomery enthusiasts certain words and expressions have become familiar from long association. Again and again in the twenty L. M.

Montgomery novels we find these words and images: spicy scent of ferns, tricksy winds, apple-green sunset skies, the fragrance of trampled mint. In fact, Montgomery, somewhat like her beloved novelist Anthony Trollope, had a penchant for repetition. She had favourite poets she liked to quote: Kipling, Tennyson, Keats, Bliss Carman, Longfellow, Thomas Gray, Milton; favourite situations she loved to conjure—lustrous-eyed, spirited girls struggling against insensitive and unthinking adults or peers. But unlike the prose-minded Trollope, L. M. Montgomery always yearned to be a poet rather than a novelist. This desire shaped her most interesting novels, for the repeated images and allusions that failed her in poetry helped to create atmosphere, enrich character, and generally modulate the tone of her prose.

Some descriptions in her novels are overdrawn or sentimental, but many do achieve a poetic harmony that eluded her successfully in poetry itself. In 1916, L. M. Montgomery published her only book of poetry, *The watchman and other poems*, a tame volume that shows all too clearly that she did, as she freely admitted to Ephraim Weber, fit in the rhymes later with the help of a rhyming dictionary. In 1917, she produced another novel, (what was to be in the completed series the fifth Anne book), *Anne's house of dreams*, potentially the most sentimental of any of her books since it deals with the long-awaited marriage of Anne Shirley and Gilbert Blythe. It is remarkably interesting and readable. Its success as a book is not found in Anne's and Gilbert's honeymoon, nor even primarily in the presence of spry Captain Jim or mysterious Leslie Moore, but in its tone. The same kinds of images and expressions used in numerous poems of *The watchman* reappear in *Anne's house of dreams*, but in the novel, they work.

L. M. Montgomery was passionately fond, as all the *Watchman* poems show, of the colour purple, of skies like cups or flagons, of flowers as cups, of "elfin" and "silver" and "gold" and "crystal." Many of the ninety-three poems, songs to the sea, hills, and woods, are marred by an ill-judged concentration of archaic or descriptive words borrowed liberally from Tennyson and Browning ("flagon," "gramarye," "shallop," "wold," "elfin," "weklin"). In *Anne's house of dreams* a preoccupation with the sea and the woods and hills also produces descriptions full of colour, jewels, stars, airy wine, and elfin things. Some of the word choices, admittedly, are as irksome as they are in the poems. For example, once when Captain Jim visits Anne, the narrator carols: "The garden was full of moist, scented air of a maritime spring evening. There was a milk-white mist on the edge of the sea, with a young moon kissing it, and a silver gladness of stars over the Glen" (pp. 164–65). More often, however, the love of metaphors, similes, jewels, and colours that stifled her poetry, brings life to the prose. ⟨. . .⟩

Anne's house of dreams is not wholly made up of starshine, vibrant colours, and beacon flashes, nor is it merely a prettily illustrated tale of love and fulfillment. In it, as in all of her good novels, L. M. Montgomery catches life. She heightens the colours occasionally and indulges in favourite images and elements, but she knows how to make the characters breathe. In this book the rapturous songs of sea, wood, and hill are balanced by humorous characters and incidents so that poetry and everyday life rest comfortably together. The characters themselves are frequently laughing, and two sober-faced ones, Susan Baker and Miss Cornelia Bryant, unconsciously provide mirth for other characters and for the reader. In her descriptions of them, Montgomery makes fun of her own self-conscious style and keeps her writing from becoming embarrassingly sentimental or self-indulgent. ⟨. . .⟩

Anne's house of dreams, potentially mawkish because of its subject, works as a novel because L. M. Montgomery is able to control its tone throughout. The familiar poetic expressions and favourite pictures of nature help to unite the characters with their physical surroundings. Leslie is the sea mists and red poppies; Captain Jim is the lighthouse beacon and the gentle harbour sunsets; Anne is the brilliant colours and the quiet shadows. At the same time, Cornelia Bryant, Susan Baker, and steady young Dr. Blythe himself are constant reminders that prose, too, has its advantages.

—Elizabeth R. Epperly, "L. M. Montgomery's *Anne's House of Dreams*: Reworking Poetry," *Canadian Children's Literature* 37 (1985): 40–41, 44–45

T. D. MacLulich

Montgomery inherited a tradition of juvenile fiction that had become prominent in the later years of the nineteenth century, and was well-established by the time she began to write. It is quite natural that Montgomery's novels should bear a closer resemblance to nineteenth-century girls' books than they do to the boys' books written by Twain and other male authors. In fact, Montgomery's two best books, *Anne of Green Gables* and *Emily of New Moon* (1923), belong to a tradition that descends from one of the most important books in nineteenth-century children's literature, Louisa May Alcott's *Little women* (1868). The heroines of Montgomery's two books are examples of a particularly interesting character who was first introduced into children's fiction in Alcott's story, the aspiring young writer or literary heroine. ⟨. . .⟩

The writers of girls' books often used literary ambition as a clear sign of a heroine's reluctance to submit to all the restrictions imposed by her society. In consequence, the literary heroine usually experiences a conflict between her desire for personal autonomy and her reluctance to upset her family by opposing the conventional social proprieties. The literary heroine is therefore a potential rebel, for the logical outcome of her youthful protests would be a systematic rejection of the values and attitudes that prevail in the heroine's male-dominated society. But the literary heroine's rebellion is never carried through into adult life. Instead, she resolves her inner conflict in favour of sub-

mission to social convention. That is, although the creators of literary heroines attach considerable importance to the right of children to follow their
own bent without undue restraint, they cannot allow adult women the same
freedom to express themselves in socially unconventional ways.

Even Jo March, the most original of all literary heroines, moves towards
conventionality as she ages. The lapse into propriety is even more striking in
the stories of subsequent literary heroines. The most conspicuous of Jo's suc-
cessors are probably Rebecca Rowena Randall in Kate Douglas Wiggin's
Rebecca of Sunnybrook Farm (1903) and Anne Shirley in Montgomery's *Anne of
Green Gables*. Like Jo March, these heroines are also given to impulsive behaviour and occasional acts of rebellion. But as they grow older, Rebecca and
Anne increasingly yield to social pressures. Above all, they start to take care
of other people, as respectable women are supposed to do. In later life, then,
the unconventionality of these literary heroines narrows to a single trait, a
penchant for literary self-expression. And in the end, like most other fictional
heroines, even Rebecca and Anne must be married off—although this conventional denouement is postponed to the sequels of the stories in which these
literary heroines make their debuts. ⟨. . .⟩

Wiggin and Montgomery do not make their fiction illustrate a systematic
feminist theory, as Alcott did. Wiggin does make her youthful heroine complain: "Boys always do the nice splendid things, and girls can only do the nasty
dull ones that get left over. They can't climb so high, or go so far, or stay out
so late, or run so fast, or anything" (*RSF* 13). But Rebecca, and Anne as well,
soon abandon their incipient feminism as they approach maturity. Yet Wiggin
and Montgomery are not entirely innocent of ideas. Examined carefully, their
fiction embodies a view of human nature that differs markedly from Alcott's
view. I mean that Montgomery and Wiggin understand their heroines primarily from a psychological perspective, whereas Alcott understood her characters primarily in moral terms. In other words, Rebecca and Anne are not
presented as "little women" but as children: they are part of a separate class of
humanity, with special emotional and intellectual needs that adults have a duty
to meet. However, Rebecca and Anne lose their privileged status as they
approach maturity; Wiggin and Montgomery could never allow an adult the
latitude that they permit to their juvenile protagonists.

—T. D. MacLulich, "L. M. Montgomery and the Literary Heroine: Jo, Rebecca, Anne, and
Emily," *Canadian Children's Literature* 37 (1985): 5, 9–11

SUSAN DRAIN

Finding one's rightful place in the social fabric is part of the challenge of growing up, and as such, it is an important focus of many books for and about chil-

dren. An entire tradition of nineteenth- and early twentieth-century "orphan tales" is explicitly concerned with the problem of identifying and occupying that rightful place. In books, like *The Wide, Wide World* (1850), *Elsie Dinsmore* (1867), and *Pollyanna* (1913), an orphaned or motherless heroine finds herself in a new and strange situation; the novel traces the course of events and adjustments which are made to ensure that the heroine takes her proper place at last. These adjustments usually work in one of two ways: either the child is subdued to the pattern of the adults, as in *The Wide, Wide World* (a book which is in this way not much more than a Sunday school tract), or like Elsie and Pollyanna, the child manages by the sweetness of her character and the power of her example to transform the narrow and bitter adults around her. In either case, belonging actually means conformity; the only question which remains is who is to conform to whom. The more realistic, and not coincidentally, the better-known, books in this tradition accept that the process of adjustment is a mutual one, in which both the stranger and the community are changed by their contact with each other. Adoption, in short, means adaptation.

Lucy Maud Montgomery's *Anne of Green Gables* is one of these more realistic orphan tales. The very title of the book suggests how important belonging is. The heroine's identity is defined not by her deeds, not even by a name which is particularly and essentially individual, but by the name of the household of which she is a part. From its title and from its initial pattern of movement—the entrance of a stranger into a small and literally insular community—the reader may expect the novel to deserve its frequent epithet "heart-warming". For *Anne* is one of those well-loved children's books the virtues of which are obscured by the very affection in which they are held. Its popular appeal, and its reputation even among those who have not read the book, mean that it requires a strong as well as a sensitive reader to see past the expected patterns to appreciate the subtleties and complexities of the experience the book presents. Any novel, however, which begins with three successive chapters entitled "Mrs. Rachel Lynde is Surprised", "Matthew Cuthbert is Surprised", and "Marilla Cuthbert is Surprised" ought to alert the reader to the possibility that this novel will confound expectation as often as confirm it.

Although the novel does trace stages in the mutual adaptation of individual and community, stages by which the one comes to belong to the other, it exhibits a more complex pattern than one of moving inward, of increasing conformity and stability. Instead, an essential part of belonging is the movement outward, for it is only with the independence made possible by the security of belonging that the fullest meaning of belonging can truly be realized. Beneath its heart-warming popular image, in short, *Anne* presents a vision of the relation between community and individual which is complex as well as close, challenging as well as comfortable.

If the title suggests that individuality is less important than community, the first chapter of the book seems to confirm that suggestion, for it is an introduction not to the eponymous protagonist, but to the community to which she is to belong. What is important to notice about this introduction is twofold: first, it is clear that belonging to Green Gables necessarily means belonging to the larger Avonlea community, and second, it is implied that "belonging" is a more complex relationship than one might initially expect— not one of subordination, possession, or conformity, but of interdependence and tension.

—Susan Drain, "Community and the Individual in *Anne of Green Gables*: The Meaning of Belonging," *Children's Literature Association Quarterly* 11, no. 1 (Spring 1986): 15–16

CAROL GAY

When *Anne of Green Gables* was first published in 1908, there had been nothing like it in children's literature since Alcott's *Little Women. Little Women* spawned the so-called "family story"—*The Five Little Peppers* and such—but no one until Montgomery took the female protagonist and, with the realism that Alcott had pioneered, created a worthy successor to Jo March. It had been a long time for readers to wait, and perhaps this is one reason why the response to *Anne of Green Gables* was so immediately strong and to Montgomery, so unexpected.

But it is not Alcott who comes to mind when one is reading *Anne*. It is Sarah Orne Jewett and her superb *The Country of the Pointed Firs*, written in the tradition of the New England local colorists with its depiction of "a rural realm that existed on the margins of patriarchal society, a world that nourished strong, free women" and which "created a counter-tradition to the sentimental/domestic convention that dominated American women's writing through most of the nineteenth century" according to Josephine Donovan's recent *New England Local Color Literature*. Unlike Jewett's women, Alcott's Jo is clearly constrained within a patriarchal world. She doesn't succumb, but she doesn't overcome it either. This is the paradox (and tragedy) of Alcott and Jo. They remain the perennial tomboy. But not Anne; she's always a girl.

Anne's sorrows are not those that come from chafing against her womanhood and the deprivation this entails in a man's world; her sorrows are those of womankind: the death of a child, the loneliness of old age, separation from a child, the loss of a beloved. For Anne lives in a woman's world. Not that men disappear. There are a few, Matthew, for instance, and Gilbert, of course, and Mr. J. A. Harrison, and Captain Jim and Owen Ford and a few others, but they, most of them, are "kindred spirits" who share traditionally women's values and who, without becoming emasculated, share with Anne the world she inhabits.

That world is a very real one, situated squarely on Prince Edward's Island's rocky coast with its fruit trees and farms and woods that still thrill with their beauty. Here, in a realistic credible world, the reader is introduced to an extra-ordinarily rich menage of female characters.

Few writers can characterize so adeptly, so quickly, and frequently, so poignantly, as Montgomery. She does it as well as Jewett and better than Harriet Beecher Stowe. And she has a sense of humor. There are always the shifting groups of girls, and, later, women, which Anne draws around her wherever she settles. And there are the memorable individuals that stand out so clearly. There is Rachel Lynde, who appears on the first page of *Anne of Green Gables*, "notable housewife," "one of those capable creatures who can manage their own concerns and those of other folks into the bargain." There are also Janet Sweet, in *Anne of Avonlea*, who waited twenty years for John Douglas to propose; Miss Lavender, whose pride let her lover leave her over a petty quarrel and who then retires to a life of solitude; Leslie Moore of *House of Dreams*, the gorgeous beauty married to a husband with the mind of a five-year-old; Mrs. Allan, of *Green Gables*, the minister's young wife, whose joy of following her husband to his next parish is marred by the grief of abandoning the grave of her first-born. Or Miss Patty, age seventy, and Miss Maria, age fifty, in *Anne of the Island*, who live together contentedly and quietly in a house called "Patty's Place" until one day they up and go to Europe. As Miss Patty declares, "I daresay I'd gone to Europe before if the idea had occurred to me." When they hear of Anne's approaching marriage they write in *House of Dreams*: "We send you our best wishes. Maria and I have never married, but we have no objection to other people doing so." And there is Miss Cornelia Bryant who knows everyone around Four Winds Harbor in *House of Dreams* and hates all men.

The life stories of these women, joyful and tragic, do not disturb the plot line of the novels. They are, indeed, the fabric of Montgomery's work, for the novels depend not on plot, but on the even flow of life, women's life. They revolve around a steady pattern of breakfast, dinner, and supper, and the intricate relationships between neighbors, mothers and sons, mothers and daughters, and the problems of growing up and raising children.

—Carol Gay, "'Kindred Spirits' All: Green Gables Revisited," *Children's Literature Association Quarterly* 11, no. 1 (Spring 1986): 10–11

JANET WEISS-TOWN

Anne of Green Gables is not a sexist book. But it *is* a girl's book; at least L. M. Montgomery saw it as a girl's book. "I thought girls in their teens might like it but that was the only audience I hoped to reach," she wrote, astounded at the book's instant success when it was published in June 1908 ⟨Mollie Gillen, *The Wheel of Things*, 1975, 26⟩.

⟨. . .⟩ *Anne* has the sort of plot usually found in girls' books, a plot quite different from a boy's book like *Treasure Island*. The girl's book occurs, basically, in a safe, domestic setting; the boy's book is an adventure, set against a backdrop of action and violence. But despite this gender difference, they both operate as wish fulfillment fantasy for children. The child in each book has the capability or power to change the lives of the adults they touch.

Anne can't help but affect those she touches for the better. Her ecstatic buoyancy and nature-loving spirit melt the heart of even Marilla; a person, we are told, "always slightly distrustful of sunshine, which seemed to her too dancing and irresponsible a thing for a world which was meant to be taken seriously" (4). Anne's imagination not only enriches her own life, but helps others to see the world in a new and better light. Anne is a nurturer. She enriches the lives of those around her emotionally and spiritually. The nurturing role is traditionally an adult female role.

If Anne's role is that of the nurturer, Jim Hawkins of *Treasure Island* acts as a protector and provider for the adults in his life. You would expect that as the only child in *Treasure Island*, amidst cut-throats and pirates, Jim would require the protection, but not so. ⟨. . .⟩ Jim is responsible, because of his actions, for the safety and well being of the captain, the squire and the doctor. He is, in a sense, their protector. He is also responsible, more than anyone perhaps, for their finding the treasure which provides each of them with a handsome financial reward. He is, therefore, their provider. The adult male member of a household is traditionally the protector and provider.

In a peculiar way, both Anne and Jim's innocence and youth are precisely the characteristics which allow them to obtain these adult roles. Were Anne an adult, she would be considered a frivolous scatterbrain. Those same characteristics which are so endearing in the young Anne, appear quite foolish in an adult. Were Jim an adult, he would never have been able to abandon the group: helping himself to food and pistols, to steal over the wall and eventually recapture the ship. As a child he can get away with it. ⟨. . .⟩

Anne and Jim, as children, share a common, innocent and romantic way of viewing their respective adventures. Though both are touched by death, neither is ultimately damaged by it. In fact they see death quite romantically. When Jim discovers that the pirates have taken over the block house with no sign of his friends, "I could only judge that all had perished, and my heart smote me sorely that I had not been there to perish with him" (168). There's a certain romance in dying bravely with your friends. Or in Anne's case, dying bravely *for* your friends:

> I was thinking the loveliest story about you and me, Diana. I thought
> you were desperately ill with smallpox and everybody deserted you,

but I went boldly to your bedside and nursed you back to life; and
then I took the smallpox and died and I was buried under those
poplar trees in the graveyard and you planted a rosebush by my grave
and watered it with your tears; and you never, never forgot the friend
of your youth who sacrificed her life for you. (309)

Anne and Jim each represent a delicate balance: they are both children
with the power of adults and the security of being children. Anne can be a nurturer; Jim can be a protector and provider. But when the story is over, they
both go back home, as all children do, because home is, after all, where security lies for most children. They do go home changed, but there is no real
sense that their childlike sense of innocence about the world has entirely vanished.

Anne of Green Gables is not, then, a sexist book. It is merely a typical children's book. As with most children's storybook heroes and heroines, there may
be some sense of Jim and Anne having reached maturity at the end of the
story; but we are still left with that ambiguous mixture of part child and part
adult.

—Janet Weiss-Town, "Sexism down on the Farm? *Anne of Green Gables*," *Children's Literature
Association Quarterly* 11, no. 1 (Spring 1986): 14–15

Bibliography

Anne of Green Gables. 1908.
Anne of Avonlea. 1909.
Kilmeny of the Orchard. 1910.
The Story Girl. 1911.
Chronicles of Avonlea. 1912.
The Golden Road. 1913.
Anne of the Island. 1915.
The Watchman and Other Poems. 1916.
Anne's House of Dreams. 1917.
Rainbow Valley. 1919.
Further Chronicles of Avonlea. 1920.
Rilla of Ingleside. 1921.
Emily of New Moon. 1923.
Emily Climbs. 1925.
The Blue Castle. 1926.

Emily's Quest. 1927.
Magic for Marigold. 1929.
A Tangled Web. 1931.
Pat of Silver Bush. 1933.
Courageous Women (with Marian Keith and Mabel Burns McKinley). 1934.
Mistress Pat. 1935.
Anne of Windy Poplars. 1936.
Jane of Lantern Hill. 1937.
Anne of Ingleside. 1939.
The Alpine Path: The Story of My Career. 1974.
The Road to Yesterday. 1974.
The Doctor's Sweetheart and Other Stories. 1974.
The Selected Journals of L. M. Montgomery (two volumes). 1985, 1987.
The Poetry of Lucy Maud Montgomery. 1987.
Akin to Anne: Tales of Other Orphans. 1988.
Along the Shore: Tales by the Sea. 1989.
Among the Shadows: Tales from the Darker Side. 1990.

Edith Nesbit
1858 – 1924

EDITH NESBIT was born August 15, 1858, the sixth child of Sara Alderton and John Collis Nesbit, an agricultural chemist. John Nesbit died when Edith was four, leaving Sara to raise her six children alone. At eight, Edith was sent to one of the many boarding schools she would attend, and it was at about this time that Sara had to move the family from their home at the Agricultural College where John, and later, she, had served as administrator, because one of the older children, Mary, came down with consumption. With Mary's death in 1871, Sara Nesbit rented a house in Kent and recalled her children from boarding school; during this relatively happy time Edith had some of her verses first published in periodicals. After four years in Kent, however, the family moved to London because of financial trouble.

Edith was seven months' pregnant when, in April of 1880, she married the father of her child, Hubert Bland, the son of a clerk. The unorthodox circumstances of the marriage were heightened by the fact that Hubert was already engaged to his mother's long-time companion, with whom he would later father a son; this sort of infidelity persisted throughout the couple's marriage despite Hubert's pose as a conservative. Edith had given birth to three children by 1885, when her fourth child was stillborn. The Blands asked a friend of theirs, Alice Hoatson, to nurse Edith through her grief. Within a year, however, Alice herself was pregnant with an illegitimate child, and only after Edith had offered to raise the child as her own and to have Alice live with them as a housekeeper did she discover that the child, Rosamond, was fathered by Hubert. Nonetheless, she adopted Rosamond, as she later adopted Alice and Hubert's son, John. Alice continued to live with the Blands as a housekeeper.

The strain these arrangements caused Edith and her conspiracy in concealing them are recorded by her admirer and frequent visitor, H. G. Wells. He had met the Blands through the Fabian Society, which the Blands had helped to found. The society brought many interesting people into the Bland household (Well Hall), among whom were George Bernard Shaw, Annie Besant, Beatrix Potter, and Joseph Conrad. Edith, who was Bohemian in her dress and appearance, was admired for her flamboyance, wit, and playfulness and became tangled up in several affairs with members of the society. She later used the names of some of her suitors in her children's books.

The majority of Nesbit's writing at this time was popular verse and fiction for adults. She supported her family by publishing her work, which was fortunate as Bland, despite his conservative stance, failed to make any money at his short-lived attempt at business. Though Edith's verse was mediocre, she would prove to be a remarkable fantasy writer for children and is often credited with defining the conventional limitations of magic's efficacy in children's literature. The first of 16 installments of her children's novel *The Story of the Treasure Seekers* appeared in the Christmas supplement of the *Illustrated London News* in 1897. Despite this success, Nesbit suffered in her personal life: in October of 1900, her son Fabian died, and the loss left Nesbit grief-stricken and affected all her subsequent writing. In the years following Fabian's death, however, she gained some economic stability with the publication of *The Book of Dragons* (1900) and a serialized version of her novel *The Five Children and It* (1902).

Over the next eight years, Nesbit's fantasy novels evolved into more psychologically compelling works and included such books as *The Railway Children* (1906), *The Story of the Amulet* (1906), and *The Enchanted Castle* (1907). But after this period, her work seems to have suffered, possibly on account of the financial pressure intensified by her husband's blindness and heart trouble. Two years after her final children's novel, *Wet Magic*, was published (1912), with the onset of World War I and Hubert's death, Edith suffered a collapse in her health and in her economic stability. She would continue to be financially troubled, but her later years were relatively contented: her marriage in 1917 to marine engineer Thomas Terry Tucker seems at last to have been a happy one. Edith Nesbit died in 1924.

Critical Extracts

H. G. WELLS

The Blands were almost the first people I met at all intimately, who were fundamentally intricate, who had no primary simple idea. They had brains as active and powerful as most other brains in my world, but—as I began to realize only after some disconcerting experiences—they had never taken them down to any sort of philosophy; they had never focussed them on any single objective, and they started off at all sorts of levels from arbitrarily adopted fantasies and poses.

The incongruity of Bland's costume with his Bohemian setting, the costume of a city swell, top-hat, tail-coat, greys and blacks, white slips, spatter-dashes and that black-ribboned monocle, might have told me, had I had the ability then to read such signs, of the general imagination at work in his *persona*, the myth of a great Man of the World, a Business Man (he had no gleam of business ability) invading for his own sage strong purposes this assembly of long-haired intellectuals. This myth had, I think, been developed and sustained in him, by the struggle of his egoism against the manifest fact that his wife had a brighter and fresher mind than himself, and had subtler and livelier friends. For many years, says ⟨the biographer Doris Langley⟩ Moore, she carried on a long correspondence with Laurence Housman and I guess that Bland had had to protect his self-esteem against many such intimations of insufficiency in his own equipment. He could not pervade her. That particular correspondence, the biographer relates, was ended when E. Nesbit, against her character and disposition, followed Bland on the anti-feminist side of the suffrage dispute.

In the end she became rather a long-suffering lady, but her restless needle of a mind, her quick response, kept her always an exacting and elusive lady. It was I am convinced because she, in her general drift, was radical and anarchistic, that the pose of Bland's self-protection hardened into this form of gentlemanly conservatism. He presented himself as a Tory in grain, he became—I know of no confirmation—a man of good old family; he entered the dear old Roman Catholic church. These were all insistencies upon soundness and solidity as against her quickness and whim. He was publicly emphatic for social decorum, punctilio, the natural dependence of women and the purity of the family. None of your modern stuff for *him*. All this socialism he assured you, so far as it was any good, was a reaction from nineteenth century liberalism to the good old social organization that flourished in England before the days of Adam Smith.

She acquiesced in these posturings. If she had not, I suppose he would have argued with her until she did, and he was a man of unfaltering voice and great determination. But a gay holiday spirit bubbled beneath her verbal orthodoxies and escaped into her work. The Bastables are an anarchistic lot. Her soul was against the government all the time.

—H. G. Wells, *Experiment in Autobiography* (New York: The Macmillan Company, 1934), 514–15

BARBARA SMITH

The most obvious stereotypes in E. Nesbit's writing are not of poor people or of women, but of minority groups. Jews, Indians, "savages," and Blacks all merit a derogatory phrase or two. In *The Story of the Treasure Seekers* the children visit a moneylender, Z. Rosenbaum, whom they believe to be a generous benefactor. Mr. Rosenbaum has "a very long white beard and a hookey nose—like a falcon" and he says that he can lend the children a pound at sixty per cent interest, payable when they are twenty-one (p. 105). Oswald remarks, "And all the time he was stroking the sovereign and looking at it as if he thought it very beautiful." ⟨. . .⟩

In *The Story of the Amulet*, which makes the most positive statement of any of the works about the need for social reforms, there is nevertheless an adventure in the financial district in which Old Levinstein and another Mr. Rosenbaum are portrayed as being selfish, usorious, and incapable of speaking "decent" English ⟨172-74⟩.

The expression "nigger" is used indiscriminately in several of the works. In *The Story of the Treasure Seekers* the Indian uncle compliments Oswald by saying ". . . he's a man! If he's not a man, I'm a nigger! Eh!—what?" (p. 198). In a recent edition of *The Conscience Pudding*, excerpted from *The New Treasure Seekers*, the word nigger is deleted. Obviously it had little negative significance to white people at the time that E. Nesbit was writing, but merely expressed the attitudes that she and her audience shared about the negligibility of dark-skinned people.

In *The Phoenix and the Carpet*, one of the children suggests that they can escape from a band of savages by going into the water, because, as he explains, "I've—heard—savages always—dirty" ⟨70⟩. In this case the children have been negatively indoctrinated, whereas in the case of the first Mr. Rosenbaum, they were innocent about the attitude they were expected to hold.

These incidents and phrases are hardly essential to the total conceptions of the works as a whole, yet they do indirectly reflect the attitudes of the society in which Nesbit did her writing, if not her personal opinions. Indeed, it is very difficult to pin down E. Nesbit's attitudes on any of these matters. Is she serious or satirical in her statements about the role of women? Is she in fact more sympathetic toward her bungling wouldbegoods' efforts to alleviate the sufferings of the poor than she is toward the poor themselves? To what degree are her attitudes affected by her own experience of social reform movements and by her husband's encouragement of her commitment to certain causes? Do any of these matters bear consideration when it is known that E. Nesbit usually wrote under the constraint to earn money and therefore to please her publishers and the public, if not always herself?

These questions are partly answered in her later works, in which, as Moore points out, she is much less subtle in expressing her personal views, often to the detriment of her story. In *The Story of the Amulet* (1906) there is, however, a skillful blending of a children's magical adventure and a clear-cut statement of E. Nesbit's social concerns. This is the most philosophical of the three magic books about the children Cyril, Anthea, Robert, and Jane, and it is also the most fascinating on an adult level. Her magical plot device, the idea of travel through time, enables her to explore themes which go beyond a mere fantasy for children. The amulet, which transports the children to different civilizations of the past, is much more complex in its magic than the Psammead or the Phoenix and the carpet, because it requires a highly abstract understanding of the dimension of time. The children gradually learn to think of time in unconventional ways, following the advice of the Psammead that "Time and space are only forms of thought" (p. 61). Not only does their understanding of the particular concept grow, but in all the three magic books they seem to increase in wisdom as a result of their magical adventures.

In the first of the series, *The Five Children and It*, the children are quite thoughtless in the wishes they ask the Psammead to grant them and they usually suffer more than they benefit from the magic they have at their disposal. In *The Phoenix and the Carpet* the children get into just as much trouble, although there is the added excitement of being instantly transported in space to a new setting. The Phoenix has the role of a semi-adult figure and provides both instruction and entertainment for the children. In both these works they learn to take into account the feelings of others, since the Psammead as well as the Phoenix are demanding and self-centered. In *The Story of the Amulet* the children have reached the stage at which they can appreciate the lessons of "history" and carefully follow the directions which safe use of the amulet requires.

—Barbara Smith, "The Expression of Social Values in the Writing of E. Nesbit," *Children's Literature* 3 (1974): 160–61

FRED INGLIS

I take ⟨as my subject⟩ *The Railway Children* because it is so well known and well filmed, and because along with *The Secret Garden*, *Alice*, *The Wind in the Willows*, much of Walter de la Mare, Kipling's 'English' stories (like *Puck*), Little Grey Rabbit and Christopher Robin, it lives in that breathing-space forced by men's imaginations and by their struggles and sacrifices, between the family home and the world of work, production, money-making, or the creation of surplus value. These children's writers, in the wake of both poets and politicians, saw the freedom of the countryside as both fact and metaphor for the restoration of a humanness in danger of killing divisions from home and work. It is no accident that so many of these writers were women (or self-consciously separate and 'impractical' men like Dodgson, de la Mare, Kipling). The women saw the separation of manly and feminine virtues as deadly, and attempted to free children from the results of this split. The children (in *The Wind in the Willows*, the animals) have to work out their lives away from parents and placed in the space between home and work. The railway children, for instance, have lost caste when their father is (wrongfully) imprisoned. Their mother must work at her writing to make ends meet. Freed from the moral divisions of labour in the family, with mother ruling at a distance but perfectly combining justice with mercy, the three children set out to make their own moral and political economy.

⟨. . .⟩ They construct that moral economy in a landscape memorably uniting culture and nature. As nowhere else, the railway is at home in the Yorkshire dales where the cuttings follow the natural line of the dale, and the stations are tucked so neatly into the lip of the bank, their fluttering ribbons of barge-boarding setting off so prettily gritstone building and steep beds of wallflowers. The children's first productive move is to steal coal. They are caught by the station master and put to rights about *that*. In a rather touching scene a little later, Peter ensures that the kindly, authoritative station master really knows that it is the erstwhile coal-miner whom he greets so benignly on his way down to work ⟨. . . .⟩ It is well done. Edith Nesbit restores Peter to the company of honourable men; the station master has the dignity and the office to be unselfconsciously generous and courteous in all encounters. Like Mr Perks, he has to be highminded to do this, and it is the strenuous highmindedness of the book which, as with the others of the Victorian and Edwardian era, may sometimes become irksome. But the highmindedness coincides with great humour and finesse. The second stage of their economy-building is to go to the kindly old gentleman for aid.

The kindly old gentleman has beamed his rubicund way through many a novel since Mr Brownlow rescued Oliver in *Oliver Twist*. In the case of *The Railway Children* I don't think there is any need to say, in a beady-eyed way, that a philanthropic railway director could only have the money to be so philanthropic if he snatched the bread from the bleeding lips of the starving proletarians. In *The Railway Children*, the old gentleman represents the possibility of a prompt and rational altruism, the possibility, even the likelihood, of which we would always seek to urge upon children. Odd though it now sounds to say so, it is the dream hidden in the idea of a welfare state; the institutions of health and shelter were intended to carry those qualities of care, magnanimity, and understanding which the old gentleman has the power to display.

It is important in the simple moral patterning of the novel that the children, upheld by the altruism of so many people—old gentleman, railwaymen, doctor—which their own earnest commitment to goodness may be said to have called out, themselves go on to act philanthropically. In the third stage of their economy, they make a collection of birthday presents from the villagers to give to their honoured friend Mr Perks the porter at the station. But

Mr Perks, in his self-reliance and self-respect, is deeply affronted by the impli-
cation of a condescending charity and by the view he understandably
imputes to the villagers that he cannot meet his proper domestic responsibilities ⟨. . . .⟩

The best of liberal values lies in that touching passage. The children, in
their innocence, have come up against the lines of class in Edwardian England
which they hardly knew to be there, but because their innocence is such that
they have themselves created a different structure of moral intention in all the
villagers, the new economy may fit the best terms of the old morality. Perks's
self-respect matches the children's goodness. Mrs Nesbit sums the lesson up
with great tact at the end of the chapter:

> When the clergyman called on Mrs Perks, she told him all about it. 'It
> *was* friendliness, wasn't it, Sir?' said she.
>   'I think,' said the clergyman, 'it was what is sometimes called loving-
> kindness.'
>   So you see it was all right in the end. But if one does that sort of
> thing, one has to be careful to do it in the right way. For, as Mr Perks
> said, when he had time to think it over, it's not so much what you do,
> as what you mean. (p. 162)

Speaking in this way of this fine novel makes it too much into an Edwardian
moral homily. In the reading Edith Nesbit's tone is light and blithe and brisk;
she very rarely lapses into the gushingness to which her combination of moth-
erly earnestness and uplift inevitably tend. My brief analysis perhaps serves to
show how these novels commend to children the best versions of the values
made possible by Victorian society, and how the novelists brace those values
against both the family and the big world in the creative effort of all writers
to transcend division and find a new unity of culture and being.

—Fred Inglis, *The Promise of Happiness: Value and Meaning in Children's Fiction* (Cambridge:
Cambridge University Press, 1981), 113–17

HUMPHREY CARPENTER

Children's books featured among ⟨Edith Nesbit's⟩ hack-work from quite early
on; they had such titles as *Pussy Tales* and *Doggy Tales*. She was in the
Molesworth tradition, a competent, professional, entirely uninspired lady children's author. Then the *Girl's Own Paper* commissioned her to write some rem-
iniscences of her childhood, and this, coupled with the appearance a few
months later of Grahame's *Dream Days*, seems to have suggested to her the idea
of writing something rather new in English children's fiction. Some of the stories which afterwards made up *The Treasure Seekers* appeared in magazines dur-

ing 1898, and the book itself came out a year later. Suddenly her name was made.

The Story of the Treasure Seekers, to give it its full title, seemed entirely new in its predominantly *comic* treatment of children. Nesbit had taken the formula of *The Golden Age* and *Dream Days*—a family of children able to conduct their lives with very little adult supervision—and used it for a series of comic set-pieces. The comedy was achieved partly through the characters of three of the children: the idealistic poet Noël, the would-be-heroic Oswald, and the youngest, H.O. (Horace Octavius); another brother, Dicky, and the girls, Dora and Alice, are less sharply characterised. But the chief source of humour is the narration; Oswald himself tells the story, though he tries to disguise his identity and to praise 'Oswald' dispassionately as though he were not himself:

> It is one of us that tells this story—but I shall not tell you which:
> only at the very end perhaps I will . . . It was Oswald who first
> thought of looking for treasure. Oswald often thinks of very interest-
> ing things . . .

The sustained humour of *The Treasure Seekers* may be original; the device of child as narrator is not. It was used in several children's books which preceded Nesbit's, most notably Dickens's *A Holiday Romance* (1868) and Mrs Ewing's *A Great Emergency* (1877), and the Ewing book has something of the flavour of the Bastables. Yet the fact that Oswald is telling the story, funny as it may be, disguises the true nature of *The Treasure Seekers*, which is as condescending towards children as are any of the Beautiful Child books of the Molesworth era. ⟨. . .⟩

In fact *The Treasure Seekers* is a strikingly old-fashioned book. Underneath the comedy, the Bastables are steadily being schooled in the accepted adult virtues. Not only do the adults patronise them; they never hesitate to deliver little moral lectures. Albert-next-door's uncle, the adult most involved with their games, is also the one most ready to be plainly didactic:

> Albert's uncle came in next day and talked to each of us separately.
> To Oswald he said many unpleasant things about it being ungentle-
> manly to spy on ladies, and about minding your own business . . .

> When Albert-next-door had gone his uncle sat in the Guy Fawkes
> armchair and took Alice on his knee . . . At last he said —
>   'Look here, young 'uns. I like to see you play and enjoy yourselves
> . . . But what about Albert's mother? Didn't you think how anxious
> she would be at his not coming home?' . . . He only talks like that
> when he is very serious, or even angry.

Very often there is no need for adults to impress the desirability of virtuous behaviour on the Bastables—they are aware of it already. Stricken with conscience because Alice has knowingly used a 'bad sixpence' to pay for a telegram, they make every effort to raise money and replace it with a good one, even to the extent of Oswald putting on ragged clothes and selling flowers outside a railway station. One might suppose from passages such as this that the book is at its heart an old-fashioned moral tale, with the children eventually reaping the reward of good conduct, were it not for the fact that the dénouement (the showering of a fortune on the family by the children's 'Indian Uncle') is chiefly the result not of their virtues but of their simple-mindedness.

The truth is that Nesbit was essentially a late Victorian writer, who accepted the attitude, prevalent in the 1870s and 1880s, that children are delightfully naïve.

—Humphrey Carpenter, *Secret Gardens: A Study of the Golden Age of Children's Literature* (London: George Allen & Unwin, 1985), 132, 134–35

U. C. KNOEPFLMACHER

Nesbit ⟨. . .⟩ is hardly as different from her Victorian peers as she might seem. She, too, remains an anti-fantastic fantasist who derives much of her power from her ambivalence about the female imagination she sets out to reappropriate. Yet, in one significant respect, Nesbit does differ from the "mentorias" before her. Her resistance to the magical realms she domesticates and controls through irony does not stem from the moral inhibitions that had weighed so heavily with earlier women writers. If their incursions into fairylands terrified them because they released pleasurable wishes at odds with the moral order they had agreed to uphold as "the real," her own flights of fancy raised more personal fears about abandonment and dissolution. These fears were rooted in the traumas of an early childhood that she dramatically revived in "My School-Days," the twelve-part series of autobiographical vignettes she published in *The Girl's Own Paper*, from October 1896 to September 1897, just before her first major success as a children's author with *The Treasure Seekers* (1899). ⟨. . .⟩

⟨. . .⟩ In her wishful attempts to repair her sense of incompleteness and loss through the agency of a new female magic, the writer often saw herself as an impostress of sorts. Her ability to view her own enterprise with absolute clarity is evident in her 1901 story of "Fortunatus Rex & Co, or, The Mystery of the Disappearing Schoolgirls." In that wonderfully clever tale, she blended theosophy with humor as a commentary on her inventive efforts to reclaim a territory for the female imagination.

"Fortunatus Rex" playfully recombines some of the same ingredients found in "My School-Days," *Five Children and It*, and *The Story of the Amulet*. The disappearance of Princess Daisy, the youngest of the seven princesses at Miss

Fitzroy Robinson's "Select Boarding Establishment for the Daughters of Respectable Monarchs," is mourned by her inconsolable father King Fortunatus, though not at all by the matter-of-fact Queen whose housekeeping chores do not leave her "much time for weeping" ⟨*E. Nesbit's Fairy Stories*, 1980, 134⟩. Yet if Princess Daisy's magical disappearance and restoration involve a comic fantasy that reprocesses the narratives relied upon by "Daisy" Nesbit to account for her own separation from a too busy mother, the emphasis of the fairy tale falls neither on her nor on the six older princesses who have been similarly abducted, but rather on the figure of their deliverer, Miss Fitzroy Robinson herself. It is this updated version of a fairy godmother that gives "Fortunatus Rex" its delicious vitality.

A composite of the pompous schoolmistresses of Nesbit's youth, of the mother who vainly tried to run the school John Nesbit had set up, and, most importantly, of E. Nesbit herself as a money-making, Psammead-like dispenser of illusions, Miss Robinson profits from her ability to make others believe in her fictions. Though little actual teaching goes on at her permissive educational establishment, she has so impressed "all the really high-class kings" with her phony credentials that they "were only too pleased to be permitted to pay ten thousand pounds a year for their daughters' education" (p. 127). But if, as an educator, Miss Robinson seems far more interested in investing "in land" than in her pupils, her powers as an illusionist nonetheless prove to be deservedly impressive. It is as a magician who can command more powerful spells than her former male instructor in white and black magic that she manages to reclaim the princesses from her rival's enchantment and to demand that, in recompense, King Fortunatus make "green again" the land that his building company has ruthlessly cut into squares for ugly housing developments (p. 144). Secluding herself in seven acres—which she wanted to be walled in a circular structure much like the one housing the Amulet—Miss Robinson zealously guards her orchard. There, she preserves the seven golden apples that imprison Daisy and her six fellow-princesses until each is kissed seven times by six eager princes and Daisy's loving little brother. Just as the green light of the Amulet can mend broken halves, so does Miss Robinson extend her greening powers beyond her seven acres of garden. The male magician that she has cut and placed into two separate geographical globes can fuse his severed halves as soon as the six princesses join their grooms.

Miss Robinson, then, whose name "Fitzroy" would reappear in the city address of the children in *The Story of the Amulet* and whose watch-dog "Martha" bears the name of the children's rural guardian in *Five Children and It*, becomes the preserver and restorer of a female terrain. She is, simultaneously, an impostress and a figure of enormous power, laughable yet awesome. If her momentary negligence causes her wards to disappear, it is Miss Robinson's activation of a magic misused by males that makes her superior to her chief foils—the enchanter who tries to possess her school and its female inmates, and the King whose acquisition of more and more land becomes just as much an act of possession that she must resist.

By asserting Miss Robinson's superiority to these two male rivals, Nesbit signifies her own reappropriation of a literary province. That reappropriation is made possible by the balance she asks us to value in a figure that is neither as power-hungry as the magician who tries to wrest away her pupils nor as sentimental as the King who must mutilate the countryside in order to find compensation for the loss of little Daisy. As enamoured of little girls as Lewis Carroll and other male child-lovers, Fortunatus finds little comfort "in the fact that his other child, Prince Denis, was spared to him. Denis was all very well and a nice little boy in his way, but a boy is not a girl" (p. 134). Nesbit enlists Miss Robinson to reclaim the King as much as his daughter. He must learn that material power cannot compensate him for emotional loss.

Nesbit's shrewd correction of the male fantasists who had adopted forms not their own to sustain their loss of the feminine could come only from one who had achieved a full understanding of the compensatory nature of her own art as a fantasist. As she realized, only the wishful structures of a fully balanced, mature woman could bring home a little girl lost.

—U. C. Knoepflmacher, "Of Babylands and Babylons: E. Nesbit and the Reclamation of the Fairy Tale," *Tulsa Studies in Women's Literature* 6, no. 2 (Fall 1987): 302, 321–23

ALISON LURIE

The typical Victorian fantasy for children, though it may begin in the real world, soon moves into some timeless Wonderland or country at the back of the North Wind. One of Nesbit's most brilliant innovations was to reverse the process and bring magic into modern London. (In this, it has been pointed out, she may have been following the lead of a contemporary writer of adult fantasy, F. Anstey.) She was the first to imagine, for a child audience, what would be the actual consequences of the delivery by magic carpet of 199 Persian cats to the basement dining room of a house in Camden Town, or of the transformation of one's brother into a ten-foot boy giant.

Even Nesbit's short tales, though they may contain magicians and dragons and kings and queens, clearly take place in the present. The details of the stories, and the language in which they are told, are always up-to-date. Discarding the romantic diction of the fairy tale and its conventional epithets—the golden hair and milk-white steeds—she uses contemporary juvenile slang and draws her comparisons from the Edwardian child's world of experience. The dragon in "Uncle James" has "wings like old purple umbrellas that have been very much rained on," and the court officials in "The Book of Beasts" wear "gold coronets with velvet sticking up out of the middle like the cream in the very expensive jam tarts." The hands of the unpleasant Miss Minto in *Five of Us, and Madeline* are "like hot goldfishes, red and wet."

Though we tend to take it for granted, the importance of magic in juvenile literature needs some explanation. Why, in a world that is so wonderful and various and new to them, should children want to read about additional, unreal wonders? The usual explanation is a psychological one: magic provides an escape from reality or expresses fears and wishes. In the classic folktale, according to this theory, fear of starvation becomes a witch or a wolf, cannibalism an ogre. Desire shapes itself as a pot that is always full of porridge, a stick that will beat one's enemies on command, a mother who comes back to life as a benevolent animal or bird. Magic in children's literature, too, can make psychological needs and fears concrete; children confront and defeat threatening adults in the form of giants, or they become supernaturally large and strong; and though they cannot yet drive a car, they travel to other planets.

Magic can do all this, but it can do more. In the literary folktale, it often becomes a metaphor for the imagination. This is particularly true of Nesbit's stories. "The Book of Beasts," for instance, can be read as a fable about the power of imaginative art. The magic volume of its title contains colored pictures of exotic creatures, which become real when the book is left open. The little boy who finds it releases first a butterfly, then a bird of paradise, and finally a dragon that threatens to destroy the country. If any book is vivid enough, this story says, what is in it will become real to us and invade our world for good or evil.

—Alison Lurie, *Don't Tell the Grown-ups* (Boston: Little, Brown and Company, 1990), 110–11

ANITA MOSS

An heir to Romantic conceptions of nature, art, imagination, and the child, Nesbit celebrated creative activity of all kinds and stressed the imagination's capacity to infuse life with meaning and value. Hostile to the industrial invasion of England, Nesbit often expressed nostalgia for the past. She explored the limits of time and space, dimensions which take an inward turn in her children's stories, just as they do in many Romantic works of literature. While Nesbit abhorred the ugliness of industrial England and praised the value of life close to nature, she nevertheless exhibited an enduring fascination with science and a decided taste for a sophisticated cultural life available only in great cities.

Despite the numerous oppositions readily apparent in her life and children's stories, Nesbit managed to liberate herself and children's books from Victorian constraints. She become the most famous Edwardian writer for children and breathed new and vital life into the Romantic child with the publication of her "Bastable Stories"—*The Story of the Treasure Seekers* (1899), *The Wouldbegoods* (1901), and *The New Treasure Seekers* (1904). *The Story of the Treasure Seekers* stands squarely between Victorian and modern children's literature and has been acclaimed by critics as ushering in the "Nesbit Tradition" in twentieth-century children's literature, a vision that owes much to Romantic conceptions of childhood and imagination 〈. . . .〉

The most significant way that Nesbit's child characters liberate themselves from static myths of childhood is by seizing control of their own stories to become makers and creators. Unlike Wordsworth's child characters, Nesbit's are highly literate. Although they retain intuitive ways of knowing, the activities of reading, thinking, fabricating, and even artful lying help them to evade sentimentality, constraints, and aggressions of adults. While Wordsworth and MacDonald celebrate the simplicity and innocence of children, Lewis Carroll and Nesbit rejoice in their complexity, intelligence, and experience. Nesbit encourages her child characters and her readers to transcend literary and social convention, to speak in radically new voices, and to create new idioms and myths of childhood, just as Nesbit herself broke free of some rather stifling conventions of Victorian children's literature. 〈. . . C〉hildren in Romantic and Victorian children's literature have been entrapped in texts; it is a telling metaphor that Philip Haldane frees creatures from texts in *The Magic City*— frees both monsters and marvels, transforms them, and sends them back again. Similarly Nesbit releases her child characters and her child readers from such imprisonment. While Oswald Bastable had feared "grown-upness," Philip Haldane and Lucy of *The Magic City* and Gerald of *The Enchanted Castle* just grow. In her later fantasies Nesbit does not lock magic behind the golden gates of childhood but makes it available within the context of mundane reality. Her characters make the magic for themselves through the creative acts of storytelling and art. Finally, each of these fantasies ends with a reunited family experiencing a sense of renewal and anticipating a future of creative labors together. Implicit in all of Nesbit's children's stories is her profoundly optimistic belief in the human capacity for transformation. New societies may emerge from the ruins of the old, she suggests, just as new stories may be constructed from the worn-out fragments of literary convention.

—Anita Moss, "E. Nesbit's Romantic Child in Modern Dress," in *Romanticism and Children's Literature in 19th-Century England*, ed. James Holt McGavran, Jr. (Athens, GA: University of Georgia Press, 1991), 225–26, 245

SARAH GILEAD

In Edith Nesbit's *Enchanted Castle* (1907), magic represents the power and dangers of desire, as it does in many other fairy tales, including Nesbit's better-known *Five Children and It* (1902). The plot traces the effects of the children's use and final renunciation of a wishing ring. Simultaneous with this renunciation is the achievement of the book's secondary 'adult' plot, a rather predictable romance of thwarted but true love between an English lord and a French governess. The episodic magic plot is replaced by a more conventional linear plot of courtship and marriage. The two stories are linked causally and thematically: the first produces and completes the second, and both are based on wish fulfillment. This double plotting invokes the familiar process of socialization, in which an anarchic childhood realm is replaced by a social world dominated by middle-class events and morality. In the Hall of Psyche, also the Hall of Granted Wishes, Psyche speaks through the governess's lips and teaches the children that wishing exacts a deadly price: death or madness. 'Granted wishes' organize the fantasy plot, but her Psyche renounces the misrule of desire in favour of inner organization by retributive guilt. The main plot has repeatedly demonstrated that children pay a severe though lesser price for wishing. The only free wish is the last, at once renouncing unregulated desire and turning it into a different sort of magic. The governess's final wish is to undo all the magic that the ring has performed and to convert the ring into 'a charm to bind [her and her lover] together for evermore' (Nesbit 1956: 252).

The children's discovery of the ring reflects their deep wish to diversify and enliven reality. On holiday, as the protagonists so often are in children's literature (and in Nesbit, in particular), the children long to loosen or defer the tightening ties to social reality that characterize growing up. The ring they find also embodies narrative desire and energy, producing story patterns without tedious repetition, as various individuals wear the ring, have adventures, and get into trouble. Narrative thrust and the wishing ring disappear simultaneously.

Each fresh episode is at first deliciously unmoored from the ordinary constraints of reality. But if the ring dissolves the barriers between desire and reality, it also operates against desire by showing the crude and troublesome ways that desire obtrudes on reality. ⟨. . .⟩

Where is magic's residue in the ordinary reality that follows the enunciation of magic? After an oneiric feast with the statue gods, the children awaken to a chill, grey day; they stand in brambles and coarse grass. 'There was no smooth lawn, no marble steps, no seven-mooned fish ponds. . . . [I]t was very cold' (Nesbit 1956: 211). But only a few pages later they enjoy a real but idyllic picnic: 'a tea for the gods!' (ibid.: 225). Is unenchanted reality capable after all of engendering its own enchantments? When the wishing ring is replaced by a wedding ring, is egotistical childhood replaced by a satisfying adult moral and social (and sexual) reality? While empowered by the ring, the children enjoy a kind of comical authority over governesses, policy officers, aunts and servants. Without the ring, the adults take over the story and resume their customary dominance over the children. The return to reality is also a turning to sentimentality: do adult wishes only arbitrarily replace the child's? Does the transparent wishfulness of the cliché-ridden romance plot compensate for the loss of the ever-changing fantasy world? Is ordinary reality shown to be intolerable unless softened by such romance? Given its most polarized interpretation, the ending on the one hand insists that desire must be renounced but that the sacrifice is recompensed by personal maturity and social integration and on the other hand provides, more implicitly, covert valorization of anarchic desire; for without anarchic energy, all that is left of desire is a sentimentalized, softened version. The opening framing segment shows the children playing 'The Sleeping Beauty'. The concluding romantic plot is an obvious version of 'Cinderella' (see page 122, where the governess is transformed from sad spinsterhood to beauty and luxuriant sexuality). Thus, the socialization plot the children complete by abjuring magic is itself a fairy tale combined with popular romance. Officially, the ending defines wishing as puerile, dangerous and useless, except as a tool for promoting adult projects such as marriage. But the narrator mocks the reader's naive expectations that the ending will satisfy and exposes the fictionality that underlies all literary realism: 'it is all very well . . . to pretend that the whole of this story is my own invention: facts are facts, and you can't explain them away' (ibid.: 253). 'Facts' refers to the mysterious disappearance, reported in the evening newspaper, of 'Mr. U. W. Ugli', the Ugly-Wugly 'who became real' at the Hall of Granted Wishes, then unreal when wishing was abjured. Playfully addressing the fantasy-reality crux of her own story, Nesbit links the 'realistic' conclusion to an entirely fictional-fantastic 'factuality'. If the socialization plot finally conquers escapist fantasy, fantasy continues to exert ironic pressure on that plot.

—Sarah Gilead, "Magic Abjured: Closure in Children's Fantasy Fiction," in *Literature for Children: Contemporary Criticism*, ed. Peter Hunt (London: Routledge, 1992), 92–95

MARIA NIKOLAJEVA

The key figure of modern fantasy, Edith Nesbit, is a gratifying object for intertextual studies, partly because her works magnificently summarize earlier children's literature, and partly because they pave the way for many English-language children's writers. ⟨. . .⟩

Nesbit's dialogic link to her various predecessors is probably seen best in her full-length fantasy novels, starting with *Five Children and It* (1902). British scholars have pointed out various sources for this text. One is Mary Molesworth's *The Cuckoo Clock* (1877), where a wooden cuckoo plays the part of a good fairy for the child, but there are also two adult novels by F. Anstey: *Vice Versa* (1882) and *The Brass Bottle* (1900). In the first book, father and son in London change places through a magic wish, whereupon the father in his son's image endures the humiliations of a boarding school, while the son is forced to take upon himself the responsibilities of a grownup. *The Brass Bottle* depicts a young London architect who by chance sets free a genie. The genie tries hard to grant his deliverer all his wishes, but everything turns into a big mess. The absurd idea of letting magical figures and objects appear in modern London, and the inability of modern humans to make use of magic are thoughts which appealed to Nesbit, and this is what all of her children's books are based on.

Following Anstey, Nesbit "deconstructs" folktale patterns. Naturally, young readers lack a significant layer of meaning in Nesbit's texts if they are not familiar with folktales. The type of fantasy Nesbit has created is sometimes (quite wrongly, I think) labeled "humorous fantasy" or even "nonsense." The humorous effect depends on the reader having folktales as intertext. In addition to its literary models Molesworth and Anstey, *Five Children and It* refers to the well-known folktale about three wishes in which the third wish must be used to eliminate the devastating consequences of the first two ⟨. . .⟩

⟨Likewise,⟩ the impact of Edith Nesbit on English-language fantasy cannot be overestimated. As Marcus Crouch puts it in a volume characteristically entitled *The Nesbit Tradition*: "no writer today is free from the debt to this remarkable woman." ⟨. . .⟩

The most interesting aspects that are unveiled in intertextual studies, however, are not superficial similarities in plot, motifs, characters or attributes between Nesbit and her followers. More exciting are the hidden echoes from Nesbit which are exposed through serious examinations of the entire genre of fantasy in which she did most of her work. Such studies help us to appreciate Nesbit's enormous contribution to the evolution of fantasy and can provide insights into what this evolution actually involved.

Because Edith Nesbit was the first to develop a "theory" of magical time travel it was she who more or less created this specific subgenre of fantasy. It was developed further in works by many later writers in Britain and other English-speaking countries. All these writers, without referring to Nesbit, accept her "rules" for magical travel in time as if these rules really existed: primary time stands still while the travelers enter other chronotopes; travelers cannot carry objects between chronotopes; travelers have no difficulty understanding and speaking foreign languages; and most important, travelers can in no way interfere with history. Nesbit chooses this principle because the purpose of her time adventures is to present history in an exciting manner; she does not want to get involved with the consequences of such an interference. The confidence of young readers in the permanence of the universe must not be shattered.

—Maria Nikolajeva, *Children's Literature Comes of Age: Toward a New Aesthetic* (New York: Garland Publishing, Inc., 1996), 159, 161, 164, 168

Bibliography

Fading Light: Verses by E. Nesbit. n.d.

Apple Pie. n.d.

Miss Mischief. n.d.

Fairies. n.d.

The Prophet's Mantle (with Hubert Bland as Fabian Bland). 1885.

Lays and Legends. 1886.

River Sketches. 1887.

The Lily and the Cross. 1887.

The Star of Bethlehem. 1887.

All Round the Year (with Caris Brooke). 1888.

The Better Part, and Other Poems. 1888.

Easter-tide: Poems by E. Nesbit and Caris Brooke. 1888.

Landscape and Song. 1888.

The Message of the Dove. 1888.

Leaves of Life. 1888.

Corals and Sea Songs. 1889.

The Lilies Round the Cross (with Helen J. Wood). 1889.

Song of Two Seasons. 1890.

The Voyage of Columbus: Discovery of America. 1891.

Sweet Lavender. 1892.

Lays and Legends: Second Series. 1892.

Grim Tales. 1893.

Something Wrong. 1893.

A Family Novelette (with Oswald Barron). 1894.

The Butler in Bohemia (with Oswald Barron). 1894.

The Marden Mystery. 1894.

Pussy Tales. 1895.

Doggy Tales. 1895.

Rose Leaves. 1895.

A Pomander of Verse. 1895.

Holly and Mistletoe: A Book of Christmas Verse by E. Nesbit, Norman Gale, and Richard Le Gallienne. 1895.

As Happy as a King. 1896.

In Homespun. 1896.

Tales Told in the Twilight. 1897.

The Children's Shakespeare. 1897.

Romeo and Juliet, and Other Stories. 1897.

Dog Tales, and Other Tales (with A. Guest and Emily R. Watson). 1898.

A Book of Dogs: Being a Discourse on Dogs, with Many Tales and Wonders Gathered by E. Nesbit. 1898.

Songs of Love and Empire. 1898.

Pussy and Doggy Tales. 1899.

The Story of the Treasure Seekers: Being the Adventures of the Bastable Children in Search of a Fortune. 1899.

The Secret of Kyriels. 1899.

The Book of Dragons. 1900.

Nine Unlikely Tales for Children. 1901.

The Wouldbegoods: Being the Further Adventures of the Treasure Seekers. 1901.

To Wish You Every Joy. 1901.

Thirteen Ways Home. 1901.

The Revolt of the Toys, and What Comes of Quarrelling. 1902.

Five Children and It. 1902.

The Red House: A Novel. 1902.

The Rainbow Queen, and Other Stories. 1903.

The Literary Sense. 1903.

Cat Tales (with Rosamond Bland). 1904.

The Phoenix and the Carpet. 1904.

The New Treasure Seekers. 1904.

The Story of the Five Rebellious Dolls. 1904.

Pug Peter. 1905.

Oswald Bastable and Others. 1905.

The King's Highway (with Dorothea Deakin). 1905.

The Railway Children. 1906.

The Story of the Amulet. 1906.

The Incomplete Amorist. 1906.

Man and Maid. 1907.

The Enchanted Castle. 1907.

The Magician's Heart. 1907.

Twenty Beautiful Stories from Shakespeare: A Home Study Course, Being a Choice Collection from the World's Greatest Classic Writer, William Shakespeare, Retold by E. Nesbit. 1907.

The Old Nursery Stories. 1908.

The House of Arden: A Story for Children. 1908.

Jesus in London. 1908.

Ballads and Lyrics of Socialism. 1908.

Harding's Luck. 1909.

These Little Ones. 1909.

Daphne in Fitzroy Street. 1909.

Salome and the Head: A Modern Melodrama. 1909.

Cinderella: A Play with Twelve Songs to Popular Airs. 1909.

Garden Poems. 1909.

The Magic City. 1910.

Children's Stories from English History (with Doris Ashley). 1910.

Children's Stories from Shakespeare. 1910.

Fear. 1910.

The Wonderful Garden, or the Three C's. 1911.

Ballads and Verses of the Spiritual Life. 1911.

Dormant. 1911; reprinted as *Rose Royal,* 1912.

The Magic World. 1912.

Unexceptionable References. 1912.

Wet Magic. 1913.

Wings and the Child; Or, the Building of Magic Cities. 1913.

The Incredible Honeymoon. 1916.

The New World Literary Series, Book Two. 1921.

The Lark. 1922.

Many Voices: Poems. 1922.

To the Adventurous. 1923.

Five of Us—and Madeline. 1925.

The Complete History of the Bastable Family. 1928.

Long Ago When I Was Young. 1966.

Katherine Paterson
b. 1932

KATHERINE PATERSON was born Katherine Womeldorf on October 31, 1932, in Tsing Tsiang Pu, by the Yellow Sea, amidst the struggle for power between the Chinese Communists and the Kuomintang government forces. Her father, George Raymond Womeldorf, and mother, Mary Goetchius Womeldorf, had come to this part of China as missionaries of the Southern Presbyterian Church. Unlike most missionary families, Katherine's lived almost exclusively among the Chinese on a school campus. As a result, many of Katherine's earliest memories are associated with a language she learned in infancy and later lost, and with the food and textures of a culture in which she participated so briefly.

When Katherine was five, the Japanese advanced rapidly upon Shanghai, compelling the family to retreat to the United States. A year later, however, the Womeldorfs returned to China, but only George could travel to the village in which they had formerly lived, on account of the danger. In 1940, the family moved permanently to the United States. Their life continued to be nomadic, though: during Katherine's childhood, they moved 15 times among different parts of Virginia, North Carolina, West Virginia, and Tennessee. Throughout this time, Katherine wrote stories and plays. She attended King College in Bristol, Tennessee, from 1950 to 1954 and later earned a master's degree in English Bible from the Presbyterian School of Christian Education in Virginia.

Like her parents, Katherine also went to the Far East to work as a missionary, only she chose to go to Japan. From 1957 to 1959, she studied Japanese, and she worked as a missionary for the next five years. She left Japan to get her second master's degree, in religious education, at the Union Theological Seminary in New York, in 1962. That same year, she met and married the Presbyterian minister John Barstow Paterson.

Over the next 10 years, Katherine and John Paterson raised their two sons and two adopted daughters in Tacoma Park, Maryland. Katherine wrote for the Presbyterian Church of the United States but she also continued to write stories—although she did not attempt to publish them. With the encouragement of her husband and children, however, she wrote three novels and had them published. These first novels are all set in Japan. One of them, *The Master Puppeteer* (1976), was awarded the National Book Award in Children's Literature in

1976. Her second novel, *Bridge to Terabithia* (1977), grew out of her observations of her son's grief over the sudden death of his best friend and her own near-fatal encounter with cancer. In 1978 the novel was awarded the Newbery Award, as was her novel *Jacob Have I Loved* (1980) three years later. Most of her work for children both presents compelling plots and deals with subtle issues of faith and mystery that have been Paterson's lifelong concerns.

After publishing several more books, including *Come Sing, Jimmy Jo* (1985), Katherine and her husband moved to Vermont, where together they wrote *Consider the Lilies* (1986). In addition to her own books for young readers, Paterson has translated several tales from Japanese and continues to write book reviews, articles, and essays— many dealing with the issues involved in writing for children.

Critical Extracts

M. SARAH SMEDMAN

In her writings and conversations about her work, Katherine Paterson repeatedly raises issues which emerge as artistic challenges for her. Among these are her commitment to the young reader's right to an absorbing story and her difficulties with plotting. Herself imbued with the Christian spirit, all Paterson's stories—whether they are set in feudal Japan or World War II Chesapeake Bay—dramatize a young protagonist's encounter with the mysteries of grace and love. Her published work reveals that many of Paterson's problems with plot may derive from the challenge of discovering and sequencing a series of episodes that will present honestly and nondidactically a theme that has no sequence in it, something "other than a process and much more like a state or quality." A plot, as C. S. Lewis says, "is only really a net whereby to catch something else" ⟨*Of Other Worlds*, 1966, 18⟩. For Paterson in her latest novel, *Jacob Have I Loved*, that something else is the experience of swift and sudden release from hatred and vengefulness through the acceptance of and cooperation with selfless love. ⟨. . .⟩

Typically Patersonian, *Jacob Have I Loved* is a tightly woven novel; each character, each episode, each speech, each image helps to incarnate that which the author is imagining. The net which catches and binds together the whole is her adroit manipulation of several levels of story: the story which the adolescent Sarah Louise ("Wheeze") Bradshaw tells of and to herself in her attempt to comprehend the meaning of the life she is daily living; the story that the young mother and midwife Sarah Louise tells through the configuration of characters and events she selects from her memory of her tumultuous teen years rounded by the insights and incidents she adds from a maturer perspective; and the Bible stories of Jacob and Esau in the Old Testament and the birth of Christ in the New, which provides an allusive frame for the other two story levels, and which add resonance to, universalize, Louise's personal experience. ⟨. . .⟩

It goes without saying that the young reader need not be consciously aware of the ironies and complexities of the novel to sense and be satisfied by the rightness with which they are integrated into a whole. The power of *Jacob Have I Loved* does not depend upon the reader's discerning the third level of story. Nor is the novel's effect diminished if a reader rejects Christianity. Paterson's subtle art incorporates the third dimension inobtrusively, to be discovered and to enrich the story. For those who do not discover it, the story still works. Without violating the norms of realism, though perhaps stretching them to include a coincidence more possible than probable, it incorporates the wisdom of myth and fairy tales. Like them, *Jacob* expresses what G. K. Chesterton has identified as the sense that life is not only a pleasure but a kind of eccentric privilege. One way of accounting for this world, which does not after all explain itself, the one which Paterson as well as Chesterton seems to accept, is that it may be a miracle with a supernatural explanation. People must be humble and submit to the limitations of the world, limitations which they may not understand.

—M. Sarah Smedman, "'A Good Oyster': Story and Meaning in *Jacob Have I Loved*," *Children's Literature in Education* 14, no. 3 (1983): 180–81, 186–87

JAMES HOLT MCGAVRAN JR.

Paterson has said that she writes in hope, but she seems quite unable, in *Jacob* at least, to found that hope in this world or its words. Echoing another devoutly Christian writer of our time, Flannery O'Connor, Paterson says she considers the novel to be "incarnational" ("Place and Idea"); by this she means that in the writer's hands the Word must become flesh through such elements of fiction as those mentioned above. But O'Connor must have felt less doubt, less guilt than Paterson about assuming the godlike and traditionally male role of authorship; and O'Connor gives so much life and freedom to characters like the grandmother and the Misfit in "A Good Man Is Hard to Find" that many readers, unaware that they are experiencing what O'Connor intended as the old lady's salvation in a swift moment of grace, still enjoy this and her other stories for their structure, their imagery, and their psychological as opposed to spiritual insights.

Paterson, on the other hand, seems determined in *Jacob* to deny Wheeze any mortal powers of seeing and naming and knowing. Surrounding her island home is the immortal sea of Romantic tradition, the powerful Jungian arche-type of death, rebirth, and consciousness; but Paterson, often as she sends Wheeze out crabbing or oystering, allows her really to see the sea and expe-rience its mysteries only when it is too late for vision to free her from the trap of her adult life. Throughout the book, Wheeze struggles with words to artic-ulate her conflicting feelings, gasping—as her nickname implies—to find a voice. In this too, however, she is thwarted, partly perhaps by the intensity of her own emotions, but more, it seems, by the author and her angry God. Instead of using her maritime setting as a symbolic source of vision and self-transcendence through the power of words, Paterson turns it into a Slough of Despond where sin, finally confronted and confessed, can be washed away only by brutal self-sacrifice. In the book's worst moment, Wheeze is literally hit on the head with the Word that was in the beginning, beaten into accept-ing the Peace that passes human understanding. In her grandmother's twisted hands, the Bible, deprived of its rich mystery, becomes hard, monolithic, love-less—a weapon to hit a sinner with—not an intricate contrapuntal harmony of many voices—historians, prophets, evangelists, martyrs, visionaries—that sing like the waves of the sea. Worst of all, one feels that in using the Bible to violate Wheeze's imagination, Paterson is actually crippling her own. ⟨. . .⟩

Now clearly Paterson is not at all comfortable with the idea of didacticism in children's literature, let alone brutal didacticism. In the 1981 Newbery speech, she speaks disparagingly of the widespread attitude that "while adult literature may aim to be art, the object of children's books is to whip the little rascals into shape" ⟨*Gates of Excellence*, 1981, 124⟩; and she insists in her speeches and essays that she always tries to keep the story, not the message, foremost in her books. However, she has also spoken, in "A Song of Innocence and Experience," of her belief "that those of us who have grown up have some-thing of value to offer the young. And if that is didacticism, well, I have to live with it" (*Gates*, p. 49). In deeply felt sympathy for all children's suffering, she has written:

> I cannot transmute their pain to joy, but I shall continue to try to
> provide a space where they can, if they wish, lay down a burden. I
> want them to know that despite all the evidence that the world seeks
> to crush them with, there is room for hope. That the good life, far
> from ending in childhood, barely begins there. (*Gates*, p. 52)

But the space she opens for Sara Louise and her readers in *Jacob* does not give room for personal vision or self-knowledge, and certainly not for female authorship. Instead, all of her good intentions notwithstanding, Paterson rather stingily affords Wheeze a glimpse or two of heaven in a perforce often hellish world, having first truncated her hopes and crushed her spirit—using the Good Book literally to whip her little rascal into shape.

   —James Holt McGavran Jr., "Bathrobes and Bibles, Waves and Words in Katherine Paterson's *Jacob Have I Loved*," *Children's Literature in Education* 17, no. 1 (1986): 4–5, 13

KATHERINE PATERSON

Several years ago I read an article about writing for children in which the writer said that her qualification for writing for children lay in her photographic memory. She had never forgotten anything that had happened to her as a child, and therefore she could write meaningfully for children. I have typically forgotten who the writer was and where the article appeared, and the only reason I remember the statement at all is that it made me resolve all over again not to read any more articles on the qualifications needed to be a writer for children.

Indeed, as I was writing *Jacob Have I Loved*, I was carrying on a running quarrel with Louise Bradshaw. I wanted to write the book in the third person because I knew perfectly well that no one—well, no one I knew—could remember her past in the kind of detail that Louise was pretending to. I was very nervous about this since I know I have a poor memory for specific events. When I am called upon to tell about something from my past, I find myself wondering, midstory, how much of what I seem to be remembering actually occurred. Gilly Hopkins would probably say that I lie a lot, but I assure you that I do not lie intentionally. I seem incapable, however, of separating the bare facts from my constantly enlarging perception of those facts. It is part of what makes me a writer of fiction, for a writer of fiction is never content with mere fact but must somehow find a pattern, a meaning, in events.

Of course, this is what Louise Bradshaw has done from the vantage point of age. She has scooped out a hunk of her youth and molded it into a story. The differences between writing a story and simply relating past events is that a story, in order to be acceptable, must have shape and meaning. It is the old idea that art is the bringing of order out of chaos, and it is interesting to me how much I crave that order. ⟨. . .⟩

I believe it is the job of the novelist to shape human experience so that a reader might be able to find not only order but meaning in the story. It seems to me, also, that the way a writer shapes human experience depends to a great extent on her history—all those forces, most of which she had nothing to do with, that made her what she is. In speaking of those forces, we are speaking of our human heritage, our particular family history, and our individual past

experience. These are the memories that we call up consciously or unconsciously as we write.

> —Katherine Paterson, "Sounds in the Heart," in *Innocence & Experience: Essays & Conversations on Children's Literature*, ed. Barbara Harrison and Gregorie Maguire (New York: Lothrop, Lee & Shepard, 1987), 22–23

SARAH SMEDMAN

The quest for the father—or the mother—is a recurrent theme and structural pattern in the novels of Katherine Paterson. Whether it is paramount or sub-ordinate in any given story, whether its object is living or dead, a known actual presence or a fantasized one, that quest infuses Paterson's stories with a meta-physical meaning reflective of her values as well as providing her work with a principle of unity. A particular family, however impaired, provides a frame-work that anchors fiction after fiction in concrete reality, simultaneously enabling meaning to transcend the limitations of historical time and cultural locale. In Paterson's work the bruised or broken family and the search for the father become milieu and metaphor for the archetypal heroic quest, the end of which, according to Joseph Campbell's theory of the monomyth ⟨in *Hero with a Thousand Faces*⟩, is that moment of enlightenment when the hero attains "transpersonal centeredness," that is, when he or she penetrates beyond the limits of the human organs of comprehension to the source of life, transcends the individual self and achieves atonement (at-one-ment) with the universal will, a ubiquitous power out of which all things rise (i.e. the father, or mother). Paterson's protagonists do discover the parent-power for whom they search though that father or mother may not be the one they set out to find. For Paterson, the quest for the father becomes a metaphor for the soul's journey, a vehicle for the dramatization of spiritual development and increased under-standing of that inscrutable father, whose thoughts, as Biblical literature attests, are more marvelous than human thoughts, the depth and richness of whose knowledge, wisdom, and judgments are ultimately incomprehensible by human power (Isaiah 55: 8–9; Romans 11:3). Consequently, though indi-vidual Patersonian heroes achieve what Campbell variously names the meet-ing with the *Magna Mater*, atonement with the Father, and the Ultimate Boon, because the ways of the Father are finally "unsearchable," the search for the father is for the author an inexhaustible vein, conducive to continual, prof-itable mining.

> —Sarah Smedman, "The Quest for the Father in Katherine Paterson's *Of Nightingales That Weep*," in *The Child and the Family: Selected Papers from the 1988 International Conference of the Children's Literature Association*, ed. Susan R. Gannon and Ruth Anne Thompson (Charleston, SC: 1988), 59

JOEL D. CHASTON

Not surprisingly, *Bridge to Terabithia* now occupies a prominent position on a number of bibliographies about death. Masha Kabakow Rudman's *Children's Literature: An Issues Approach* (1984) discusses the novel as an example of one of many books whose "characters do not respond heroically or admirably to death" (337). It is a useful book, she implies, because it depicts a child who "passes through all of the stages of mourning . . ." (338). ⟨. . .⟩

Paterson, however, is bothered by the inclusion of *Bridge to Terabithia* on "death lists." While not entirely opposed to recommending a book to readers with special problems, she is wary of bibliotheraphy. She writes:

> The first time I was told that *Bridge to Terabithia* was "on our death list,"
> I was a bit shaken up. There follows, you see, the feeling that if a
> child has a problem, a book that deals with that problem can be
> given to the child and the problem will be cured. As Jill Paton Walsh
> points out, only children's books are used this way. "One does not,"
> she says, "rush to give *Anna Karenina* to friends who are committing
> adultery, or minister to distressed old age with copies of *King Lear.*"

Paterson goes on to address what she sees as shallowness in "problem novels" for children, arguing that the best a writer can do is to "share with children works of the imagination—those sounds deepest in the human heart, often couched in symbol and metaphor." These works, she continues, don't give children ready-made answers, but invite them "to go within themselves to listen to the sounds of their own hearts" (34–35). In other words, books like *Bridge to Terabithia* should not be used as a cure for or fast solution to the problems children face. It is only when literature stimulates readers to look within themselves and search their hearts for their own solutions to problems that it is effective.

A close reading of *Bridge to Terabithia* reveals that these same ideas are present in the novel itself. This book, which is so often featured on "death lists," can be read as an argument against attempting to solve children's problems through literature. According to the novel, stories, whether written or oral, are no substitute for real experience; no amount of literary exposure to death, for example, can prepare Jess for Leslie Burke's death. When such works help readers "listen to the sounds of their own hearts," however, they are valuable indeed. At the same time, through its allusions to other death stories, *Bridge to Terabithia* shows how its own treatment of the subject is distinctive, suggesting a movement towards a new kind of death literature.

—Joel D. Chaston, "The Other Deaths in *Bridge to Terabithia*," *Children's Literature Association Quarterly* 16, no. 4 (Winter 1991/92): 238–39

JOEL D. CHASTON

In Katherine Paterson's first collection of essays, *Gates of Excellence* (1981), she compares writing fiction for children to playing a musical instrument. She feels that one of the few limitations of her choice of audience has to do with the intricacy, density, and design of what she writes. She compares great novels for adults, such as Mary Lee Settle's *Blood Tie*, Anne Tyler's *Celestial Navigation*, and John Fowles's *Daniel Martin*, to "a symphony orchestra." On the other hand, she calls her own *Bridge to Terabithia* "a flute solo, unaccompanied." Even when she is dealing with complicated situations, "through all the storm and clamor" of her books, she hears "a rather simple melody" (36). 〈. . .〉

〈. . . But〉 Paterson is careful to make the point that she does not write down to her readers, that simplicity is not a matter of readability. She also maintains that simple melodies can strongly affect the listener and reader, once again using music to talk about literature. It requires, however, some effort on the part of the audience. She quotes Frances Clarke Sayers, who talks of "the shattering and gracious encounter that art affords." But, Patterson goes on to explain, it is "only when the deepest sound going forth from my heart meets the deepest sound coming forth from yours—it is only in this encounter that the true music begins" (*Spying Heart* 37). Continuing with her musical imagery, Paterson explains that she wants to be one of the "scarlet tanagers, who . . . rise up, sing, and fly free" (171).

Critics of Paterson's work have often commented on the "simplicity" of her books and her interest in form. Patricia Craig maintains that her second novel, *Of Nightingales that Weep* (1974), "has something of the formality and simplicity of a retold folk tale" 〈*Books and Bookmen*, 1977, 66〉. Writing about *Jacob Have I Loved* (1980), Sarah Smedman argues that it is a "tightly woven novel; each character, each episode, each speech, each image helps to incarnate what the author is imagining" 〈*Children's Literature in Education*, 1983, 181〉.

Since Paterson views herself as a musician, a flute soloist who provides "shattering encounters" for her readers, it should not be surprising that her fiction is filled with descriptions of powerful, yet simple songs. For example, Okada, the blind writer of puppet plays in *The Master Puppeteer* (1975), is said to sing his plays to those who transcribe them. In *The Sign of the Chrysanthemum* (1973), *Of Nightingales that Weep*, and *Rebels of the Heavenly Kingdom* (1983), music helps to heal or restore the listener. At the end of *The Sign of the Chrysanthemum*, Fukuji sings of the cycle of life, his voice shimmering "in the night air—the voice bright above the zither's chords like raindrops on a spider web" (130). The young emperor in *Of Nightingales that Weep* discovers a healing power in Takiko's songs of the Dragon King and longs to learn how to play the flute so he too can make music. 〈. . .〉

Paterson's most developed use of music, however, occurs in *Jacob Have I Loved* and *Come Sing, Jimmy Jo* (1985). In these works, she once again celebrates the power of simple music and its effect on both the listener and the performer. ⟨. . .⟩ Paterson uses music as a metaphor through which she defends her own writing, both what she sees as its basic simplicity, as well as her decision to write for children and young adults.

—Joel D. Chaston, "Flute Solos and Songs That Make You Shatter: Simple Melodies in *Jacob Have I Loved* and *Come Sing, Jimmy Jo,*" *The Lion and the Unicorn* 16 (1992): 215–17

PERRY NODELMAN

Several things intrigue me here ⟨in examining Ursula Le Guin's *Very Far Away from Anywhere Else* and Suzanne Newton's *I Will Call It Georgie's Blues*⟩: the peculiar coincidence of the discovery of music and the denial of fathers; the relation of music to a safe space away from a distressing world, a place that represents a paradoxical conflation of perfection and selfhood, both utopia and what one secretly actually is; and music's connection with femininity, a feminine order which a male chooses as an act of defiance against his father's conventional male values. These boys become triumphantly themselves by choosing the secret music of the female space over a silence or cacophony identified with the male authority that the world expects of them. A female music represents the essence of their presumably male selfhood.

Other young adult novels about performers make similar connections between music and gender. For instance, *Come Sing, Jimmy Jo,* by Katherine Paterson, is about a musician named James, who to begin with makes music only in his grandmother's house (another private space controlled by a woman). A male intruder into this space, an agent representing the commercial interests of the big world outside, forces the reluctant James to perform in public—the move that occurs near the end of the two other novels—where he learns to preserve the values of the female space even in a world at odds with them. But while *Jimmy Jo* makes the same connections among femininity, music, and private space, and between maleness and public space, it tells the next part of what appears to be a common story: what happens to a male performer *after* what now begins to seem like a gestation period, after the performer is born out of the protective private female space into a world where others, either males or women seduced by male values, claim him and try to control and change him. Furthermore, one of those others in *Jimmy Jo* is James's actual father, who tries to replace the man James has always lived with and thought of as his father, and who also feels allegiance to the grandmother's traditional music. As in *Far Away* and *Georgie's Blues,* this novel implies connections between the acceptance of music associated with a female and with a family one isn't actually related to and the denial of one's own real father. And also as in Le Guin and Newton's books, *Jimmy Jo* ends with a performance in the midst of family disruption that signals the triumph of a different sort of family, one created through music: James's mother may be having an affair with his uncle, the family group may be about to break apart, but James's singing and playing bring his audience into an unbroken circle of love.

The obvious questions raised here are these: Why is the performance of music opposed to conventional paternal male authority? And why is it associated with femininity and with spaces controlled by females? ⟨. . .⟩

The supposed femininity of a secret self is most apparent in *Jimmy Jo*, in which James's music, called "comfort" music, represents a loving concern for his audience of a sort that is conventionally equated with femaleness; he sees these people "full of love, looking up at him . . . like little children on Christmas morning—waiting all full of hope for a present. And he had the gift" (178). Just as he was the object of his grandmother's maternal concern and comfort earlier, he now becomes something like a consoling mother himself—perhaps specifically, in terms of the Christmas morning metaphor, like the ultimate symbolic mother, the Virgin Mary.

Yet paradoxically, the actual music these novels describe tends to be identified with males and masculinity: the classical composers in *Far Away* and the jazz artists *Georgie's Blues* mentioned as symbolic peers, are all males; James's comfort song is identified more with his grandfather than his grandmother. In theory, at least, the nurturing women in these novels merely provide a space in which the boys can discover their connections to traditions that, despite their difference from their own culture's definitions of acceptable masculinity, are inherently masculine.

In other words, these novels present a shifty response to the question how can you be both musical and masculine. On the one hand, you can't; you must accept and express your femininity. On the other hand, you can; in expressing that supposed femininity you will merely be acting like a genealogy of male musicians who actually represent your true spiritual family—you can act like a woman because these great men of the past did too.

In either case, masculinity is redefined; it is no longer the pragmatic, deliberately insensitive, anti-intellectual aggressiveness that we usually identify as machismo and understand as being driven and excused by male sexuality. Indeed, the denial (or simple disregard) of that sort of sexuality is a significant thread in all of these novels ⟨. . . .⟩

—Perry Nodelman, "Males Performing in a Female Space: Music and Gender in Young Adult Novels," *The Lion and the Unicorn* 16 (1992): 224–26

Bibliography

Who Am I? 1966.

Justice for All People. 1973.

The Sign of the Chrysanthemum. 1973.

To Make Men Free. 1973.

Of Nightingales That Weep. 1974.

The Master Puppeteer. 1976.

Bridge to Terabithia. 1977.

The Great Gilly Hopkins. 1978.

Angels and Other Strangers: Family Christmas Stories. 1979.

Jacob Have I Loved. 1980.

The Crane Wife (translator). 1981.

Fates of Excellence: On Reading and Writing Books for Children. 1981.

Rebels of the Heavenly Kingdom. 1983.

Come Sing, Jimmy Jo. 1985.

Consider the Lilies: Plants of the Bible (with John Paterson). 1986.

The Tongue-cut Sparrow (translator). 1987.

Park's Quest. 1988.

The Spying Heart: More Thoughts on Reading and Writing Books for Children. 1989.

The Tale of the Mandarin Ducks. 1990.

The Smallest Cow in the World. 1991.

Lyddie. 1991.

The King's Equal. 1992.

Flip-Flop Girl. 1994.

Beatrix Potter
1866 – 1943

BEATRIX POTTER was born July 28, 1866, and until she was in her thirties, she was cloistered in her nursery with little social contact. Her father, Rupert Potter, was a barrister and solicitor with an amateur talent in photography. Beatrix's mother was the less affectionate of her parents, spending most of her time making calls and sewing. With the birth of Beatrix's brother, Bertram, when she was five, her loneliness was abated. The children shared many interests and talents, including painting. But when Bertram was of age, he was sent to school, and Beatrix remained alone in the nursery.

The greatest delight in Beatrix's life as a child was her family's summering in Perthshire. From these visits, she and Bertram secretly created a menagerie of rabbits, mice, rats, newts, a bat, a toad, snails, lizards, a kestrel, an owl, a jay, and various insects, which Beatrix tended in the nursery while Bertram was at school. They also collected dead animals to dissect or boil down in order to reconstruct the skeletons. Beatrix created her own classification system for the fossils and used Bertram's microscope to make detailed observations, and for her powers of observation she received the passing praise of the painter Sir John Everett Millais, an acquaintance of her father.

This enthusiasm for scientific observation developed into an intensive study of fungi. Although Beatrix was encouraged by several people—including her uncle, a knighted scientist—her discoveries were dismissed by experts as the work of an amateur. In the face of these discouragements, Beatrix struggled against depression, nervous headaches, rheumatic fever, insomnia, and faintness; she despaired of escaping her parents' house, blaming her own shyness and insufficient beauty as well as her parents' rigidity. Nevertheless, she continued working and had a strong sense of her own interests and goals.

When Beatrix was in her twenties, a vicar of Windermere, where the Potter family now spent their holidays, admired her watercolors and suggested that she make illustrations for cards and nursery rhymes; her brother then helped her sell her first efforts. Though Beatrix enjoyed the slight independence this work gave her, the inanity of her employers' assignments was discouraging. She returned to her own world in her nursery, sharing her work with only a few relatives and with her former governess's children.

The first incarnation of *The Tale of Peter Rabbit* was an illustrated story-letter Beatrix sent to one of her governess's little boys in 1893.

Eight years later, again at the vicar's suggestion, Beatrix revised the piece and sent the manuscript to six different publishers. When it was rejected, Beatrix in 1901 published the book with her own money, quickly selling 250 copies to relatives and friends. But its popularity was such that she had to print another 200 within the year. Encouraged, Beatrix approached the most gracious of the publishers she had solicited earlier, Frederick Warne & Co., who now accepted her book provided that she use her own text rather than the verse version supplied by the vicar.

Through their correspondence over the book, Beatrix and her editor, Norman Warne, became friendly. Just before the Warne edition of *The Tale of Peter Rabbit* was issued, Beatrix finished *The Tailor of Gloucester*, which she again published on her own. She sent Norman a copy of the new book and her plans for another book on a squirrel. Both *The Tailor of Gloucester* and *The Tale of Squirrel Nutkin* were published by Warne the following year. Although her parents disapproved of her friendship with Norman Warne, Beatrix was acquiring the confidence and money to win her independence. She bought property in Sawrey, a countryside she had come to love from her family's holidays, and she and Norman were engaged in August of 1905. They by now had collaborated on *The Tale of the Two Bad Mice* (1904), *The Tale of Benjamin Bunny* (1904), and *The Tale of Mrs. Tiggy-Winkle* (1905). But less than a month after their engagement, Norman died of leukemia.

During the months of grief and illness that followed Norman's death, Beatrix continued to work on a new book she had planned with him, *The Pie and The Patty-Pan*. Her other consolation was her purchase of a farmhouse on the Sawrey property; as her success continued, she invested more and more of her life and earnings there. Through these business transactions she met the solicitor William Heelis, who in 1912 proposed to her. That same year, Beatrix published what many consider her masterpiece, *The Tale of Mr. Tod*.

Potter and Heelis were married after fighting her parents' disapproval, many arguments, and her nearly fatal illness. The couple moved into the farmhouse in Sawrey, and, in addition to continuing to produce books for children, Beatrix lived and farmed with her husband for the remaining years of their lives. Beatrix Potter Heelis died in 1943.

Critical Extracts

GRAHAM GREENE

Looking backward over the thirty years of Miss Potter's literary career, we see that the creation of Mr Puddle-Duck marked the beginning of a new period. At some time between 1907 and 1909 Miss Potter must have passed through an emotional ordeal which changed the character of her genius. It would be impertinent to inquire into the nature of the ordeal. Her case is curiously similar to that of Henry James. Something happened which shook their faith in appearances. From *The Portrait of a Lady* onwards, innocence deceived, the treachery of friends, became the theme of James's greatest stories. Mme Merle, Kate Croy, Mme de Vionnet, Charlotte Stant, these tortuous treacherous women are paralleled through the dark period of Miss Potter's art. 'A man can smile and smile and be a villain'—that, a little altered, was her recurrent message, expressed by her gallery of scoundrels: Mr Drake Puddle-Duck, the first and slightest, Mr Jackson, the least harmful with his passion for honey and his reiterated, 'No teeth. No teeth. No teeth', Samuel Whiskers, gross and brutal, and the 'gentleman with sandy whiskers' who may be identified with Mr Tod. With the publication of *Mr Tod* in 1912, Miss Potter's pessimism reached its climax. But for the nature of her audience *Mr Tod* would certainly have ended tragically. In *Jemima Puddle-Duck* the gentleman with sandy whiskers had at least a debonair impudence when he addressed his victims ⟨. . . .⟩

But no charm softens the brutality of Mr. Tod and his enemy, the repulsive Tommy Brock. In her comedies Miss Potter had gracefully eliminated the emotions of love and death; it is the measure of her genius that when, in *The Tale of Mr Tod*, they broke the barrier, the form of her book, her ironic style, remained unshattered. When she could not keep death out she stretched her technique to include it. Benjamin and Peter had grown up and married, and Benjamin's babies were stolen by Brock; the immortal pair, one still neurotic, the other knowing and imperturbable, set off to the rescue, but the rescue, conducted in darkness, from a house, 'something between a cave, a prison, and a tumbledown pig-sty', compares grimly with an earlier rescue from Mr MacGregor's sunny vegetable garden:

> The sun had set; an owl began to hoot in the wood. There were
> many unpleasant things lying about, that had much better have been
> buried; rabbit bones and skulls, and chicken's legs and other horrors.
> It was a shocking place and very dark.

But *Mr Tod*, for all the horror of its atmosphere, is indispensable. There are few fights in literature which can compare in excitement with the duel between Mr Tod and Tommy Brock (it was echoed by H. G. Wells in *Mr Polly*):

> Everything was upset except the kitchen table.
> And everything was broken, except the mantelpiece and the kitchen fender. The crockery was smashed to atoms.
> The chairs were broken, and the window, and the clock fell with a crash, and there were handfuls of Mr Tod's sandy whiskers.
> The vases fell off the mantelpiece, the canisters fell off the shelf; the kettle fell off the hob. Tommy Brock put his foot in a jar of raspberry jam.

Mr Tod marked the distance which Miss Potter had travelled since the ingenuous romanticism of *The Tailor of Gloucester*. ⟨. . .⟩

(NOTE. On the publication of this essay I received a somewhat acid letter from Miss Potter correcting certain details. ⟨. . .⟩ She denied that there had been any emotional disturbance at the time she was writing *Mr Tod*: she was suffering however from the after-effects of flu. In conclusion she deprecated sharply 'the Freudian school' of criticism.)

—Graham Greene, "Beatrix Potter" (1933), reprinted in *Only Connect: Readings in Children's Literature*, ed. Sheila Egoff, T. G. Stubbs, and L. F. Ashley (Toronto: Oxford University Press, 1969), 295–98

FRED INGLIS

In an ideal reading course for the very earliest years onwards, Beatrix Potter offers herself as the best first fiction for so many of the reasons for which I have commended Lewis Carroll, and she exemplifies here the grammar of literature for Victorian children at its most elementary. She perfects the conventions for the very young in the scale of her books, the delicate adjustment of water-colours to narrative, the grave tone, the careful examination of vocabulary. The imagery of Beatrix Potter's world balances a colonized, accomplished horticulture and agriculture, and the stable but mysterious Nature which lies untamed beyond the garden wall. Everybody's daydream of a perfect holiday for children occurs in such a scene. For the grown-up such a holiday, a pastoral idyll beside the sea or up the dale, lies always glowing at the horizon of memory, twenty, thirty, forty years back. For a nation or for a class, it lies just over the rim of its oldest members' memories—Edwardian summers, the old Queen's last Jubilee, the *fin de siècle*.

The world of Beatrix Potter lives in that geography: Lewis Carroll sent Alice paddling down the Cherwell in the south of the same limitless blue afternoons. But like Carroll, Beatrix Potter peopled her county in a very dry-eyed and dry-toned style. The awful antics of the fubsy little animals in the pages of her latter-day imitators cannot be made her responsibility. On the contrary, the stern and dangerous world in which Jemima Puddleduck is almost eaten by Mr Fox, and Squirrel Nutkin loses his tail as a punishment for cheeking Old Brown the owl, is marked by what we might now think of as a distinctly Victorian moral realism, its sanctions and severities. At the same time, Beatrix Potter, in her tiny compass, has quite enough strength to give her characters life and idiosyncrasy such that it is clear that these creatures are part of Lewis Carroll's or Dickens's society too. In *The Tale of Mrs Tittlemouse* alone, we have the heroine's neurotic over-cleanliness, Mr Jackson's sodden, genial, and repulsive bulk—'tiddley widdley widdley, pouff, pouff, pouff'—and the mad, importunate assortment of unwanted guests. A critical child's-eye view is given plenty to dislike from an early age. And the same eye and imagination can feed delightedly on every little girl's favourite game of a hole-home, wonderfully safe *underground*, with 'her own little box bed'.

Beatrix Potter sets down, in the thoroughly settled farmlands, gardens, and villages of Westmorland, the colour and variety of Victorian society, its firm structures, its strong base in home and family, its disobedient heroes, its polite little girls, its rich patterns of gentility and roguery. Young readers can best begin there: she includes so much of the great abstractions—history, morality, class, work—and gives them her special vividness, in both words and water-colour.

I have made this short digression into Beatrix Potter in order to stress her affinity with Lewis Carroll. Both are Victorians, and great ones in their way. There is much more to Carroll, of course, but my immediate point is to stress what a powerful image of the world they hold out to children, and how much there is for children to *recognize* there. Both writers have that peculiar strength of those who are intensely, if variously, attuned to a child's-eye view (Beatrix Potter could be a tough old egg): they can invent a world in which children can immediately pick up their bearings, find experiences and characters presented on their own, the children's terms ('You are *not* to go into Mr Macgregor's garden . . . but Peter, who was very naughty . . .'), and go on to find the world of the book deepening, shaping and altering the world outside the book. A child who begins with the secure social structure, the settled place, the regular patterning of bravery and retribution in Beatrix Potter is doing far more than meet the conventional fixities of Victorian England. The bold imagery and striking, simple narratives carry with them a staid, strong version of what to do and how to act. By the time the child gets to *Alice*, he or she finds the house of fiction a much more ambiguous and subversive and wildly comic place.

—Fred Inglis, *The Promise of Happiness: Value and Meaning in Children's Fiction* (Cambridge: Cambridge University Press, 1981), 109–11

SETH SICROFF

Beatrix Potter's prose style bears a resemblance to Mrs. Tiggywinkle's plain print frock; underneath the deceptively simple dress there are prickles. The apparently simple, guileless point of view of the narrator is betrayed by an understated humor which depends on the complications of word games and the interplay between details of text and illustration. The premise of anthropomorphism is not accepted and ignored, but continually recalled to mind by sly references and incongruities. To see the importance of the deliberately bland and aphoristic sentence structure, one need only compare the taut understatement of Potter's "your Father had an accident there; he was put in a pie by Mrs. McGregor" with the wordy French translation: "Un accident affreux arriva a votre pauvre père dans ce maudit jardin. Il fut attrapé et mis en pâté par Madame McGregor." In this case, less *is* more.

Beatrix Potter has a feel for unusual words, which glow "with a hard and gem-like flame" against the backdrop of deliberate simplicity. In most of the books, there are one or two of these elegant words: Tommy Brock snored "apoplectically" in *The Tale of Mr. Tod*, and in *The Tale of the Flopsy Bunnies*, the effect of the lettuce is very "soporific." In these passages, the word draws attention to an important idea. The soporific effect of eating lettuce is responsible for the rabbits' capture; Tommy Brock's deceptively apoplectic appearance encouraged Mr. Tod to risk setting the booby trap. In most cases, these incongruously elegant words are used in such a way as to emphasize the incongruity of the characterization. Jemima's high aspirations move her to complain of the "superfluous hen." The technical language in *Ginger and Pickles* suggests the awesome complexity of the problems besetting the dog and the cat: "Send in all the bills again to everybody, 'with compts', replied Ginger."

Potter indulges in a number of little games which remind the reader of the ambiguous position of her inventions, between man and beast. An important trick is juxtaposition, as in *Mr. Tod*:

> Mr. Tod was coming up Bull Banks, and he was in the very worst of tempers. First he had been upset by breaking the plate. It was his own fault; but it was a china plate, the last of the dinner service that had belonged to his grandmother, old Vixen Tod. Then the midges had been very bad. And he had failed to catch a hen pheasant on her nest.

Sentimental human regrets are set cheek by jowl with the practical concerns of a predator.

—Seth Sicroff, "Prickles under the Frock: The Art of Beatrix Potter," in *Reflections on Literature for Children*, ed. Francelia Butler and Richard Rotert (Hamden, CT: Library Professional Publications, 1984), 39–40

HUMPHREY CARPENTER

The Tale of Peter Rabbit itself, though her most famous book, is actually almost her least remarkable, certainly one of her least ambitious. Yet its single theme is a dark one, familiar in folk-tales: the pursuit of a hapless individual (Peter) by a vengeful giant (Mr McGregor the gardener). Peter is the youngest of his family and should therefore, according to fairy-tale principles, be the luckiest; but he is a fourth child, not a third, and the luck has passed him by. The nature of the threat is made clear to him at the beginning: 'Your Father was put in a pie by Mrs McGregor.' But he ignores this old legend, and ventures, Jack-and-the-beanstalk fashion, into the ogre's very castle ⟨. . . .⟩ He begins to help himself to the giant's treasure ('First he ate some lettuces and some French beans; and then he ate some radishes'), but comes face to face with the giant and takes to his heels. Strikingly, his eventual escape is utterly unheroic; no folk-tale hero would arrive home in a pathetic condition and be put to bed by his mother as a punishment; moreover she

> made some camomile tea; and she gave a dose of it to Peter! 'One table-spoonful to be taken at bed-time.' But Flopsy, Mopsy, and Cottontail had bread and milk and blackberries for supper.

The expectations of the folk-tale or fairy story have been upset. Instead of being presented with the ordered, utopian universe of folklore, where heroes can be heroes and giants are properly defeated, we have a much more true-to-life account of an individual's unpleasant encounter with a force greater than himself. *Peter Rabbit*, though slight, is an ironic comment on the giant-killer stories.

The other three books which concern Peter Rabbit himself continue to develop this theme. *The Tale of Benjamin Bunny* (1904) and *The Tale of the Flopsy Bunnies* (1909) are progressive stages in the defeat of Mr McGregor, who by the end of *Flopsy Bunnies* has been made into a proper fool, just as giants should be. But there are enemies even more unpleasant than giants, traitors among one's own race. *The Tale of Mr Tod* (1912) has for its villain somebody who should by rights be the rabbits' ally: the badger Tommy Brock, who turns ogre when they are off their guard. And in *Mr Tod*, as in *Peter Rabbit*, there is no heroic victory; the 'heroes', Peter and Benjamin, merely grab the rabbit-babies and run for their lives while Brock's attention is distracted by his enemy Mr Tod. The *Peter Rabbit* sequence ends as it began, with the ignominy of flight.

Two other Beatrix Potter stories, both early, deal with the motif of ogre and little man. *The Tale of Squirrel Nutkin* (1903) is an exercise in taking the 'hero' as close as possible to the ogre without getting eaten up. Nutkin, indeed, goes too far; while the other squirrels soberly present their tributes to Old Brown, the owl on whose island they are nutting, Nutkin behaves like a Brer Rabbit or Till Eulenspiegel, dancing up and down under Old Brown's very beak and chanting riddles at him. Instead of being content to observe time-honoured religious rituals and make sacrifice to the tribal god, he laughs in that god's very face—and Beatrix Potter is fully aware of the threatening nature of the riddle-game in which Nutkin tries to engage Old Brown:

> Nutkin was excessively impertinent in his manner. He bobbed up and down like a little red *cherry*, singing—
>
> > 'Riddle me, riddle me, rot-tot-tote!
> > A little wee man, in a red red coat!
> > A staff in his hand, and a stone in his throat;
> > If you tell me this riddle, I'll give you a groat.'
>
> Now this riddle is as old as the hills; Mr Brown paid no attention whatever to Nutkin.

The riddle, like others chanted by Nutkin, is indeed 'as old as the hills', and one of the strengths of Beatrix Potter's work is that it is rooted again and again in traditional nursery rhymes and folk-tales, from which it gains resonances beyond the immediate story.

Squirrel Nutkin fares worse than Peter Rabbit, who merely lost his clothes in the encounter with Mr McGregor; Nutkin has his tail pulled off, a castration-like calamity which ends the story with striking abruptness:

> Old Brown carried Nutkin into his house, and held him up by the tail, intending to skin him; but Nutkin pulled so very hard that his tail broke in two, and he dashed up the staircase and escaped out of the attic window. And to this day, if you meet Nutkin up a tree and ask him a riddle, he will throw sticks at you, and stamp his feet and scold, and shout—'Cuck-cuck-cuck-cur-r-r-cuck-k-k!'

The Tale of Jeremy Fisher (1906), the other story in this early group which deals with the aggressor-and-victim theme, resembles *Peter Rabbit* in that the hero escapes with no worse injury than the loss of his clothes and his possessions. On the other hand, Mr Jeremy Fisher, a frog, is actually seized in the jaws of his antagonist the trout:

> . . . a really *frightful* thing it would have been, if Mr Jeremy had not been wearing a macintosh! A great big enormous trout came up—ker-pflop-p-p-p! with a splash—and it seized Mr Jeremy with a snap, 'Ow! Ow! Ow!'—and then it turned and dived down to the bottom of the pond!

The whole of *Jeremy Fisher*, in which the story develops with sinister slowness and is pervaded by the oppressive dampness of the river atmosphere, is an accumulation of threats. More subtle in this respect than *Peter Rabbit* and *Squirrel Nutkin*, the book suggests that there are worse things than ogres. Dangers lurk around every corner, and perpetual vigilance is necessary. Long before the appearance of the trout, Jeremy Fisher has been frightened by a water-rat and injured by a stickleback which he inadvertently lands with his fishing line. Nor is it a simple matter of hero and enemies: Jeremy Fisher himself is a predator to smaller creatures, for he eats a butterfly sandwich for his lunch, and at the end of the book he dines off 'roasted grasshopper with ladybird sauce'.

    —Humphrey Carpenter, *Secret Gardens: A Study of the Golden Age of Children's Literature* (London: George Allen & Unwin, 1985), 145–47

CHARLES FREY

Both *Peter Rabbit* and *Squirrel Nutkin* tell of boys who refuse to participate in the food-gathering work of their clan and who prefer to challenge authority through selfish and somewhat atavistic behavior. The stories *seem* to disapprove of this behavior. High diction phrases such as "excessively impertinent" suggest that the narrator's view is not from the child's eye but from the adult's. Yet the birds implore Peter to exert himself toward escape, and Nutkin's narrator appears self-consciously to intervene to release Nutkin from the Owl's deadly grip. Nutkin's riddles, moreover, give him a density of language that competes with the fancy vocabulary of grown-ups. Still, at the end, he is stripped of that language just as surely as Peter Rabbit is stripped of his blue coat and buttons. With part of our hearts we applaud, perhaps, the daring of the two lads: they follow their *process* to remarkable lengths of individuation. But, underneath, the tales are deeply cautionary: the expression of all that boyish energy and challenge rouses a violently retributive response from male power in the world. Life becomes a losing: no dessert, no more happy riddles. The stories bend us through the double bind of much trenchant narrative: yes, enjoy your adventure while you can, and push it to the farthest, but at the end be prepared to take your medicine, lose your tail, and have nothing left but a stamp of your foot to your impotent shouting: "cuck!"

    Beatrix Potter specialized in ritual and semisublimated action of violent cast and fearful import. Her deft economy of narrative line, her set-piece, tableauxlike illustrations, and her zest for the most energetic issues of our desire and anger all took her, repeatedly, to the very jugular of myth and of archetypal dream. She epitomizes the still-underrated but manifest and even disturbing power of children's literature to speak to our keenest wishes and fears. Such literature might be compared to a shrouded dynamo or to a bejeweled Pandoran box.

    —Charles Frey, "Victors and Victims in the Tales of *Peter Rabbit* and *Squirrel Nutkin*," *Children's Literature in Education* 18, no. 2 (1987): 110–11

RUTH MACDONALD

Potter's unflinching use of the word "soporific" on the first page of *The Tale of the Flopsy Bunnies* (1909) is characteristic of the level of diction that Potter uses when she presents herself in her books. Through her refusal to compromise on levels of diction, she shows her respect for children in not talking down to them. She assumes that children will gather the meaning of these adult locutions, and indeed, is careful to supply contexts that will help children define those meanings, as with the word "soporific":

> It is said that the effect of eating too much lettuce is "soporific."
> *I* have never felt sleepy after eating lettuces; but then *I* am not a rabbit.
> They certainly had a very soporific effect upon the Flopsy Bunnies! (9)

The accompanying picture of the bunnies flopped in sleep around the base of a lettuce plant reinforces the sleep-inducing effect of the greens, at least upon bunnies. Thus, Potter sets up a verbal as well as a visual environment that helps to define the meaning of her adult diction in her books.

    Furthermore, in this passage Potter's articulation of her non-rabbithood might seem to make her an unbelievable narrator. She disclaims knowledge of the effect of lettuce because she is not a rabbit. But the picture confirms the old adage, and Potter's knowledge of it gives her the status of a narrator who is both reliable and knowledgeable about rabbit affairs. Throughout her books, she uses the technique of first-person narration to do just the opposite of what first-person narratives are supposed to do; instead of limiting the perspective to what one person, a human, can know, it has the effect of becoming omniscient narration, based on Potter's assertion of her knowledge about the intimate conduct of animal lives. By claiming such inside knowledge, Potter creates a credible animal universe that exists side by side with the human.

    By placing herself both in the illustration and in the narrative of her books, Potter solidifies the fantasy world of her animals. Though it would seem more likely that a human presence would destroy the fantasy, especially when the human appears in the illustration, the opposite is true with Potter. Her voice is part of the seamlessness of the animal world as it converges with the human world. In fact, her intrusions are hardly intrusions; instead, they are simply part of the telling of the story. Frequently, she uses her own voice in an aside to supply details that otherwise interrupt the flow of the narrative, as in *The*

Tale of Benjamin Bunny (1904). In this story, she explains how Mrs. Rabbit supports her family: "Old Mrs. Rabbit was a widow; she earned her living by knitting rabbit-wool mittens and muffettes (I once bought a pair at a bazaar). She also sold herbs, and rosemary tea, and rabbit-tobacco (which is what *we* call lavender)" (13). Here Potter supplies the details of rabbit life with which humans would be unfamiliar. She asserts personal knowledge of Mrs. Rabbit's wares by her purchase of them and shows her familiarity with herbal lore in the aside about lavender. Instead of betraying herself as a human, she demonstrates her ability to see things from an animal point of view. Once again, she establishes herself as more animal than human, thus creating credibility for the fantasy.

   —Ruth MacDonald, "Narrative Voice and Narrative View in Beatrix Potter's Books," in *The Voice of the Narrator in Children's Literature: Insights from Writers and Critics*, ed. Charlotte F. Otten and Gary D. Schmidt (New York: Greenwood Press, 1989), 54–55

CAROLE SCOTT

It is clear that Potter's resentments against the social conventions and constraints that are senseless and galling to children (and to others that retain an unspoiled vision) are being expressed in her characters' clothes-related adventures. The unwilling submission to the strictures of clothing exemplifies both a physical and a figurative confinement that leads to a sense of disempowerment in both personal and social terms. The disempowering sensation of being constrained in an outer covering worn for society's eyes and inappropriate to one's sense of self is perfectly portrayed in the plight of the kittens whose clothes make them awkward, clumsy, and out of control. And clothing that emphasizes a class distinction can similarly disempower, as do Jemima's poor shawl and poke bonnet which make her fair game for the well-dressed, gentlemanly fox. Perhaps the most vivid and frightening case of impotence caused by the wrong covering occurs in the *Tale of Samuel Whiskers* where the rats encase Tom Kitten in a coating of dough prior to baking and eating him.

   But Potter's ambivalence to society and the individual's relationship to it is also clearly revealed in these events. The animal characters are safe in their rebellious casting off of clothes because, unlike human children, they have their own coats underneath; Lucie, the human child, loses only nonessential articles in her handkerchiefs and pinafore. Nonetheless, the poignancy with which Potter describes the shedding of the outer, social cover is significant. Thus the sense of relief felt when Peter wriggles from his coat or Tom bursts out of his clothes is tempered by a sense of loss. As Peter escapes from the jacket entangling him in the gooseberry bush, Potter stops the action to tell us that "It was a blue jacket with brass buttons, quite new." The kittens' behavior when they are confined to their room after losing their clothes is exaggeratedly wild; thumps overhead disturb the "dignity and repose" of the tea party beneath, like echoes from a more savage sphere, and the accompanying picture shows the kittens messing about with their mother's clothes. The reader knows that punishment will surely follow this show of rebellion. Hunca Munca in *Two Bad Mice* feels she must repay with a sixpence and daily cleaning service the clothes she takes from the dolls. And when Jeremy Fisher loses his galoshes to the hungry trout, he also loses his desire ever to go fishing again.

Thus Potter reveals value as well as constraint in the relationship between self and society that clothing represents, even if, like Jeremy Fisher's mackintosh, it simply serves to keep one from being eaten alive. Though wearing the wrong clothes or wearing them unwillingly is disempowering, the right ones can bring joy and fulfillment when freely chosen. When Thomasina Tittlemouse helps save the Flopsy Bunnies from the McGregors, she is given a gift of rabbit wool to make a cloak, hood, muff and mittens. These warm, comforting and pretty clothes are not restrictive but an expression of love and gratitude. Similarly, Potter's favorite book, *The Tailor of Gloucester*, centers on the reciprocal kindness of the Tailor, and the mice who help him in his hour of need, and is expressed entirely in the fabrication of clothing.

—Carole Scott, "Between Me and the World: Clothes as Mediator between Self and Society in the Work of Beatrix Potter," *The Lion and the Unicorn* 16, no. 2 (1992): 196–97

JOHN GOLDTHWAITE

Some readers will find it too radical an assessment but, weighing the evidence, I think it is fair to say that Potter never told a wholly original tale in her life. Every plot she used was someone else's plot, and more scenes than would seem plausible were other people's scenes in paraphrase. It is simply the way she worked. To remark on it does not deny, it only serves to define, her originality. Like Lewis Carroll, or Maurice Sendak today, or even like Shakespeare and Coleridge, Potter was an eclectic reader of the world of story, a gatherer and a translator. What we find in her tales are fragments of those books she first thought merely to illustrate, and then reprocessed instead. Where the original collectors of the nursery rhymes she loved to quote were gatherers only; Potter, like Lear and Stevenson, reimagined what she found and made of it what we have come to think of as the now-and-forever Beatrix Potter tale.

Oddly, and rather sadly in retrospect, she misunderstood her own talent and to the end of her life was afraid of being caught out as a cheat. "Copying," she called it. "It is a risky thing to copy," she confided to her journal as early as 1883; "shall I catch it?" ⟨. . .⟩

There is no record of what Potter's or her father's libraries contained in 1893. We know those influences, like Caldecott and the Bible that she had credited herself, and allusions in various letters point to her having read Jane

Austen (a likely source of clarity in her style) and *Uncle Tom's Cabin*, and virtually complete editions of Mrs. Ewing and Mrs. Molesworth. All in all, the evidence suggests that the Potters' shelves boasted the notable books of the day. *Little Pig Robinson* implies not only Lear but Defoe, and a character like Mr. Jackson ("Tiddly, widdly, widdly! Your very good health, Mrs. Tittlemouse!") intimates a mimetic love of Dickens. Indeed, throughout Potter's work we find unmistakable clues that she did in fact at one time or another own a given book.

Take the narrative premise of *The Roly-Poly Pudding*, for example. Here you have an adventurous kitten downstairs and, upstairs behind the wallboards, a phlegmatic rat. How do you bring the two of them together? No one that I have read has noted the book's resemblance to that other classic of English children's literature, Kingsley's *The Water Babies*. Both are set in the North Country; both tell of a boy named Tom; in each book Tom climbs up the inside of a chimney and tumbles, covered with soot, into an upstairs chamber where he makes an unpleasant discovery—in Kingsley, the "little black ape" of his own reflection in a mirror; in Potter, that other of her Dickensian characters, Samuel Whiskers. In Kingsley a girl startled from her bed by the intrusion screams out and brings running "a stout old nurse from the next room," who "dashed at him . . . so fast that she caught him by the jacket." In Potter, Samuel Whiskers, wanting to know what Tom means "tumbling into my bed all covered with smuts," squeaks out "Anna Maria! Anna Maria!" and "an old woman rat . . . rushed upon Tom Kitten, and before he knew what was happening—His coat was pulled off. . . ." Surely Potter knew the book. This close a paraphrase cannot have been coincidental. ⟨. . .⟩

A text Potter did freely cite as an influence was the Bible, and one tale at least can be laid directly to her reading of it. *Two Bad Mice* was prompted initially by her association with her publisher's niece; it was written to celebrate a doll's house and to entertain a particular child. But now and again in Potter (as in *Squirrel Nutkin*) we glimpse an allegorical urge that is nothing if not playful. A doll's house and a child are the occasion for *Two Bad Mice*, but Genesis and the story of the Garden of Eden are the source of its style and incident. Read the two stories side by side (keeping in mind that none of this should be taken any more solemnly than Potter did herself). The doll's house is the garden (at eighteen she had eulogized her own childhood as a paradise lost); Hunca Munca and Tom Thumb, like Adam and Eve, are naked in the garden, and thereafter—a doll's clothes having been heisted—Hunca Munca at least is clothed. The policeman posted by the door following discovery of the trespass is the angel sent to guard the gates of Paradise; and the two bad mice atone for their sins in the end by sweeping up and paying a crooked sixpence as restitution for damages. It is very neatly done.

The comic effect Potter wanted to achieve is more easily heard, perhaps, if we merge her own and King James's English into a single passage:

> Such a lovely dinner was laid out upon the table! She took of the fruit thereof, and did eat, and gave also unto her husband with her; and he did eat.
>
> Then there was no end to the rage of Tom Thumb and Hunca Munca, for underneath the shining paint it was made of nothing but plaster!
>
> And the eyes of both of them were opened, and they knew that they *were* naked; and they broke up the pudding, the lobsters, the pears and the oranges; and they sewed fig leaves together, and made themselves aprons.

Knowledge gained for Potter is what we might today call getting wised up to reality. In the Bible she found and used to wry effect literature's first example of the coming-of-age novel.

Whenever we find her using a particular text as her model, we almost always find in that text some likeness to Potter herself. In Kingsley and throughout Dickens we have the stories of unloved children; in Lear, the bliss of running way. The Bible story that became *Two Bad Mice* may have called to mind her own lost childhood and provoked a desire to do to her fake existence what Tom Thumb did to fake doll's food: "bang, bang, smash, smash!" Whenever she recognizes herself in the literature, it seems, she wants to take some remembrance away with her. Perhaps, in the appropriating way of children, she was building her own world of story out of what belonged to her anyway because it *was* her.

—John Goldthwaite, *The Natural History of Make-Believe* (New York: Oxford University Press, 1996), 298, 300–2

Bibliography

The Tale of Peter Rabbit. 1901, 1902.
The Tailor of Gloucester. 1902.
The Tale of Squirrel Nutkin. 1903.
The Tailor of Gloucester. 1903.
The Tale of Benjamin Bunny. 1904.
The Tale of Two Bad Mice. 1904.
The Tale of Mrs. Tiggy-Winkle. 1905.

The Pie and the Patty-Pan. 1905.
The Tale of Mr. Jeremy Fisher. 1906.
The Story of a Fierce Bad Rabbit. 1906.
The Story of Miss Moppet. 1906.
The Tale of Tom Kitten. 1907.
The Tale of Jemima Puddle-Duck. 1908.
The Roly-Poly Pudding. Later renamed *The Tale of Samuel Whiskers.* 1908.
The Tale of the Flopsy Bunnies. 1909.
Ginger and Pickles. 1909.
The Tale of Mrs. Tittlemouse. 1910.
Peter Rabbit's Painting Book. 1911.
The Tale of Timmy Tiptoes. 1911.
The Tale of Mr. Tod. 1912.
The Tale of Pigling Bland. 1913.
Tom Kitten's Painting Book. 1917.
Appley Dapply's Nursery Rhymes. 1917.
The Tale of Johnny Town-Mouse. 1918.
Cecily Parsley's Nursery Rhymes. 1922.
Jemima Puddle-Duck's Painting Book. 1925.
Peter Rabbit's Almanac. 1928 and 1929.
The Fairy Caravan. 1929, 1930.
The Tale of Little Pig Robinson. 1930.
Sister Anne. 1932.
Wag-by-Wall. 1944, 1944.
The Tale of the Faithful Dove. 1956.
The Journal of Beatrix Potter, 1881—1897. 1966.
The Writings of Beatrix Potter. 1971.
The Sly Old Cat. 1971.
The Tale of Tuppenny. 1973.
The History of the Tale of Peter Rabbit. 1976.

P. L. Travers
1899 – 1996

P. L. TRAVERS was born Helen Lyndon Goff in Australia on August 9, 1899, the eldest of three children of Robert and Margaret Travers Goff. Her childhood was marked by a sense of the wonder and mystery of the natural world—a sense reinforced by her parents, who, she has said in interviews, offered their children few explanations. Like the children she would later write about in her famous Mary Poppins books, she and her siblings were cared for by a series of nannies. Most were Irish, like her father, and Helen early developed a taste for Irish writers such as Yeats. She was allowed to read indiscriminately among her parents' few books; of children's authors she liked Lewis Carroll, Edith Nesbit, and Beatrix Potter.

Robert Goff died when Helen was 14, and after several years of straitened circumstances, Helen left Australia for England. There she began writing seriously: she befriended the editor of *Irish Statesman*, A. E. (George William Russell), who would have a significant influence upon her thinking, and she began publishing poems in his journal. She wrote criticism as well and published reviews of books, theater, and films in *New English Weekly* from 1933 until 1949 (although, during the war, she fled England temporarily for the United States).

Although Travers has published widely, she is most well known for her Mary Poppins books. According to Travers, the idea arose spontaneously when she was pressed to amuse several children. In interviews she has insisted on the mystery of the creative process and prefers to see herself as more a conduit than a creator; she has developed this idea in her extensive thinking about the role of fairy tale and myth in our culture. The story that ultimately became *Mary Poppins* (1934) would introduce readers to a character and uses of magic that are almost archetypal. Although not without its critics–who noted, for instance, a strain of racism that Travers would later excise—the book was extremely successful and has been followed by nine others centering upon the mythical nanny.

In addition to her Mary Poppins books, Travers has written about characters in her childhood, about the fragmenting experience of war, and about the mythic figures Hanuman and Sleeping Beauty. She worked as a consulting editor for *Parabola: The Magazine for Myth and Tradition* from 1976 until her death in 1996.

Critical Extracts

RICHARD R. LINGEMAN

When asked how Mary Poppins came into being, ⟨Travers⟩ likes to quote Hendrik Willem Van Loon's remark to her: "You didn't think up Mary Poppins, but I am inclined to think she thought up you." But, 30 years ago, she said in an interview: "Not long ago I found myself left alone with two strange, rather solemn children to amuse . . . 'Listen! I've got an idea. I'll tell you a story.' And suddenly, as I said those ordinary and quite usual words, an old mood rose up in me; I felt the crash of wind and rain on a struggling wooden house, and, in spite of the sunny afternoon, it seemed to me that a soft impenetrable darkness was everywhere.

"'What about?' said the boy-child, slightly interested. The answer came involuntarily—rose up unpremeditated and swift, like an exclamation. From where it came I know not. 'About Mary Poppins,' I said. And presently the adventures unrolled, slowly and quietly as the children listened, and each adventure had as its center a figure at once implacable and tender, stern and wise, terrible and loving. And later, still wondering where she came from, I wrote out the stories and made the book of 'Mary Poppins.'"

"That explanation," says P. L. Travers now, "will do as well as any." Though herself a student of the links between myth and fairy tale, she refuses to trace the mythical—if any—origins of the character of Mary Poppins. The most she will do is quote a remark once made to her by AE ⟨George William Russell⟩: "'Popkins,' he told me—he always used to call her 'Popkins'—in any other age would have come with golden tresses and a magic wand, but this being the iron age, she had to choose the habiliments that went with it.'" ⟨. . .⟩

Commonsensical, practical Mary Poppins, who never claims to have superhuman powers, is, then, a character thoroughly grounded in ordinary life. "Only someone with his feet on earth can take off into air," says Miss Travers. "Her magic comes directly from this. . . . Ordinary life is the key to magic. If there is nothing but fairy words, what do we have?—chaos. When a fairy flies—or Peter Pan—we're not surprised when it flies. When Mary Poppins flies, one is astonished, and the absurdity of it becomes part of the magic."

Mary is a kind of modern-day, "white" witch, her powers stemming from unseen, but nonetheless real spheres of being in the universe. In a sense, too, Mary's "absurdity" is of the form of a playful metaphysical paradox. Or perhaps one of those Zen *koans*, which one might crudely put in the following way: Q.—"Can Mary Poppins fly?" A.—"Only with her feet on the ground." But perhaps her creator should have the last words on Mary Poppins's magic: "If I inquired into it I'd be knocking at a forbidden door, a door to which I don't have an open sesame. If I knew how the magic was effected it would cease to have been magic."

—Richard R. Lingeman, "Visit with Mary Poppins and P. L. Travers," *The New York Times Magazine* (25 December 1966): 28

JONATHAN COTT

Although blessed with the fascinating idea of including five other versions of the Sleeping Beauty story in translation from Germany (the Grimms), France (Perrault), Italy (Basile), Ireland (Curtin), and Bengal (Bradley-Birt), P. L. Travers ⟨in *About the Sleeping Beauty*⟩ must have forgotten to invite a fairy godmother to the christening of her own new version, tempting the fates who preside over the well-being and integrity of the literary laws of the realm of Faerie.

Aware of the risks, she writes in an Afterward: "But love of the fairy tales . . . need not require the lover to refashion them. Do they need retelling, you may ask. Does it not smack of arrogance for any writer to imagine he can put a gloss on a familiar theme? If I answer yes to both these questions I put myself in jeopardy. And yet, why should I fear? To be in jeopardy is a proper fairy-tale situation. Danger is at the heart of the matter, for without danger how shall we foster the rescuing power?"

No "rescuing power," however, can succeed if the form of the fairy tale is not respected: as C. S. Lewis described it, "its brevity, its severe restraints on description, its flexible traditionalism, its inflexible hostility to the analysis, digression, reflection and 'gas.' " Intending to "ventilate" her own thoughts about the tale of Sleeping Beauty, P. L. Travers tells us that she needed to "separate it from its attic clutter—the spinning wheel, the pointed witch cap and all the pantomime buffoonery—in order to see its meaning clear."

But instead of creating a fresh and vibrant "sub-created world"—without which, Tolkien believed, nothing either meaningful or magical could ever be communicated—P. L. Travers furnishes us with a gimcrack silk and damask Arabian court setting, inhabited by bright-liveried servants, salaaming Viziers, guests "proffering" gifts, and a "dark slave" named Bouraba who is clumsily forced to act the role of a kind of Jungian shadow or animus figure to the heroine.

Considering the fact that psychologists and writers as diverse as Erich Fromm, Robert Graves and Alison Lurie have seen in fairy tales the survivals of an ancient matriarchal culture and faith, it seems gratuitous at best for P. L. Travers to remark in an aside: "And then, since a man cannot grieve continually—though the same thing is not true of women. . . ." But what is equally disappointing is the author's frequent use of precious phrases and parodies (for example, "How far is it to fairyland? Nearer by far than Babylon" or "At last the great day—as must happen, even with small days—arrived")—and her tendentious underlinings of her "meaning" (for example, "Wit is no substitute for wisdom" or "He is himself his own weapon. The time must be ripe")—all of which cheat us of our desire to *imagine* and which further belie the promise the author makes in her "Afterword" that this "latest version of the story, true to the law of the fairy tale, makes no attempt to explain." Any author who begins her tale: "Once upon a time, a time that never was and is always"—not knowing that the four-word formula itself implies the explanation of eternity—transgresses this very law.

    —Jonathan Cott, [Review of *About the Sleeping Beauty*], *The New York Times Book Review* (28 September 1975): 27

KENNETH J. RECKFORD

⟨F⟩airy tale motifs ⟨. . .⟩ found in Old Comedy, such as talking birds and tables that set themselves with bountiful food and drink, take on special force, and special meaning, from the worship of Dionysus and from the revelry of his festival. They express, in comic and popular form, an ancient awareness of a divine energy that irrupts into the world and transforms it: an energy that, if not divine in nature, and divinely controlled, would be demonic. ⟨. . .⟩

⟨One of the Mary Poppins stories, "Full Moon,"⟩ is, in many ways, typical of that collection, written by a woman who welcomes, yet duly reveres, the power of Dionysus—or something very like it—in the world. ⟨. . .⟩

After Jane and Michael Banks are put to bed, and perhaps sleep, a voice summons them. They follow the voice, out of bed, out of their house, through the streets, until they find themselves at the familiar entrance of the Zoo. A full moon is shining. A Brown Bear welcomes them and gives them tickets. Once inside, they find various animals—wolves and a stork, a beaver and an American vulture—deep in conversation, apparently discussing somebody's Birthday; and there are other strange occurrences:

> Just by the Elephant Stand a very large, very fat old gentleman was walking up and down on all fours, and on his back, on two small parallel seats, were eight monkeys going for a ride.
> "Why, it's all upside down!" exclaimed Jane.
> The old gentleman gave her an angry look as he went past.
> "Upside down!" he snorted. "Me! Upside down? Certainly not. Gross insult!" The eight monkeys laughed rudely.
> "Oh, please—I didn't mean you—but the whole thing," explained Jane, hurrying after him to apologize. "On ordinary days the animals

carry human beings and now there's a human being carrying the
animals. That's what I meant."
     But the old gentleman, shuffling and panting, insisted that he had
been insulted, and hurried away with the monkeys screaming on his
back. ⟨. . .⟩

It turns out, when they reach the Snake House, and see Mary Poppins, and
meet the Hamadryad (who is very old, and very wise, and very dangerous),
that all these reversals of nature are taking place because it is one of the very
special times when Mary Poppins' birthday coincides with the full moon. The
Hamadryad gives her a present of his old skin, which he shrugs off, for a belt.
The climax of the festivities is a dance ⟨. . . .⟩
     As the dance moves, and the whole world seems to rock around them,
Jane and Michael (by another imperceptible transition) find themselves in
bed. When they awaken the next morning, they wonder whether they have
dreamt it all: certainly, they have had the same dream, down to every detail.
Mary Poppins, on being questioned, is very indignant at the very suggestion
that *she* could have been seen at the Zoo, and at night too! But the children
notice, quietly, that

> Round her waist Mary Poppins was wearing a belt made of golden
> scaly snake-skin, and on it was written in curving, snaky writing:
> "A Present From the Zoo."

     I have described this story partly out of gratitude, since my own appreci-
ation of comedy, and of life, is derived in large part from *Mary Poppins*, and
partly because these stories include and illustrate two key aspects of
"Dionysian fairy tale." The first is that, with Mary Poppins, a wonderful transforming energy breaks through into ordinary life, so that the Banks children
find themselves soaring through the air with balloons, or having tea parties
(with plenty of bread and jam and cake) on the ceiling, or communing with
dangerous and powerful personages—with hamadryads and with stars. The
stories bring us, delightfully, out of ordinary custom and routine (which
nonetheless remain extremely important) into a world of magic where the laws
of nature are suspended and normal relations are changed (though kindness
and decency count for much, and you must exhibit good manners at tea, even
on the ceiling). Part of the fun consists, naturally, of recognizing familiar people and things in such strange and wonderful surroundings. Still more comes
though surprise, incongruity, and reversal, as with the monkeys riding the old
gentleman, or the people in cages being fed. The fantasies are rich and fulfill-
ing. They abound in delighted laughter, of release. But they are also (and this
is their second key aspect) reassuring, ultimately safe. Daemonic energies

sometimes get loose, and they are very dangerous, as children well know; but they are always brought back under control by the protecting figure of Mary Poppins, who is surrounded by the magic and excitement that she helps generate, but never really affected or altered by it. She always guides the children home again, back to the bedroom (did they dream it all?), back to safe and known reality—though some piece of that other world can still be glimpsed and its associated memories enjoyed. The world has been transformed a little, and the children, and we, with it. That is why we can laugh so richly, and so well, after reading and rereading these stories.

Even if I were not aware that P. L. Travers was, and is, a serious student of mythology, folklore, and anthropology, and something of a mystic, I would be justified in speaking of the *Mary Poppins* stories as Dionysian. What I really want, though, is to reverse the proposition, to argue that Aristophanes' Dionysian comedies are like fairy tales.

—Kenneth J. Reckford, *Aristophanes' Old-and-New Comedy* (Chapel Hill: University of North Carolina Press, 1987), 101–4

HUMPHREY CARPENTER

A good deal in the Poppins stories is slackly derivative. The first book, "Mary Poppins," was published in 1934 and edited by Peter Lewelyn Davies, who in childhood had been one of the Lost Boys befriended and immortalized by J. M. Barrie, and it is heavily influenced by Barrie. The Banks household, with its fond but ineffective mother and blustering father, strongly suggests the Darlings, while Mary Poppins herself flies onto the scene, blown by the wind, much as Peter Pan flits into the night nursery.

The first book, however, does contain one suggestion of what is to come: the strange and rather terrifying figure of Mrs. Corry, an aged crone who, with her fat and downtrodden daughters Miss Fannie and Miss Annie, is the proprietor of a mysterious sweet shop to which Mary Poppins takes the children. Mrs. Corry breaks off her fingers and gives them to people to eat—they are made of barley-sugar, or sometimes of peppermint—and she can remember the making of the world. She takes paper-gilt stars from the wrappings of her gingerbread, climbs a ladder and fixes them in the sky, where they become real stars. There is nothing derivative about this; we are on a territory that is Miss Travers's own, an idiosyncratic blend of domestic comedy and cosmic resonance.

"Mary Poppins Comes Back" appeared in 1935, and proved much better than the first book. Strange and almost archetypal figures like Mrs. Corry began to proliferate—the grotesque Nellie-Rubina, a painted Dutch doll who herself paints animals, sky and trees in their spring colors, thereby bringing about the coming of the real spring (she turns out to be the daughter of Noah). Miss Travers's theme and purpose began to become clear. She is obsessed with the conflict between society's demand for respectability and the enormous forces of energy that lie beneath the surface of human nature—"daemonic energies," as Mr. Reckford rightly calls them. Mary Poppins herself expresses this conflict clearly. At one moment she is introducing the children to primitive forces of nature, ⟨. . .⟩ but at the next she is denying that anything out of the ordinary ever happened, and is forcing the children back into the social mold. She is most angry when the children make any allusion to magical happenings; such things may take place, but they must *never* be referred to again once it is all over. It is very like the Victorian attitude toward sex. ⟨. . .⟩

⟨. . . D⟩espite their patchy craftsmanship ⟨the Poppins books⟩ are the product of a fiery imagination, and are driven by an obsessive and invigorating interest in the unceasing conflict between social respectability and the real needs of human nature, between reason and the imagination—the theme, as historians of children's literature will know, of all great children's books.

    —Humphrey Carpenter, "Mary Poppins, Force of Nature," *The New York Times Book Review* (27 August 1989): 29

SARAH GILEAD

Like Peter ⟨Pan⟩, Mary Poppins is associated with flight and nature (the wind, animals, heavenly bodies). Her 'pop-ins' appear spontaneous, like the wind that blows her into and out of the narrative. Mary is a semidivine 'Cousin' of the zoo animals; for the children who accompany her to the transformed, moonlit, 'upside-down' zoo, she is a teacher of truths transcending adult conceptual narrowness and selfishness (Travers 1934: 134). Defying gravity, she seems also to defy adult 'gravity' (see especially Chapter 3, 'Laughing gas', where comic fantasy temporarily defeats anxieties concerning loss and death). But Mary is also a governess, a socializing agent and at times even a repressor who denies magic or uses it for punishment of moral lapses. For example, at the end of Chapter 3, the scene of the hilarious, floating tea, she sniffily denies that the incident took place. In Chapter 6 she whisks the children off to hobnob with animals, only later to use this fantasy journey, in the form of a nightmare, to punish one of her charges (ibid.: 80–1). Thus, Mary embodies the ambivalence of fantasy writing for children, now escapist and frankly unsocial (or even antisocial), now framed by the justifying context of moral didacticism.

In the overall narrative's closural frame, the fictional world is restored to its original, prefantasy condition. When Mary departs, magic, fantasy and nature myths depart too. But the child protagonists experience this departure as loss, not as restoration. Further, the meaning of the departed fantasy is not established: no particular lessons have been learned, self-concepts are not strengthened, religious truths vaguely hinted at remain unrevealed. The closure points to an absolute barrier between fantasy and reality, between childhood and adulthood; Mary's presence obscures that barrier, but her absence makes it manifest. Oddly, though, when her magic disappears, the very sense of its loss suggests that magic is an intrinsic, though ambiguous, good—not justified by, and apparently not needing to be justified by, any other frame of reference.

Like Peter Pan, Mary and her magic comes into the initial reality frame to fill a parental gap and, more broadly, to compensate for the multiple inadequacies of adult reality. In the initial frame, adult activities are presented as trivial, the adults as obtuse and selfish, remote from the children and indifferent to their needs; and these qualities are exacerbated in the closing frame (see especially pages 156–7, where Michael now fully comprehends his mother's selfishness). The closural loss of magic and of its consolations thus sharpens the critique of adults and of their version of reality and makes the loss of the fantasy world tragic. Reality is not rectified; fantasy and reality are not aligned.

The series of episodes and interpolated tales that make up the narrative mostly follow the reality-fantasy-reality pattern of the whole. Fantasy never becomes fully present; it is temporary, risky, and unstable in duration and meaning (ironically, adult reality is even more unstable and much less satisfying and comprehensible). For example, Chapter 2, 'The day out', repeats the general frame narrative in structure but opposes it in meaning. Mary's day off is indeed 'off' the plane of reality. Initially described in realistic terms, it soon enters the 'framed' world of fantasy—here, almost literally: she and her sidewalk-artist friend, Bert, 'enter' a picture he has painted, a pastoral landscape where they enjoy an idyllic tea. Returning to reality, Mary tells the children that she has been in a fairyland all her own, that is, one derived from her wishes. In the demarcated spaces of art, fantasy offers temporary gratifications for reality's omissions (the 'real' tea was foiled by Mary's and Bert's lack of money). In confusing contrast, Chapter 9, 'John and Barbara's story', shows infants outgrowing their ability to understand the speech of natural objects and creatures. In Chapter 2 Mary seems to offer fantasy as a compensatory resource. In Chapter 9 she presides over the 'natural' loss of the 'magical' delights of perceptual and cognitive unity with nature. Does her leaving reflect childhood's inevitable end? If so, why have her equivocal lessons in fantasy reinforced the children's sense of reality's inadequacy? As reality even more clearly resumes its initial shape of barren and joyless necessity, the children are left with a framed portrait of Mary and her hint of return ('au revoir').

That is, they hope that once again ordinary reality may be reduced to a mere frame around a more exciting and variable realm. Almost cruelly, Mary has forced them back to reality without reconciling them to it; she has, if anything, spoiled them for it by her tantalizing range of modes of escape and by her refusal or inability to define the uses of enchantment.

—Sarah Gilead, "Magic Abjured: Closure in Children's Fantasy Fiction," in *Literature for Children: Contemporary Criticism*, ed. Peter Hunt (London: Routledge, 1992), 98–100

PATRICIA DEMERS

Jonathan Cott's label of "cosmic" for Mary Poppins applies for several reasons. Her quickness to diagnose, assess, and measure the behavior of the Banks children, as she does in opening segments of the first three books by administering medicine, thrusting a thermometer into their mouths, and stretching a tape measure along their heights, betokens a certain righteousness on her part. Hers is an Old Testament righteousness that fills the measure and meets a standard (Deut. 25:15; Lev. 19:36). Her participation in the Hamadryad's Grand Chain ("Full Moon," *Mary Poppins*); the greeting she receives in the constellations' golden ring, "a swaying . . . mass of horns and hooves and manes and tails" ("The Evening Out," *Mary Poppins Comes Back*); her recognition at the Terrapin's party ("High Tide," *Mary Poppins Opens the Door*); and her birthday-eve celebration with shadows ("Hallowe'en," *Mary Poppins in the Park*) indicate that the powers of this nanny surpass all ordinary conventions and chronology. These celebrations are, strictly speaking, liturgical, which makes all the more sense when one traces the Hamadryad's observation "that to eat and be eaten are the same thing," to "The Hymn of Christ" in the Apocryphal *Acts of John*.

Mary Poppins seems to come from another world and time and yet to be also a futuristic model of understanding. Her syncretistic belief in unity, imagination, and wisdom inspires many like-minded friends. The Hamadryad insists that "bird and beast and stone and star—we are all one, all one." In *Mary Poppins Comes Back* when the children query the Sun about the difference between "what is real and what is not," his answer is a poetic one, "that to think a thing is to make it true." The Terrapin in *Mary Poppins Opens the Door* reminds them of the sea's importance as originator and model of their world: "the land came out of the sea . . . [and] each thing on the earth has a brother here." In *Mary Poppins in the Park* the Bird Woman lets them see the transporting value of the shadow, "the other part of you, the outside of your inside," as a way to wisdom, which goes "through things, through and out the other side." Although Mary Poppins has phenomenal abilities, such as ushering in spring overnight, and exceptional friends, she also exemplifies and extols trusted human virtues like loyalty and compassion. The offer of her handkerchief as a cushion for the sleeping Robertson Ay and her story of the Tramp-Angel's awareness of everyone's illusions (*Mary Poppins in the Park*) are moving instances of this storyteller's desire to embrace and possibly heal all.

This singular heroine also raises some questions. It is curious that this talented figure must pass through so many entrances and exits to the various episodes, as well as blow into a whirl out of the Banks family home three times. Is such narrative coming and going a reminder from Travers that this mythic creature, with a foot in reality, must also submit to the logical interrogatives of how, when, and where? Mary Poppins's peremptory refusals to answer questions and her outright denials of involvement in fantastic events raise the issue of deliberately jeopardized credibility. Is this reverse psychology? Does Mary Poppins deny so vociferously to incite readers to believe in, affirm, and acclaim her with added enthusiasm? Despite the discernment of her gimlet eyes, she proves amazingly susceptible to Michael's transparent flattery. Is this Poppins peccadillo meant to corroborate her essential childlikeness? Travers offers no answers, admitting to Jonathan Cott that "anything I write is all question."

—Patricia Demers, "P. L. (Pamela Lyndon) Travers," in *Dictionary of Literary Biography: Volume 160: British Children's Writers, 1914–1960* (Detroit, MI: Gale Research Inc., 1996), 277

Bibliography

Moscow Excursion. 1934.
Mary Poppins. 1934.
Mary Poppins Comes Back. 1935.
Happy Ever After. 1940.
Aunt Sass. 1941.
I Go By Land, I Go By Sea. 1941.
Ah Wong. 1943.
Mary Poppins Opens the Door. 1943.
Johnny Delaney. 1944.
Mary Poppins in the Park. 1952.
Mary Poppins from A to Z. 1962.
The Fox at the Manger. 1962.
A Mary Poppins Story for Coloring. 1969.
Friend Monkey. 1971.

George Ivanovitch Gurdjieff. 1973.

Mary Poppins in the Kitchen: A Cookery Book with a Story. 1975.

About the Sleeping Beauty. 1975.

Two Pairs of Shoes. 1980.

Mary Poppins in Cherry Tree Lane. 1982.

Mary Poppins and the House Next Door. 1988.

What the Bee Knows: Reflections on Myth, Symbol, and Story. 1989.

Laura Ingalls Wilder
1867 – 1957

LAURA INGALLS was born February 7, 1867, near Pepin, Wisconsin, to Charles and Caroline Lake Quiner Ingalls. In the first years of Laura's life, the family moved from Wisconsin to Missouri and from there to Kansas—richly textured episodes that Laura would later fictionalize in *Little House on the Prairie*. In 1871, when she was just four, the entire family nearly died of diphtheria and returned to their little house in the big woods of Wisconsin. In three years, however, their struggle to make a living compelled them to move again, this time to Minnesota.

The family's life continued to be difficult throughout the years they lived in Minnesota. After Charles built a house and a school, the family lost two crops to plagues of grasshoppers in successive years. In order to survive, Charles had to find work in the East for a time, and later the whole family had to spend several months in Iowa running a hotel with another poverty-stricken family. These years also saw the birth and death of Laura's brother, Charles Frederick, and of her sister Grace. In 1879 Laura's older sister, Mary, contracted scarlet fever and suffered a stroke that left her blind. When Charles was offered work building the railroad in the Dakota Territory, he quickly accepted so that he could send Mary to a college for the blind. In 1880 the whole family moved to De Smet.

After earning her teaching certificate and surviving the long winter of blizzards with all the other settlers, Laura boarded with a family outside De Smet and started to earn money teaching school. Her only pleasure during this time was her weekly ride with Almanzo Wilder back into De Smet over the weekends. In 1884 she and Almanzo were engaged, and the following year they married and settled on Almanzo's claim.

The first 10 years of the Wilders' life together were riddled with disaster. Their crops repeatedly failed; they were in debt; and two years after their daughter, Rose, was born (1886), Almanzo and Laura contracted a nearly fatal case of diphtheria. Almanzo forced himself to work his land, despite his lingering illness, but the strain proved too great and caused him to suffer a stroke that left him partially paralyzed in his arms and legs for the rest of his life. A year after they had both recovered, Laura gave birth to a son who died within 12 days. Shortly thereafter their house burned to the ground, and their crops failed once again.

After so much loss, the young family moved to Florida with the hope of better luck in a gentler climate. The weather, however, did not suit Almanzo, so they returned to De Smet in 1892. The couple took various jobs in town and saved their earnings until 1894, when they moved to Mansfield, Missouri. There they were at last fortunate, running a prosperous farm for the rest of their lives together.

Laura Ingalls Wilder's career as a writer began in Mansfield, where she became a columnist for the *Missouri Ruralist* and contributed articles to *McCall's* and *Country Gentleman* from 1911 to 1924. Her daughter, Rose, who had married and moved to San Francisco to make a career as a writer, came home periodically from 1924 to 1931 to help Laura develop her writing and encourage her emerging autobiographical narrative. Laura had come to realize that she had experienced a monumental period in American history, and she wished to record fictively her visions of this experience. She would later state that all she told of in these books was true—but she preferred the virtues of fiction to those of history in her selective telling of truth.

Harper accepted Wilder's manuscript of *Little House in the Big Woods* in 1931. Her next book, *A Farmer Boy*, was an account of her husband's childhood in New York and was published in 1933; it was followed by *Little House on the Prairie* in 1935 and soon by the others in the series. All of the Little House books were successful, and four were awarded Newbery Medals. In 1943 the whole series was reissued and newly illustrated by Garth Williams.

Almanzo died in 1949; eight years later, at the age of 90, Laura Ingalls Wilder died.

Critical Extracts

FRED INGLIS

I take *The Long Winter* because I think it is the best of an excellent series, not because it fits a thesis. Its prose is, in Rowe Townsend's memorable words, 'clear, plain, and as good as bread' ⟨*Written for Children*, 181⟩ *because* its political origins—that family, that township, those shops and schools and ways of husbandry—were as they were. Its strength in showing daughters how to become women is so much greater than that of the bestsellers, not only because the story is moved by the absoluteness of historical fact. *The Long Winter* has its force because the story and the prose in which it is told lie so close to the author's morality. There is no strain upon the writer in her seeking to commend what is beautiful and rational and good. The way the little family acts is the way it ought to act, and this congruence of culture and nature, of economics and action, means that Laura Ingalls Wilder can tell her tale quite purely. The sanctions and piety of the Ingalls are open and lovely, although they are so because they do not have to encompass the greater moral contortions of life in a more complex social structure. It is to the point to note that within the Ingalls family and their little community, we find a perfect expression of the just society, ordered on the principles of liberal theory. ⟨. . . The⟩ novelist's preoccupation with an ideal social order and the materials to hand for its creation must, as it is communicated to children, provide a picture either of an imaginable future or of a real past. *The Long Winter* and its companion books hold past and future together. Life at the Frontier really was like that, but life ought also to be like that again. The community's life is ordered by the two principles of justice: that each person is to have equal rights to the most extensive basic liberty compatible with a similar liberty for others; and that inequalities work in such an arrangement that they are to everyone's advantage and attached to offices open to all. ⟨. . .⟩

What isn't 'fair' in the book is the length and severity of the winter. The seven months' savage weather is the family's bitter enemy. But Mrs Wilder is too admirable and pious an artist not to acknowledge the bounty of nature first, and the first fifth of the book describes a rich, glowing and splendid autumn, a heavy harvest, and the joys of the hot sun on the prairie. The pleasure of reading these pages sharpens because we know what is coming. In everyday life children find it particularly pleasurable to anticipate a storm rolling in from the sea in purple dark clouds and grumbling thunder, especially when they are still in bright sun. The opening chapters of *The Long Winter* give you that feeling. When the blizzard breaks, the sensation is like that of hearing from a warm bed the rain driven onto the window pane in spatters, while the wind howls. ⟨. . .⟩

The pacing of the book is unimprovable. Each chapter is quite short, nicely adjusted to a young reader's stamina, but each shifts the story a little way on in to the long, rhythmless tedium of the winter. The family very nearly starve. They kindle for themselves a thin edge of warmth in temperatures 40° below zero, burning light sticks of tightly twisted hay. They bend a serene patience against the killing cold and their boredom. The girls' dependence on their parents is absolute, of course, but their work is essential to survival (the hay Laura brings in sees them through the last month). Father, being the only man of the family, and with a man's strength, has to face the storm most directly. His courage is of an utterly different and superior order to that of Allan Quartermain. And for all that his strength is essential to protect the weaker women, he could not live without their help, both practical and affectionate.

The love that holds the family upright against the winter is amazing; it gives endurance its meaning as experience, and as we see at the Ingalls's Christmas, it always makes happiness possible. When relief comes, the joy of the moment expresses itself in the delighted suddenness with which the rhythm and diction of the prose change ⟨. . . .⟩

> They ate the coarse brown bread and went through the dark and cold upstairs to bed. Shivering in the cold bed Laura and Mary silently said their prayers and slowly grew warm enough to sleep.
>
> Sometime in the night Laura heard the wind. It was still blowing furiously but there were no voices, no howls or shrieks in it. And with it there was another sound, a tiny, uncertain, liquid sound that she couldn't understand.
>
> She listened as hard as she could. She uncovered her ear to listen and the cold did not bite her cheek. The dark was warmer. She put out her hand and only felt a coolness. The little sound that she heard was the trickling of waterdrops. The eaves were dripping. Then she knew.
>
> She sprang up in bed and called aloud, 'Pa! Pa! The Chinook is blowing!'
>
> 'I hear it, Laura,' Pa answered from the other room. 'Spring has come. Go back to sleep.'
>
> The Chinook was blowing. Spring had come. The blizzard had given up; it was driven back to the north. Blissfully Laura stretched out in bed; she put both arms on top of the quilts and they were not very cold. She listened to the blowing wind and dripping eaves and she knew that in the other room Pa was lying awake, too, listening and glad. The Chinook, the wind of the spring was blowing. Winter was ended. (pp. 232–3)

Even then the book paces evenly to an end which insists on the continuity of life and the worthwhileness of the struggle against that dreadful winter. Supplies are delayed, and it is mid-May before town and family open the Christmas barrel.

The tale is not a lesson. It is a piece of folk-history—though perfectly accurate. Folk-history is just as scientific and ideological as academic history. The ceremonious mode of narration is necessary to give order to a dangerous and uncertain life. That life image is the best part of America, especially its womenfolk.

—Fred Inglis, *The Promise of Happiness: Value and Meaning in Children's Fiction* (Cambridge: Cambridge University Press, 1981), 166–67, 169–71

HAMIDA BOSMAJIAN

Little House on the Prairie ⟨is⟩ a book that reveals an awareness of historical and cultural discontents and at the same time reverberates with the contentment of felicitous space where one's being is housed and with the excitement of vast space wherein one's being expands.

The storyteller begins with an expansion of memory, "A long time ago," and closes with a lyrical anticipation of future possibilities, "Daily and nightly I wander with thee." The book is a daughter's fictionalized memory of her father's anticipations expressed through a phenomenology of the spaces of vastness and contraction: the prairie and the little house. Anticipation, future time, urges towards happy space, but memory knows that both the vast and the intimately contracted space have been precarious and ambiguous as values of human experience in the world. With great subtlety *Little House on the Prairie* introduces the child to the ironies of American life and history, including the American dream and the temporal and spatial horizon of the mythology of Manifest Destiny. The dreamer about the West is unaware that moving toward the westward horizon is traditionally a move toward the end of a time. The narrator, however, knows it: "That long line of Indians slowly pulled itself over the Western edge of the world. And nothing was left but silence and emptiness. All the world seemed lonely and quiet" (p. 311).

The most radical expression of vastness and contraction occurs in the chapter "Fever 'N' Ague," when the Ingalls family suffers from malaria. Laura hallucinates in her fever: "Something dwindled slowly, smaller and smaller, till it was tinier than the tiniest thing. Then it slowly swelled up again till it was larger than anything could be" (pp. 186–87). We have here what ⟨Gaston⟩ Bachelard calls a "phenomenology without phenomena" that refers us directly to "our imagining consciousness" ⟨*The Poetics of Space*, 1969, 184⟩. The minuscule intimate point that contracts into itself is a defensive energy of such density that it would collapse of its own weight unless it expanded again aggressively. Both, extreme constriction and all-filling vastness, suck in or swallow the fragile ego. These phenomena, experienced here in their sheerness, apply also to the topography of the little house and the prairie as well as to the tensions within and between characters.

Vastness and contraction have a positive and negative end on a spectrum of values. The vastness of the prairie resonates with desire and the need for expansion as these are felt by the human heart, the wandering spirit. But the sublime vastness of the prairie consumes the exploring wanderer and, since the prairie is not really level, threatens with condensed pockets of danger. To keep intact, the ego must clear a containing space, a round shelter in the vastness: the circle of the camp, the shelter of the "hut-dream" (Bachelard) which becomes the little house. The house is the most positive image of civilization in the book, although its contracted space is always endangered from without and within. The image in transit between prairie and little house is the covered wagon with Ma and Pa in front anticipating the future and Laura shaping her memories by looking back at the abandoned house through the circle of the drawn canvas cover (p. 324).

Vast and contracted space and their values become correlatives for the three character groups in the book. The Indians have their camps, but they are really housed in the vastness of the prairie. Ma and Mary desire the contracted space of the house and its civilization. Pa Ingalls and Laura hover between the values of the open prairie and the values of the house. Ma, Pa, and Laura each has a personal image that condenses these values. Laura has the word *papoose*, Ma has the small china shepherdess, and Pa has his fiddle. Vast and contracted space as well as these personal images reveal the meaning of human experience in *Little House on the Prairie*.

    —Hamida Bosmajian, "Vastness and Contraction of Space in *Little House on the Prairie*," *Children's Literature* 11 (1983): 51–53

VIRGINIA L. WOLF

⟨The⟩ movement ⟨of Wilder's Little House books⟩ involves a progression from myth to adventure toward psychological realism. The first three books focus on archetypal symbols, creating a vision of how life might be at its best. The next two portray life as it usually is, a mixture of good and bad, but yield to the child's desire for heroic triumph in adventures against formidable foes. *The Long Winter*, the sixth book, marks a transition. Like *On the Banks of Plum Creek* and *By the Shores of Silver Lake*, it ends in triumph, but not of action. Rather, it celebrates endurance, patience, courage, and those other internal values explored in the last two books. And it is the darkest book in the series, the one in which death seems closest. Here Laura learns that if she can never control nature, she can control herself. The shift to the inner voyage is completed in the last two books. The Ingallses never leave De Smet, South Dakota, and Laura here acquires her philosophy of freedom. Her statement of this philosophy gradually emerges in *Little Town on the Prairie*, and is completed in *These Happy Golden Years*, the symbolism of the first three books now "critically read" by Laura as her narration becomes Wilder's vehicle for meaning.

What Laura comes to understand is the culmination of the whole series: a philosophy unifying the contradictions of existence. But her triumph is internal, not external. It specifies a set of values, not a specific social or political stance. It, furthermore, implies less about a specific set of historical circumstances than it does about universal concerns such as love and freedom. What Wilder ultimately tells us is that life is inevitably a tension in which the individual has—at best—control over herself as she alternates between being at one and at odds with other people and nature, patiently living through the bad times but always expecting the return of the good ones. The cycle, symbolized by the circle, embodies Wilder's hope just as the tension of opposites conveys her awareness of reality. The structure of the series is a cycle, beginning with *Little House in the Big Woods* and ending with "Little Gray Home in the West," but within this cycle exists constant tension—within each book and between the books, as each book has its parallel and yet opposite in another book in the series. In the very fabric of the series, in other words, Wilder conveys the understanding that Laura will eventually communicate.

Wilder's vision exists at the level of complementary images: house and wilderness, Ma and Pa, Mary and Laura, pioneer and Indian. But careful balance of antitheses also exists in the structure of the series. The first two books balance the last two; the third book, *Farmer Boy*, actually the second one published, balances the sixth; and *On the Banks of Plum Creek* and *By the Shores of Silver Lake* occupy the center, balancing each other. In good part, the parallelism of the titles reflects this division: *Little House in the Big Woods* and *Little House on the Prairie, On the Banks of Plum Creek* and *By the Shores of Silver Lake.* The conclusive evidence, of course, is the content of the books, each set displaying the antithetical balance found in the imagery and in the series as a whole. Although within each book there are images of both freedom and security, each set of books alternates between the two, and in the last set the emphasis is reversed, *Little Town on the Prairie* being about inner freedom and *These Happy Golden Years,* about inner security. Tension thus pervades the series, oppositions balanced and contained within a cyclical pattern.

—Virginia L. Wolf, "Laura Ingalls Wilder's Little House Books: A Personal Story," in *Touchstones: Reflections on the Best in Children's Literature,* vol. 1 (West Lafayette, IN: Children's Literature Association Publishers, 1985), 294–95

CHARLES FREY

Laura's is the most active and feeling sensibility in the narrative. Although she professes to know that "nothing could hurt her while Pa and Jack were there," still she wakes in the night, repeatedly, when Mary and Carrie remain sleeping. Laura experiences more of life than any other character experiences. She turns out not to be contained or securely bound in by Pa's personality, or by Ma's. It is her story even though Pa may at times catch her in "his safe, big hug." One of Pa's typical terms of endearment for Laura—"'little half-pint of sweet cider half drunk up'"—may hint at the appetitive though affectionate relation that parents such as Pa often feel for their children whom they call "muffin" or "sugar" or such like, but still Laura's poetic perceptions of the prairie vastness and the life in nature differentiate her world from Pa's. His spirit is, to be sure, a wandering one. He has a gift for mechanical labors that Laura never relishes in herself. And his music-making and song are the counterpart, but only that, to Laura's separate drive to tell the tale of her own, very special life and to tell it in the prose-poem form of a book, something that would last, in some ways, beyond the range of Pa's makings. But still it is a book that tells in varying ways the story of Laura's affinity with and differentiation from her father. ⟨. . .⟩

A remarkable feature of the Laura books is the amount and degree of hardship depicted therein without self-pity. One sees Laura in the very process of acclimatizing herself to an alien landscape beyond her home. Surprisingly, the reader, along with Laura, tends to forget or to play down such scenes as these: "There was no place to make camp and build a fire. Everything was damp and chill and miserable in the wagon, but they had to stay in it and eat cold bits of food" (11). Such moments are never lingered over or sentimentalized, and readers are encouraged to see this family's hard, honest way of life so close to the bones of earth and sky as a good way of life, a deeply peaceful and loving way despite the length and strength of its trials. The dramatic creek-crossing of the second chapter is taut and electric in itself but it also brings out a little more of the family's emotional dynamic. Mary huddles down "afraid," "but Laura was excited; she liked the splashing." Mary trembles and lies still, but Laura wriggles and peeks; Mary hides her face but Laura rises up; Mary cries, but Laura watches and holds onto the seat. Laura's the one who thinks of Jack. When Jack is lost, Laura thinks she knows that it is "shameful to cry" though here is crying "inside her." One gets a sense of Laura as a tremendously sensitive, energetic, vibrant personality who feels more keenly than many children the burden of repressive standards for conduct. Yet Laura shows time and again that no external rules will be conceded the power to restrain her natural zest. Her story is so interesting in part because she lives her life so fully, with such strength. Laura is a child-woman, incipient in her independence, invested early on with authorial power, and therefore cast as a somewhat ambiguous and tensional presence in the family.

—Charles Frey, "Laura and Pa: Family and Landscape in *Little House on the Prairie*," *Children's Literature Association Quarterly* 12, no. 3 (Fall 1987): 126

LOUISE MOWDER

⟨In the Little House books,⟩ Mary, all blond, light pink and blue, contrasts with Laura, whose colors are brown and red. These colors also align each child with two of the primary totems within the series: the china shepherdess and the Indian. The placement of the shepherdess upon a mantel or its decorative bracket is the ritual that indicates that the Ingalls family has finally appropriated each new landscape ⟨. . . .⟩

Besides her stereotypical prettiness, the china shepherdess is distinguished by her immutability and her silence. She is manufactured, a product of civilization and its cultural standards of beauty, and imported into the landscape. Yet that importation also reorders the landscape. For, while the china woman is stock-still and voiceless, she is also the tacit referent of socialization in what otherwise is read as a barbaric landscape. She is the ultimate model of femininity within the home and the crowning marker of civilization within the wilderness. ⟨. . .⟩

If the china shepherdess is analogous to Mary, then the Indians are aligned with Laura. They too are "reddish-brown;" they live outdoors; they are enviably naked. They are natural products of the wilderness, known by their howls and cries and their reputation of acting on unbridled impulse. Laura is continually chastised for "Indian-like" traits: her rambunctious noisiness and her refusal to maintain a pale complexion. Laura is imaginatively infatuated by Indians, more fascinated than frightened; while they are a source of fear to her, they are also enviable in their autonomy.

Yet it is the Indians' autonomy and their endogeny, their native presence in the landscape, which not only fascinates the child but threatens the project of womanly domestication of the frontier. The Indians are threatening by their nature, that is, by their very existence, rather than by any specific actions; they thus must be eliminated. In the Little House books, it is the adult women who give voice most directly to the hatred of the Indians and call for their extermination.

The china shepherdess and the Indian, then, are also totems of speech and language patterns within the work, standing as they do for silence and the howl. The silence of the civilized women stands in mute yet powerful contrast to the unfathomable but eloquent howl of the wild masculine. ⟨. . .⟩

The project of American imperialism is interpreted within the Little House books as a distinctly feminine project, one that is enacted by women upon both the landscape and upon their children. The discipline of training is the same, is simultaneous, in each case. The re-ordering of the West is not the masculine version of the cowboy gunslinger and the cattle drive, but of the continual erection of new homes in which to shelter the women, of new places to spread the tablecloth and display the china shepherdess. The creation of a woman, as it is enacted in Laura, is the reordering of personality and habit from that of an active, noisy, barefoot child who craves nakedness and self-interest, to that of a quiet, well-behaved young lady, interested in books, clothes, and self-sacrifice. Ma must create civilization out of both wildernesses. The lesson of the Little House books may be that civilization—

embodied in the domestic bliss of Laura and Almanzo—cannot exist without such a transformation, but the reader can also perceive an undeniable sadness in the depiction of adult family life in the later volumes, a melancholy which is completely absent from the earlier works.

Colonialism here is the triumph of the domestic, the creation of a space in which the china shepherdess and all she represents can be enshrined. Within this space there is no room for Indians and wolves, and the true maturity of the frontier is that moment of silence when even the echoes of their cries has died away, just as true womanhood is that moment when the utterances of the child have been enculturated into silence. Laura herself is the text upon which we can read the imperial project of gendering and domestication, just as the landscape is a parallel text, where we can read the colonial project of the domestication of race and the Other. As the boundaries of the civilized nation expand, Laura's boundaries become more constricted.

This version of the American frontier, a physical and psychological ground domesticated by the women who tame and define themselves even as they act upon the landscape, is the silenced and unspoken story in American literature.

—Louise Mowder, "Domestication of Desire: Gender, Language, and Landscape in the Little House Books," *Children's Literature Association Quarterly* 17, no. 1 (Spring 1992): 16, 18

JAN SUSINA

The aural landscape of *The Little House on the Prairie* initially appears silent and devoid of sound, except for the constant blowing of the wind. The reader might be tempted to consider the Kansas prairie to be a great empty chamber waiting to be filled by sounds of Pa's fiddle, or Laura and Mary's laughter; Wilder has too perceptive an ear for such a simplistic description. While Pa and his ubiquitous fiddle form one of the major voices of the prairie, it is certainly not the only one. Wilder is especially attentive to the songs emanating from the prairie itself, and she carefully plots her story around the music produced by the various parts of this landscape.

One of the chief sources of music is the flora and fauna. The Kansas prairie is frequently personified in the novel and is capable of producing a variety of sounds ranging from "the grasses [which] seemed to sing and whisper and laugh" (Wilder 112) to the melodies of the prairie meadowlarks. For the young Laura, it is these sounds that make the prairie such a comforting locale:

> Laura was very happy. The wind sang a low, rustling song in the
> grass. Grasshoppers' rasping quivered up from all the immense prairie.
> A buzzing came faintly from all the trees in the creek bottoms. But all
> these sounds made a great, warm, happy silence. Laura had never
> seen a place she liked so much as this place. (Wilder 48–49)

It is into this melodious landscape that the Ingalls attempt to integrate. The family's primary source of music is Pa's fiddle. ⟨. . .⟩

The fiddle, which Pa had carefully packed between pillows on the wagon trip out west, represents his link with civilization and society as much as the dainty china figurine that Ma carefully unwraps and places on the mantel-shelf of the new cabin to remind herself that the family is "living like civilized folks again" (Wilder 129). Ma's china figurine is a powerful symbol of female domestication appropriately at the center of the hearth. Pa's fiddle is frequently played outside the house and its bright tunes both encourage and promote Laura's liveliness and independence.

For such a taciturn man as Pa, who tends to speak in cliches—"all's well that ends well" (Wilder 92), "Better be safe than sorry" (Wilder 153), and "There's no great loss without some small gain" (Wilder 320)—he is unusually eloquent once he puts his hand to the bow. Like a frontier version of Orpheus, no object, animate or inanimate, seems immune to his powers of music. The most dramatic example of his musical skills comes one night when he plays to the stars:

> The large, bright stars hung down from the sky. Lower and lower
> they came, quivering with the music.
>   Laura gasped, and Ma came quickly. "What is it, Laura?" she asked,
> and Laura whispered, "The stars were singing." (Wilder 50–51)

In this passage, Pa is capable of coaxing the stars into song, which ought to remind the reader that *Little House on the Prairie* is not an unvarnished pioneer account of the settling of the West, but a carefully constructed text full of literary allusions. Wilder referred to this mixture of fact and fancy in her "Book Fair Speech," in which she suggested "Every story in this novel, all the circumstances, each incident are true. All I have told is true, but it is not the whole truth" (220). Pa's ability to create the music of the spheres suggests how well the Ingalls have adapted into their new landscape.

—Jan Susina, "The Voices of the Prairie: The Use of Music in Laura Ingalls Wilder's *Little House on the Prairie*," *The Lion and the Unicorn* 16, no. 2 (1992): 159–61

SUSAN NARAMORE MAHER

Crossing a border both threatens and liberates, silences and opens one up to new expression. In the world of children's literature, growing up itself proves a crossing of borders. Young protagonists negotiating the increasing complexities of life face uncertain thresholds—entries to possible damnation, illumination, or both. Add to this inevitable maturation a move, a displacement, from the known to the unknown; then, children, while gaining through parents the traditions of other places, must still respond to the imperatives of new ground. Amid the uncertainties of growing up and resettlement ⟨. . .⟩ American childhoods are shaped.

The American West, in particular, has provided children's writers a wealth of border crossings. ⟨. . .⟩ Gender roles themselves underwent considerable revision. Settlers' daughters enjoyed the outdoors, contributed to men's work, felt themselves part of a national experiment. These daughters of "first wave women" questioned their mothers' practices and often identified strongly with the male members of their circles—fathers, brothers, and uncles.

Little House on the Prairie and ⟨Carol R. Brink's⟩ *Caddie Woodlawn*, both published in 1935 and subsequently honored by the Newbery Award committee, share a common narrative: they present heroines trying to negotiate public and private spheres, to redefine gender lines, and to come to terms with the liberating spaces around them. Kathryn Adam claims the "rhythm of the Little House books carries Laura back and forth between town and prairie, civilization and wilderness, 'stay' and 'go,' in a sense she is the living embodiment of the central tension in her parents' marriage" ⟨"Laura, Ma, Mary, Carrie and Grace," 1987, 104⟩. Brink's novel, too, shares this struggle. In attempting to modify the givens of mother-defined femininity, Laura and Caddie frustrate the domestic sphere "reconstructed" by their mothers. These prairie-nurtured girls find their fathers (and, in Caddie's case, brothers) encouraging their attempts to open up the cultural borders that restrict them. Pa Ingalls fosters Laura's explorations—both spatial and intellectual—and Mr. Woodlawn permits Caddie to romp freely with her brothers, instructs her in repairing timepieces, and sanctions her visits to the Indian camp. The fathers, consciously breaking with eastern society, become their daughters' mentors, guiding the girls' transformation as daughters of the land. The mothers, conveyors of eastern manners and fashions, of domestic protocol, modify, even hinder, the girls' attachment to the native soil. Though neither novel dismisses "womanly achievements," each presents traditional domestic work as "limiting." Finally, the girls' contacts with Native Americans further their maturation, for the differences glimpsed provide both Laura and Caddie insightful views into the confines of their own acculturation. The girls push their limits, and, in the give-and-take of growing up, learn to combine the lessons of their fathers and their mothers. Thus crossing geographical, cultural, and racial borders helps shape Laura's and Caddie's evolution and make the girls into something more than "westernized domestics." They both stand for an attempted synthesis, a paradoxically uneasy yet releasing bridging of their mothers' continuous domesticity and their fathers' westering instincts.

—Susan Naramore Maher, "Laura Ingalls and Caddie Woodlawn: Daughters of a Border Space," *The Lion and the Unicorn* 18, no. 2 (1994): 130–32

ANITA CLAIR FELLMAN

If the Little House books teach us about frontier life, the question becomes, what frontier life are we talking about? What interpretation of our past are we inculcating in our children through an uncritical acceptance of the books as history? "Frontier" as both historical phenomenon and guiding American mythology is not a self-evident concept. Over the past century it has come to be a key embodiment of American struggles to define our national identity and to shape appropriate government policy. Because of its centrality to these fundamental undertakings, interpretations of the content and meaning of the frontier have long been contested.

The notion that it was the frontiering experience—more than European inheritance, Puritan tradition, the impact of the Founding Fathers, ethnic mixture, or climate of the country—that gave America its distinctive character had long been in the air when historian Frederick Jackson Turner introduced his famous interpretation in an address at the World Columbian Exposition in Chicago in 1893. Turner, whose birth preceded that of Laura Ingalls by just six years and whose Wisconsin birthplace was only about 150 miles from hers, argued that the frontier was the dominant influence in shaping American civilization. The ability to push ever westward, away from settled areas in quest of cheap land hacked out of the wilderness, created the distinctive features of the national character: Americans were restless, innovative, individualistic, pragmatic, buoyant, and willing to take risks. The presence of the frontier was also the major determinant of the democratic character of American political institutions.

Turner's formulation, coming at a worrisome time, when the frontier appeared to be closing, struck a chord both in and out of academic life. Not only did a whole generation of American historians go to school on Turner, but Theodore Roosevelt and Woodrow Wilson took up his idea, and as Gerald Nash puts it, "within a few years writers, artists and musicians joined them until it quickly entered into national consciousness and myth" ⟨Creating the West, 1991, 3–4⟩. ⟨. . .⟩

Laura Ingalls Wilder's books, ostensibly a record of the actions and values of her pioneer family, are part of the frontier myth; I would even argue that they are a key means by which the myth gets perpetuated generation after generation, as children read them in school, borrow them from the library, or perhaps get the boxed set for Christmas or a birthday. The myth selects out portions from the vast array of pioneer experiences and projects them as the entire picture. In its focus on the individualism inherent in the settlers' values, for instance, the myth ignores the struggles to form community in regions with the ceaseless coming and going of populations. In its emphasis on self-sufficiency and on the bounty of the land, it leaves out the shaping role of government, the close economic ties of the West to the industrial order, and the dependence of many settlers upon wage labor.

The Little House books do this as well. Out of the fullness of the Ingalls's lives, Laura Ingalls Wilder and Rose Wilder Lane, her daughter and collaborator, selected elements that convey a certain portrait of their family. Their vision of the frontier was created by memory, by their gender, by the dynamics of the relationship between them as mother and daughter, by their politics, by their livelihoods, by the "frontier longings" that they shared with many of their contemporaries in the 1920s and 1930s, and by their awareness, as literate Americans, of the frontier thesis.

—Anita Clair Fellman, "'Don't Expect to Depend on Anyone Else': The Frontier as Portrayed in the Little House Books," *Children's Literature* 24 (1996): 101–2, 104

SUZANNE RAHN

Forthright tone, transparent style, episodic narrative, and details we can touch and taste create the illusion of untrained honesty in the Little House books—the sense that we are simply living Laura Ingalls Wilder's life. As we read through the series, Laura's memories become ours as well. It always comes as something of a shock when we uncover the craft, purpose, and design that transformed Wilder's life into art. *Little Town on the Prairie*, published in 1941, is a prime example of this transformation. Here, in contrast to the strongly focused structure of the preceding volume in the series, *The Long Winter*, Wilder appears merely to be highlighting the most interesting and amusing incidents of two years in Laura's early teens. Yet by the end of the book, both Laura and her Little Town have grown up, and what "grown up" means in America has been carefully defined. For where *The Long Winter* is essentially about being human—surviving the winter as a human being rather than an animal—*Little Town* is specifically about being an American. In linking Laura's maturation with that of her country, however, Wilder may have revealed more than she intended. Beneath the thematic structure of *Little Town*, two very different concepts of history are at war. ⟨. . .⟩

In effect, *Little Town on the Prairie*—I believe, unconsciously—undermines its own thematic structure. What Wilder wants to show is that America and its people should be "free and independent," that what they need most is the self-discipline to become truly self-sufficient. What she actually shows—based on what actually happened when she was a teenager—is individual farmers and storekeepers bonding into a community. An isolated young girl becoming thoroughly socialized. And a chapter of American history in which there are

no "great men"—only men, women, and children, all essential to the creation
of a frontier outpost of Western civilization—a little town on the prairie.

What really happens in *Little Town on the Prairie* is worth noticing, these
cracks of self-contradiction running through the plaster of a series that has
become an icon of conservative political and family values in America—for
the cracks hint at subsurface strains. But even more worth noticing is what *Little
Town* shows us about history. *Little Town* sets two definitions, old and new, side
by side: what Laura has been taught about America and its history, and what
she experiences herself without realizing her own experience. The one,
shaped to articulate meaning with perfect clarity. The other, a silent, shape-
less, private stream of happening whose meaning we have to seek out ourselves. We can see them both now, after fifty years.

> —Suzanne Rahn, "What Really Happens in the Little Town on the Prairie," *Children's Literature*
> 24 (1996): 117, 125

Bibliography

Little House in the Big Woods. 1932.
Farmer Boy. 1933.
Little House on the Prairie. 1935.
On the Banks of Plum Creek. 1937.
By the Shores of Silver Lake. 1939.
The Long Winter. 1940.
Little Town on the Prairie. 1941.
These Happy Golden Years. 1943.
*On the Way Home: The Diary of a Trip from South Dakota to Mansfield,
    Missouri.* 1962.
The First Four Years. 1971.